AAT

INTERMEDIATE

NVQ AND DIPLOMA PATHWAY
(ADVANCED CERTIFICATE)

COURSE **COMPANION** Units 6 and 7

Costing & Reports
and Returns

BPP

PROFESSIONAL EDUCATION

Fifth edition April 2006
First edition 2001

ISBN 0 7517 2610 9 (previous ISBN 0 7517 1759 2)

British Library Cataloguing-in-Publication Data
A catalogue record for this book is available from the British Library

Published by

BPP Professional Education
Aldine House
Aldine Place,
London
W12 8AW

Printed in Great Britain by WM Print
Frederick Street
Walsall
West Midlands, WS2 9NE

CONTENTS

INTRODUCTION

BPP's innovative Companions range of AAT materials offers a concise and compact alternative, for students who like to get to grips with the essentials and study on the move.

The range comprises

- **Course Companions**, covering all the technical content and theory needed by students, with numerous illustrations, practical examples and activities for students to use to consolidate their learning.

- **Revision Companions**, ideal for classroom courses, which contain an additional range of graded activities and answers for each chapter of the Course Companion, plus specially written practice assessments and answers for the Unit, including a selection of AAT assessments up to December 2005.

- **Tutor Companions**, providing a further bank of questions, answers and practice assessments for classroom use, available separately only to lecturers whose colleges adopt the Companions for the relevant Unit.

This Course Companion, *Costing & Reports and Returns* (for Unit 6 Recording and Evaluating Costs and Revenues and Unit 7 Preparing Reports and Returns of the NVQ) has been written specifically to ensure comprehensive yet concise coverage of the Standards of Competence and performance criteria. It is fully up to date as at April 2006 and reflects both the Revised Standards of Competence and the assessments, so far under those standards.

Each chapter contains:

- clear, step by step explanation of the topic

- logical progression and linking from one chapter to the next

- numerous illustrations and practical examples

- interactive activities within the text of the chapter itself, with answers at the back of the book

- a bank of questions of varying complexity, again with answers supplied at the back of the book

The emphasis in all activities and questions is on the practical application of the skills acquired.

Diploma pathway

Please note that under the Diploma Pathway students do not need to study Unit 7, as the content is included in Diploma Unit 31, Accounting Work Skills. Diploma pathway students, therefore, need only study chapters 1 to 9 of this book.

STANDARDS OF COMPETENCE

The structure of the Standards for Intermediate Units

Each Unit commences with a statement of the knowledge and understanding which underpin competence in the Unit's elements.

The unit of Competence is then divided into elements of competence describing activities which the individual should be able to perform.

Each element includes:

- A set of **performance criteria** which define what constitutes competent performance

- A **range statement** which defines the situations, contexts, methods etc in which competence should be displayed

The elements of competence for Unit 6: Recording and Evaluating Costs and Revenues and Unit 7: Preparing Reports and Returns are set out below. Knowledge and understanding required for the units as a whole are listed first, followed by the performance criteria, and range statements for each element. Performance criteria are cross-referenced below to chapters in this Course Companion.

Unit 6: Recording and Evaluating Costs and Revenues

Unit Commentary

This unit is concerned with how organisations record, analyse and report current and future costs and revenue data for use within the organisation. You will need to know that organisations build up costs and revenues in different ways. The way costs are recorded vary with the type of industry as well as the measurement rules chosen by the organisation. You have to understand the meaning and consequence of these different ways of recording costs and revenues and be able to apply them in relevant circumstances.

There are three elements. The first element focuses on direct costs and revenues, the second on overheads. You will need to apply both types of costs to the reporting of the organisation's expenses. In addition, you will need to apply both types of costing to the recording and analysing of unit and departmental costs. The third element is concerned with using cost and revenue information to help organisations make decisions. You will need to know about cost behaviour and apply it appropriately to managerial decisions for both short - and long-term planning purposes.

Elements contained within this unit are:

Element 6.1   Record and analyse information relating to direct costs and revenues

Element 6.2   Record and analyse information relating to the allocation, apportionment and absorption of overheads costs

Element 6.3   Prepare and evaluate estimates of costs and revenues

Knowledge and understanding

To perform this unit effectively you will need to know and understand:

The business environment	Chapter
1 The nature and purpose of internal reporting (Elements 6.1, 6.2 & 6.3)	1, 6, 8, 9
2 Management information requirements (Elements 6.1, 6.2 & 6.3)	1, 8, 9
3 Maintaining an appropriate cost accounting system (Elements 6.1 & 6.2)	2, 3, 4, 6, 7

Accounting techniques

4 Recording of cost and revenue data in the accounting records (Elements 6.1 & 6.2)	2, 3, 4, 7
5 Methods of stock control and valuation including First In First Out, Last In First Out and Weighted Average Cost (Element 6.1)	2
6 Methods for and calculation of payments for labour (Element 6.1)	3
7 Procedures and documentation relating to expenses (Element 6.1 & 6.2)	3

Chapter

Accounting principles and theory

The Organisation

Element 6.1 Record and analyse information relating to direct costs and revenues

Performance criteria   **Chapter**

In order to perform this element successfully you need to:

A   Identify **direct costs** in accordance with the organisation's costing procedures   2, 3, 6

B   Record and analyse information relating to direct costs   2, 3, 6, 7

C   Calculate direct costs in accordance with the organisation's policies and procedures   2, 3, 6

D   Check cost information for **stocks** against usage and stock control practices   2

E   Resolve or refer queries to the appropriate person   2, 3

Range statement

Performance in this element relates to the following contexts:

Direct costs:

- Materials
- Direct labour costs

Stocks:

- Raw materials
- Part-finished goods
- Finished goods

Element 6.2 Record and analyse information relating to the allocation, apportionment and absorption of overhead costs

Performance criteria   **Chapter**

In order to perform this element successfully you need to:

A   Identify **overhead costs** in accordance with the organisation's procedures   4, 6

B   Attribute overhead costs to production and service cost centres in accordance with agreed **bases of allocation and apportionment**   4

C   Calculate overhead absorption rates in accordance with agreed **bases of absorption**   4, 6

D   Record and analyse information relating to overhead costs in accordance with the organisation's procedures   4, 5, 6, 7

E   Make adjustments for under and over recovered overhead costs in accordance with established procedures   4, 7

F   Review methods of allocation, apportionment and absorption at regular intervals in discussions with senior staff and ensure agreed changes to methods are implemented   4

G   Consult staff working in operational departments to resolve any queries in overhead cost data   4

Range statement

Performance in this element relates to the following contexts:

Overhead costs:

- Fixed

- Variable

- Semi-variable

Bases of allocation and apportionment:

- Direct methods

- Step down methods

Bases of absorption

- Labour hour methods

- Machine hour methods

Element 6.3 Prepare and evaluate estimates of costs and revenues

Performance criteria	Chapter

In order to perform this element successfully you need to:

A	Identify information relevant to estimating current and future revenues and costs	8, 9
B	Prepare **estimates** of future income and costs	8, 9
C	Calculate the effects of variations in capacity on product costs	8
D	Analyse critical factors affecting costs and revenues using appropriate accounting techniques and draw clear conclusions from the analysis	8, 9
E	State any assumptions used when evaluating future costs and revenues	8, 9
F	Identify and evaluate options and solutions for their contribution to organisational goals	8, 9
G	**Present** recommendations to appropriate people in a clear and concise way and supported by a clear rationale	8, 9

Range statement

Performance in this element relates to the following contexts:

Estimates

■ Short term decisions:

- Break-even analysis
- Margin of safety
- Target profit
- Profit volume ratio
- Limiting factors

■ Long term decisions:

- Project appraisal using payback and discounted cash flow methods

Methods

■ Verbal presentation

■ Written reports

Unit 7: Preparing Reports and Returns

NVQ route only

Unit commentary

This unit relates to the preparation of reports and returns from information obtained from all relevant sources. You are required to calculate ratios and performance indicators and present the information according to the appropriate conventions and definitions to either management or outside agencies, including the VAT Office. The unit is also concerned with your communication responsibilities which include obtaining authorisation before despatching reports, seeking guidance from the VAT Office and presenting reports and returns in the appropriate manner.

Elements contained within this unit are:

Element 7.1   Prepare and present periodic performance reports

Element 7.2   Prepare reports and returns for outside agencies

Element 7.3   Prepare VAT returns

Knowledge and understanding

To perform this unit effectively you will need to know and understand:

The business environment	**Chapter**
1 Main sources of relevant government statistics (Elements 7.1 & 7.2)	15
2 Relevant performance and quality measures (Element 7.1)	11
3 Main types of outside organisations requiring reports and returns: regulatory; grant awarding; information collecting; trade associations (Element 7.2)	15
4 Basic law and practice relating to all issues covered in the range statement and referred to in the performance criteria. Specific issues include: the classification of types of supply; registration requirements; the form of VAT invoices; tax points (Element 7.3)	16
5 Sources of information on VAT: Customs and Excise Guide (Element 7.3)	16
6 Administration of VAT: enforcement (Element 7.3)	16, 17
7 Special schemes: annual accounting; cash accounting; bad debt relief (Element 7.3)	16,17

Accounting techniques	
8 Use of standard units of inputs and outputs (Elements 7.1 & 7.3)	11
9 Time series analysis (Element 7.1)	14
10 Use of index numbers (Element 7.1)	14

Knowledge and understanding, continued

The Organisation

Element 7.1 Prepare and present periodic performance reports

Performance criteria

In order to perform this element successfully you need to: **Chapter**

A   Consolidate **information** derived from different units of the organisation
into the appropriate form   10

B   Reconcile **information** derived from different information systems within
the organisation   10

C   Compare results over time using an appropriate method that allows for
changing price levels   14

D   Account for transactions between separate units of the organisation
in accordance with the organisation's procedures   10

E   Calculate **ratios** and **performance indicators** in accordance with the organisation's
procedures   11

F   Prepare reports in the appropriate form and present them to management
within the required timescales   12, 13

Range statement

Performance in this element relates to the following contexts:

Information:

- Costs
- Revenue

Ratios:

- Gross profit margin
- Net profit margin
- Return on capital employed

Performance indicators

- Productivity
- Cost per unit
- Resource utilisation
- Profitability

Methods of presenting information

- Written report containing diagrams
- Table

Element 7.2 Prepare reports and returns for outside agencies

Performance criteria	Chapter
In order to perform this element successfully you need to:	

A   Identify, collate and present relevant information in accordance with the conventions and definitions used by outside agencies — 15

B   Ensure calculations of **ratios** and performance indicators are accurate — 15

C   Obtain authorisation for the despatch of completed **reports and returns** from the appropriate person — 15

D   Present **reports and returns** in accordance with outside agencies' requirements and deadlines — 15

Range statement

Performance in this element relates to the following contexts:

Ratios:

■   Gross profit margin
■   Net profit margin
■   Return on capital employed

Reports and returns

■   Written report
■   Return on standard form

Element 7.3 Prepare VAT returns

Performance criteria   **Chapter**

In order to perform this element successfully you need to:

A   Complete and submit VAT returns correctly, using data from the
appropriate recording systems, within the statutory time limits   17

B   Correctly identify and calculate relevant **inputs and outputs**   16, 17

C   Ensure submissions are made in accordance with current legislation   17

D   Ensure guidance is sought from the VAT office when required, in a
professional manner   16, 17

Range statement

Performance in this element relates to the following contexts:

Recording systems:

- Computerised ledgers
- Manual control account
- Cash book

Inputs and outputs

- Standard supplies
- Exempt supplies
- Zero rated supplies
- Imports
- Exports

chapter 1:
MANAGEMENT INFORMATION AND COST ACCOUNTING

chapter coverage 📖

This first chapter of the text introduces you to the concept of management information and some of the basics of cost accounting. The topics covered in this chapter will be used and expanded upon in later chapters of the text. The topics to be covered are:

✍ management information

✍ cost accounting

✍ the uses of cost information

✍ classification of costs

✍ the difference between capital and revenue expenditure

✍ classification of costs according to their function

✍ classification of costs as direct or indirect costs

✍ classification of costs according to their behaviour

✍ finding the fixed and variable elements of a semi-variable cost

✍ the unit cost card

✍ revenue

Unit 6

knowledge and understanding – the business environment

1   the nature and purpose of internal reporting

2   management information requirements

knowledge and understanding – accounting techniques

15   the identification of fixed, variable and semi-variable costs and their use in cost recording, cost reporting and cost analysis

13   analysis of the effect of changing activity levels on unit costs

knowledge and understanding – accounting principles and theory

24   cost behaviour

MANAGEMENT INFORMATION

In order to run their business the management of an organisation will need detailed and up to date information about the costs and revenues of the business on a regular basis. The managers of an organisation will have many roles but their three main functions in terms of ensuring that the business is run efficiently and at a profit are:

- ■ ˙decision making
- ■ planning
- ■ control

The cost and revenue analyses and reports produced by the information system will focus upon providing information in order that the management can carry out these three important functions.

Management information is a very wide term and can cover many differing areas, for example market research results, specifications for a new computer system, surveyor's reports on a building that is to be purchased, staff appraisal reports, pricing policies of competitors and much, much more. In this text however we will be concentrating on the provision of information to management regarding the costs and revenues of the business. This is done in the form of COST ACCOUNTING.

COST ACCOUNTING

Cost accounting is an area of accounting that is mainly concerned with the recording of cost information and its use in the efficient running of the business. It answers an important question: "How much does it cost to......mine a tonne of coal?......carry a passenger on a train journey?.........build an office block?........carry out a kidney transplant?.......make 1,000 shirts?.......etc"

So far in your studies you will have met various aspects of FINANCIAL ACCOUNTING which records the commercial transactions of a business for the purpose of the preparation of the annual financial statements. These 'accounts' have to be prepared and sent to the shareholders of limited companies by law, and their layout and contents are also governed by law and various Accounting and Financial Reporting Standards. The accounts are also used by other groups, such as the Government for the preparation of statistics, the Inland Revenue for taxation purposes and banks who have been asked for a loan. Because of this, businesses that are not limited companies also produce accounts which comply with the law and Accounting and Financial Reporting Standards.

Cost accounting is different, though. The emphasis here is not just on recording historical information, but on using it to run the business. A key aspect of cost accounting is that it will go on to be used to plan the activities of the business for the future. The cost information produced does not have to comply with any regulations, and it does not have to be sent to anyone outside the business (although there may be some situations when this is the case, for example the bank may request certain costing information if a loan has been applied for to fund the purchase of some new equipment). The management of the business requires the information that is most helpful to it. As this text will show, there is a certain amount of information that will be vital for the purpose of managing a business, and cost accounting functions will aim to produce this.

The main differences between cost accounting and financial accounting are summarised in the table below.

Cost accounting	Financial accounting
Used within the business for management purposes	Used to prepare the financial statements which are for use outside the business
Cost information is not specifically required by law	Financial statements are required by law for limited companies
The way in which the costing information is recorded and presented is up to the management	The content and layout of the financial statements must be in the manner required by the law and Accounting and Financial Reporting Standards
Cost information includes the recording of historical information and the use of this information to produce future plans	Financial accounting records the historical information only

THE USES OF COST INFORMATION

Every organisation needs to know how much it costs to produce their products or perform their services. Costs are recorded so that this information can be found. But it doesn't stop there. It is then used by management for three specific purposes.

- decision-making
- planning
- control

Decision-making

Knowing the cost of a product can help in the decision as to how much to charge for it and how much profit will be made. Alternatively, if there is a lot of competition such that the selling price is set by the market, the business can decide whether the product is going to be profitable (based on estimated costs) and therefore worth making in the first place. Deciding between two products is sometimes necessary if a shortage of resources, such as production capacity or materials, means that only one can be made. The decision will be based on profitability, for which cost information is needed. These types of decisions will be covered in more detail in Chapter 8.

Planning

Once a decision has been taken to make a new product in the coming period, or to continue making an existing one, a plan or BUDGET will be drawn up. The budget will contain details of the quantities and costs involved and a timetable for production. The quantity that can be sold is often the limiting factor on production, and once this is established by market research or past experience, the production quantity can be set. From this, budgets will be produced for the materials that need to be purchased, the number of hours of labour and machine time needed, and their costs. Expenses and income will also be considered, and the level of debtors, creditors and cash, of course. This may indicate that more machinery needs to be purchased and workers employed, and the business may need to raise funds to finance its plans. All this will be set out in the budget, on a month-by-month basis, so that the business knows what it has to do to achieve its aims, and when.

Control

The budget will forecast the costs and quantities expected, and once the plan is put into action, the actual figures can be recorded. The actual results are monitored and discrepancies, or variances, between these and the budgeted figures may then come to light. Some minor discrepancies are bound to occur, but the business will investigate those which exceed pre-set tolerance limits.

Say a business found that the labour cost for a particular month was a lot higher than expected. If this were due to a pay rise that had not been foreseen in the budget, then the budget would need to be revised for future periods or else a discrepancy would show up every month. If, on the other hand, it was because there was insufficient unskilled labour to do an unskilled job and skilled workers had had to be used, the business might decide to employ more unskilled workers to keep costs down. Another possible cause could be a machine breakdown leading to workers being idle, in which case the maintenance procedures might need looking into or the purchase of a new machine could be necessary. This illustrates that there are many courses of action that may arise from investigation of differences between budgeted and actual figures.

CLASSIFICATION OF COSTS

A business will incur many different types of cost from day to day. For cost accounting purposes it is useful to group or classify these costs. There are, however, a number of different ways of doing this.

CAPITAL AND REVENUE EXPENDITURE

The expenses of a business can be categorised as either capital or revenue.

CAPITAL EXPENDITURE includes

- the purchase of fixed assets
- the improvement of the earning capability of fixed assets

FIXED ASSETS are assets that are used in the business for more than one accounting period to provide benefits. These benefits are (we hope!) the profits earned from using the fixed assets in the business. Plant and machinery, land and buildings, office equipment and motor vehicles are all examples of fixed assets that play their part in earning profits by being used within the business rather than being bought to make profit on their resale.

REVENUE EXPENDITURE includes

- the purchase of goods for resale
- the maintenance of the existing earning capacity of fixed assets
- expenditure incurred in conducting the business

Capital expenditure is shown as a fixed asset in the balance sheet, whilst revenue expenditure is charged as a cost in the profit and loss account. In costing terms, capital expenditure would not be included in the cost of a product: only revenue expenses are included. It is therefore important to distinguish correctly between capital and revenue items, as this could hit profit quite hard given the relatively large figures involved where fixed assets are concerned. It would also mean that the balance sheet did not show the correct cost of assets used by the business. For costing purposes it would mean that the amounts included in the calculations of product costs would be inaccurate.

Some tricky items you might come across when deciding between capital and revenue categories often involve changes to fixed assets:

	Capital	Revenue
Extension to a building	✓	
Repairs to a building or machine		✓
Legal costs of buying a new factory	✓	
Installation of new machinery	✓	
Redecorating offices		✓

Activity 1

Explain why an extension to a building is treated as capital expenditure, but a repair to a building is treated as revenue expenditure.

Depreciation

Although a fixed asset is capitalised in the balance sheet, it would not be realistic to leave it there forever. After all, as the asset is used, part of the cost of the asset is "used up". This is a cost that should be charged as an expense in the profit and loss account and included in the cost of products made. This cost is depreciation, and it is calculated so as to spread the cost of a fixed asset over the periods benefiting from its use. So, as the capitalised fixed asset is used in the business, part of its cost is effectively converted to a revenue item and transferred to the profit and loss account each year as a depreciation charge. This will be dealt with in more detail in Chapter 3.

CLASSIFICATION OF COSTS BY FUNCTION

Revenue expenditure can be further classified according to the function that causes the cost. The main functions within a manufacturing business will give rise to the following cost categories.

- **Production costs.** Materials and labour used to make the products, maintenance costs of the machinery and supervision of the workforce are examples of costs caused by the production function of a business.

- **Selling and distribution costs.** Advertising, delivery costs and sales staff salaries would be caused by the selling and distribution function.

- **Administration costs.** The administration function gives rise to management, secretarial and accounting costs in coordinating the other functions of the business.

- **Financing costs.** The financing function gives rise to all the expenses associated with raising money to finance the business, such as a loan or overdraft.

The distinction between these categories is not always clear, particularly when we are talking about administration costs, as there are no rules or regulations to follow: just common sense. What's more, these are not the only possible functions within a business. Large companies often have a research and development function, or a training function; it depends on the type of business.

Activity 2

Look at the list of costs below and decide whether each one would be classified as a production cost, a selling and distribution cost or an administration cost.

- a) Factory rent
- b) Managing Director's salary
- c) Sales Director's salary
- d) Depreciation of office equipment
- e) Depreciation of plant and machinery
- f) Petrol for delivery vans
- g) Factory heating and lighting

DIRECT AND INDIRECT COST ELEMENTS

A different way of classifying revenue expenses looks at the three major cost elements.

- materials
- labour
- expenses

Each category is then sub-divided into

- DIRECT COSTS: costs which can be directly identified with a particular unit of production or service provided

- INDIRECT COSTS: costs which cannot be directly identified with a unit of production or service

It is usually easy to identify the amount of a direct expense that is spent on one unit, but it is more difficult to do so with indirect costs as they are not spent directly on one unit: they are usually spent in relation to a number of units.

The resulting six cost elements, and examples of these costs are shown in the table below.

Direct materials	Materials that are incorporated into the finished product, e.g. wood used in the construction of a table.
Indirect materials	Materials that are used in the production process but not incorporated into the product, e.g. machine lubricants and spare parts. Insignificant costs that are attributable to each unit are sometimes included in indirect materials for convenience, e.g. nails and glue.
Direct labour	Wages paid to those workers who make products in a manufacturing business (e.g. machine operators) or perform the service in a service business (e.g. hairdressers in a hair salon).
Indirect labour	Wages and salaries of the other staff, such as supervisors, storekeepers and maintenance workers.
Direct expenses	Expenses that are identifiable with each unit of production, such as patent royalties payable to the inventor of a new product or process.
Indirect expenses	Expenses that are not spent on individual units of production, e.g. rent and rates, electricity and telephone.

In costing, the three types of indirect cost are often lumped together and called overheads.

OVERHEADS = indirect materials + indirect labour + indirect expenses.

Activity 3

A building contractor employs a painter to paint the exterior and interior of the buildings they have built. Explain whether this is a direct or an indirect cost.

FIXED AND VARIABLE COSTS

Costs can also be classified by their BEHAVIOUR, how the total cost is affected by a change in production level or activity level.

VARIABLE COSTS vary according to the level of production or activity. Each unit of output causes the same amount of cost to be incurred, so the total cost increases in proportion to the increase in output.

HOW IT WORKS

Toys 4 U is a company that makes children's toys. One of their top selling lines is a "Chunker", a chunky plastic car that can be assembled by a child. The plastic components are bought-in from China at a cost of 90p per car. The company packages these in boxes which cost 20p each. The labour used for the packaging operation costs 12p per unit. A royalty of 8p is paid to the inventor of the toy for each unit produced.

Each Chunker made will have a variable cost of:

	£
Direct materials (plastic components and packaging)	1.10
Direct labour	0.12
Direct expenses	0.08
Variable cost	1.30

If Toys 4 U made no Chunkers at all, there would be no cost at all. If it made 10 Chunkers, it would cost £13. If it made 5,000 Chunkers, it would cost the company £6,500, and so on.

If a graph were plotted of the variable cost on the y-axis and the level of output on the x-axis, an upward-sloping straight line would be obtained which passes through the origin (0,0).

Graph of variable costs

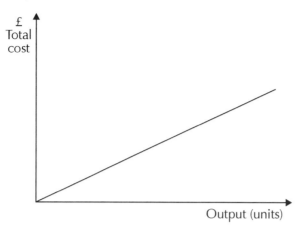

Direct costs are generally variable, although bulk purchase discounts and economies of scale may affect them. As a general rule, though, as the direct cost is spent directly on each unit of production, this will be the same amount for each unit, so a graph of **unit cost** against level of output would be a horizontal line; no matter how many are produced, it will cost the same for each unit.

Graph of variable cost per unit

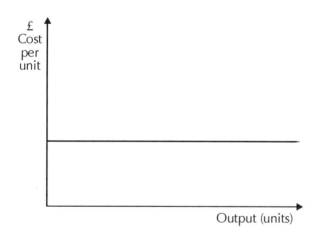

Some indirect costs may also vary in line with output, for example maintenance costs of a machine will increase if it is used more.

FIXED COSTS are not affected by changes in production level. They remain the same in total whether no units are produced or many units. They are incurred in relation to a period of time rather than production level, and are often referred to as PERIOD COSTS. This is the case with the salary of a supervisor, the rent of a factory or straight-line depreciation of plant and machinery.

A graph of fixed costs against output level would produce a horizontal line.

Graph of fixed costs

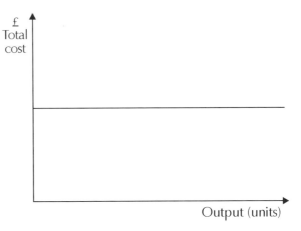

One important point to make at this stage is that because fixed costs remain the same at different output levels, if a fixed cost per unit is calculated, this will decrease as output increases. This gives management an incentive to increase production as it will mean that each unit is cheaper to produce. This is demonstrated in the graph below.

Graph of fixed cost per unit

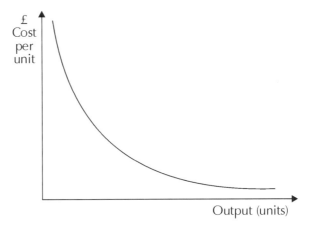

There are problems with calculating a fixed cost per unit. Some of these will become apparent later in the text, but one arises because many fixed costs are only fixed over a certain range of output. If the business decides to expand beyond a certain level, there will be a sudden jump in the cost to a new fixed amount. Such costs are STEP FIXED COSTS; the graph below demonstrates how they got their name. The rental of an extra factory unit, or the employment of another supervisor as the workforce increases beyond the limit which can be managed efficiently by one supervisor would give rise to step fixed costs.

Graph of step fixed costs

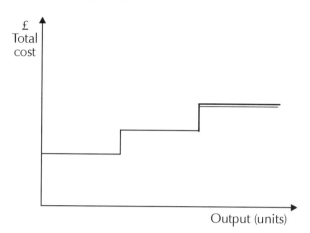

Activity 4

Sleet Limited makes garden benches and incurs fixed costs of £20,000 per year. Calculate the fixed cost per garden bench at the following output levels:

a)   1,000 units
b)   10,000 units
c)   20,000 units
d)   100,000 units

A SEMI-VARIABLE COST is one which has a fixed element as well as a variable element.

Graph of semi-variable costs

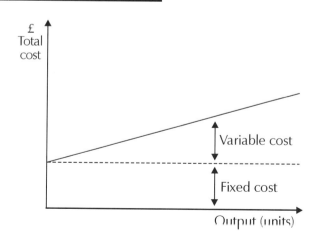

Calculating the fixed and variable elements of semi-variable costs

The HIGH LOW TECHNIQUE can be used to estimate the fixed and variable parts of a semi-variable cost. It requires several observations of the costs incurred at different output levels, such as would be recorded over a number of accounting periods. This data can then be used to predict costs that would be incurred at other output levels.

HOW IT WORKS

Over the last 5 years, Stormbreak Limited has recorded the following costs.

Year	Output (units)	Total cost £
2001	32,000	505,000
2002	37,000	583,000
2003	48,000	754.000
2004	53,000	820,000
2005	51,000	798,000

Stormbreak Limited wants to estimate the cost for 2006, when they expect to produce 52,000 units.

This problem can be tackled by following 4 steps.

Step 1   Identify the high and low output and associated costs

Look carefully at the information given and identify the highest and lowest output levels. Write these down, along with the total costs at those levels. (Don't be put off by any other information, such as the year, or the order in which the data is given; even if the cost column is given first, it is the highest and lowest output that matter.)

	Output (units)	Total cost £
Highest	53,000	820,000
Lowest	32,000	505,000

Step 2   Deduct the lowest output/costs from the highest output/costs.

	Output (units)	Total cost £
Highest	53,000	820,000
Lowest	32,000	505,000
Increase	21,000	315,000

This tells us that an increase of 21,000 units has led to an increase in costs of £315,000. This is due to the variable costs only, and gives us the figures we need for the next step.

Step 3   Calculate the variable cost per unit.

$$\text{Variable cost per unit} \;=\; \frac{\text{High cost - low cost}}{\text{High output - low output}}$$

$$=\; \frac{£315,000}{21,000}$$

$$=\; £15$$

Step 4   Find the fixed costs at one of the output levels used in the above calculations.

Choose either the highest or the lowest output level; both will give the same result. Calculate the variable cost by taking the cost per unit from step 3 multiplied by the number of units of output. Deduct this from the total cost at the same level of output and you will be left with the fixed cost.

At 53,000 units:

	£
Total cost	820,000
Less: variable cost (53,000 x £15)	795,000
= fixed cost	25,000

At 32,000 units (as a check):

	£
Total cost	505,000
Less: variable cost (32,000 x £15)	480,000
= fixed cost	25,000

Now we are in a position to answer the actual question asked, which is "What are the expected costs when output is 52,000 units?" All we need to do is build up the total cost from the fixed and variable elements at this level of output.

	£
Fixed cost	25,000
Add: variable cost (52,000 x £15)	780,000
= total cost	805,000

Activity 5

Sunny Limited has recorded the following total costs over the past 6 months.

Month	Production volume (units)	Total cost £
January	3,500	44,500
February	2,900	41,000
March	3,300	43,500
April	3,700	48,000
May	4,200	54,000
June	4,000	51,000

Estimate Sunny Limited's fixed costs using the high/low technique.

Cost behaviour and levels of activity

Knowledge of cost behaviour is essential when a business is planning its production levels and costs for the coming period. Estimates of the numbers of units of product that can be made and sold can never be accurate, and it is often helpful to look at a range of options.

HOW IT WORKS

Cloudy Limited makes pencils and operates from a factory which costs £40,000 per annum to rent. The production line is largely mechanised and the depreciation of the machinery amounts to £15,000 per annum. These costs are fixed over the range of output levels under consideration.

The variable costs per box of 100 pencils are:

- raw materials and packaging, £1.20
- labour, £1.60
- expenses, £0.20

An overseer is employed to supervise the production line and inspect samples of the product. If production exceeds 500,000 boxes per annum another overseer has to be employed on a salary of £18,000 per annum.

Cloudy Limited produced 400,000 boxes of pencils last year, but hope to increase this to 600,000 next year as they have had enquiries from new customers. However, there is a threat of industrial action by one of their major raw material suppliers, and if they can't source their raw materials from elsewhere, they will have to cut production by 50% to 200,000 boxes.

To analyse the effect of these possible activity levels on costs, a budgeted production schedule can be drawn up. Variable costs can be found by multiplying the units of output by the variable cost per unit. Fixed costs remain the same at each output level. The amount included for the overseer's salary will be one salary for 200,000 and 400,000 units, but two salaries if production is 600,000 units. This is a step fixed cost.

The estimated costs for the three possible production levels are as follows.

BUDGETED PRODUCTION COSTS

Units	200,000	400,000	600,000
	£	£	£
Costs			
Variable			
(units x (£1.20 + £1.60+ £0.20))	600,000	1,200,000	1,800,000
Fixed	55,000	55,000	55,000
Step fixed	18,000	18,000	36,000
Total production cost	673,000	1,273,000	1,891,000
Cost per unit	£3.37	£3.18	£3.15

Activity 6

Malylong Ltd had budgeted to produce 100,000 jugs in 2007. Sales demand could be as high as 150,000 units, but may fall to only 75,000 units. Each jug costs £5 in materials, and takes 3 labour hours, at a rate of £7.50 per hour. Once production exceeds 100,000, direct cost overtime premium of £2 per hour will need to be paid. Direct expenses will be £1.50 per jug. Fixed overheads are budgeted at £80,000 currently; increasing production to 150,000 units will incur extra fixed costs of £20,000.

Calculate the estimated total and unit costs at each level of production.

Units made	75,000	100,000	150,000
Costs	£	£	£
Variable costs:			
Direct material			
Direct labour			
Direct expenses			
Prime cost			
Fixed costs			
Overheads			
Production cost			
Cost per unit			

THE UNIT COST CARD

A COST UNIT is a unit of product or service to which costs can be attached. It could be a single item such as a table, or a batch of items such as 200 loaves of bread. A batch is a more useful cost unit if the items are made in a batch and/or the individual cost of an item is very small: fractions of a penny, for example. For a hotel, a cost unit would be a guest night and for a taxi service, a passenger mile.

The cost of a cost unit is an important piece of costing information which will be used in many different ways. The cost is built up on a **cost card**, which groups the costs using the categories that we have just looked at.

COST CARD	£
Direct materials	X
Direct labour	X
Direct expenses	X
Prime cost	X
Production overheads	X
Production cost	X
Non-production overheads	
– selling and distribution	X
– administration	X
– finance	X
Total cost	X

The cost card has two sub totals

- PRIME COST is a term used for the total of the direct costs.

- PRODUCTION COST is the total of the manufacturing costs. It is this cost that would be used for reporting purposes, in other words for the valuation of stock in the balance sheet and the cost of goods sold in the profit and loss account. In cost accounting the non-production overheads are included to give the full cost, shown as total cost here, so that the business can ensure that all costs are covered by the selling price and that a profit is being made.

There are a number of different ways in which the values of materials, labour and overheads on the cost card are found. For a one-off job made to a customer's individual specifications, all the costs can be identified with that particular job. This method is known as JOB COSTING. If the product is made in batches of identical items, the costs of producing a batch would be found, which is called BATCH COSTING. The cost of an individual item within a batch can be found, if this is meaningful, by dividing the batch cost in total by the number of items in the batch. Chapters 2, 3 and 4 detail how materials, labour and overhead costs are recorded. Chapter 6 looks at job and batch costing in a little more detail together with a further costing system known as process costing.

The way in which a production overhead cost per cost unit is found is known as ABSORPTION COSTING. This technique aims to attach an appropriate amount of each type of overhead, such as lighting, heating, power, depreciation and maintenance, to the products made. It is dealt with in detail in Chapter 4.

REVENUE

The emphasis in this chapter has been on the costs incurred by a business as this will be of prime importance to management. However, they will of course also be interested in the revenue earned by the business. Unit 6 is entitled "Recording and Evaluating Costs and Revenues" and therefore revenue cannot be ignored. In particular management will be concerned to ensure that enough units are sold at the right price in order to cover all costs and therefore make a profit. We will consider this area in more detail in Chapter 8.

CHAPTER OVERVIEW

- managers will require a wide range of information in order to be able to carry out their three main functions of decision-making, planning and control

- cost accounting differs from financial accounting in that a business records historical cost information and generates future expected cost information for use in the management of the business. Financial accounting is geared towards recording historical information for the purpose of the financial statements

- a key piece of cost information is the cost of making an individual product

- cost information is used for decision-making, planning and control

- costs are either capital or revenue in nature. Revenue expenditure is included in the cost of a product, but capital expenditure is not. Capital expenditure is converted to revenue expenditure in the form of depreciation

- revenue costs can be classified by several methods

  - by function: production, selling and distribution, administration and finance

  - by element

Direct	Materials
	Labour
	Expenses
Indirect	Materials
	Labour
	Expenses

  - by nature or cost behaviour: fixed, variable, step-fixed, semi-variable

KEY WORDS

Cost accounting recording costs and using cost information to manage the business. This will involve decision-making, planning and control

Financial accounting recording transactions and the preparation of the financial statements in accordance with the law and Accounting Standards

Budget a plan of the activities of the organisation for a future period, covering expected quantities and values of sales, production, assets and liabilities

Control investigating variances between actual and expected costs (and income), and taking any necessary action

Capital expenditure purchases of fixed assets or the improvement of the earning capability of fixed assets

Fixed assets assets used in the business for a period longer than one accounting period to bring benefits

Revenue expenditure

- purchase of goods for resale
- maintenance of the existing earning capacity of fixed assets
- expenditure incurred in conducting the business

Depreciation a measure of the cost of a fixed asset that is used up in a period, and is calculated so as to spread the cost of the fixed asset over the periods benefiting from its use

Direct costs can be directly identified with a unit of production or service

Indirect costs cannot be directly identified with a unit of production or service

Overheads indirect costs (i.e. indirect materials, labour and expenses)

Cost behaviour the way a cost changes as production quantity or activity level changes

Variable costs vary according to the level of production

Fixed costs (period costs) do not vary with changes in production level. They are incurred in relation to a period rather than a product

CHAPTER OVERVIEW cont.

- the high-low technique can be used to find the variable and fixed elements of a semi-variable cost by identifying the costs at the highest and lowest levels of output

- at different production levels:

  - variable costs will change in line with the quantity produced, but fixed costs will remain the same

  - the variable cost per unit will be the same, but the fixed cost per unit will fall as the quantity produced increases

- a cost card builds up the total cost of a product using the following cost categories and sub-totals:

  - direct materials
  - direct labour
  - direct expenses
  - prime cost
  - production overheads
  - production cost
  - non-production overheads
  - total cost

KEY WORDS

Step-fixed costs   costs which are fixed over a certain range, but when output increases beyond a certain level, there will be a sudden jump in cost to a higher fixed amount

Semi-variable (or semi-fixed, or mixed) costs costs which have both a fixed element and a variable element

High-low technique   a method for estimating the fixed and variable parts of a semi-variable cost

Cost unit a unit of product to which costs can be attached

Prime cost   the total of direct costs

Production cost   the total of manufacturing costs

Job costing the method of costing an individual job made to a customer's own requirements

Batch costing   the method of costing a batch of identical items

Absorption costing   a method for finding an appropriate amount of overheads to be included in the cost of a product

HOW MUCH HAVE YOU LEARNED?

1 What is cost information used for?

2 Study the list below and decide which items are capital and which are revenue. Tick the appropriate box.

	Capital	Revenue
A new telephone system		
Depreciation of vehicles		
Salesman's car		
Road fund license for delivery van		
Telephone bill		
Computer software		
Repairs to the Managing Director's company car after an accident		

3 Complete the following sketch graphs:

a) **Fixed costs**

b)   Fixed cost per unit

4   Look at the following sketch graph and then decide which of the suggested costs could account for that shape of graph.

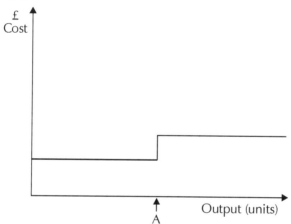

	Cost behaviour	
	Does fit the graph shape	**Does not fit the graph shape**
a) Plastic used in the manufacture of moulded plastic furniture. A bulk-buying discount is given at point A on the graph.	....	....
b) Straight-line depreciation of a freehold factory. A new factory is bought at point A.	....	....
c) Rent of a warehouse. A further warehouse is rented at point A.	....	....
d) Electricity costs which have a standing charge and a cost per unit of power used. At point A the level of production reaches the point where a nightshift is required, which uses electricity at a cheaper rate.	....	....

5 Use the high-low technique to predict the costs at a production level of 12,000 units, given the observed data in the table below.

Year	Production level (units)	Total cost £
2002	9,000	24,000
2003	6,500	17,500
2004	13,500	31,500
2005	10,300	26,300
2006	12,600	30,200

6 Draw up a cost card using the following information. All costs given are per cabinet.

To make a filing cabinet, metal sheeting to the value of £3.80 is cut, formed, welded and painted by machine. A group of machines are monitored, the labour cost of which has been worked out at £0.30. Metal fixtures costing £1.80 are attached manually, and the cabinets are then assembled and packaged. The labour cost of assembly and packaging is £6.70, and the packaging materials cost £0.90. The power used by the factory gives a cost of £0.20, and delivery costs and advertising works out at £3.00.

chapter 2:
MATERIALS COSTS

chapter coverage 📖

This chapter looks at materials: obtaining, documenting, storing, valuing and controlling them. The topics to be covered are:

✍ the different types of materials

✍ the stages involved in purchasing materials including the documents relevant to costing

✍ stock and stock records

✍ stock valuation

✍ how materials movements are recorded in the costing ledger accounts, including coding and direct and indirect materials

✍ the costs associated with keeping stock

✍ control of stock levels

✍ stocktaking and its role in checking the stock records

Unit 6

knowledge and understanding – the business environment

3   maintaining an appropriate cost accounting system

knowledge and understanding – accounting techniques

4   recording of cost and revenue data in the accounting records

5   methods of stock control and valuation including First In First Out, Last In First Out and Weighted Average Cost

knowledge and understanding – accounting principles and theory

19   relationship between the materials costing system and the stock control system

knowledge and understanding – the organisation

27   the sources of information for revenue and costing data

Performance criteria – element 6.1

A   identify direct costs in accordance with the organisation's costing procedures

B   record and analyse information relating to direct costs

C   calculate direct costs in accordance with the organisation's policies and procedures

D   check cost information for stocks against usage and stock control practices

E   resolve or refer queries to the appropriate person

MATERIALS

The term 'materials' encompasses:

- raw materials and components which are incorporated into products made by a manufacturing business

- goods bought for resale by a retail or wholesale business

- goods bought for consumption by a business

Raw materials and components used by a manufacturer would be classified as direct costs for costing purposes. Examples are fabric in a tailoring company, paper in a printing company and electrical components in a manufacturer of electrical goods.

A retailer, such as a shop, and a wholesaler, which acts as a 'middle man' between the manufacturer and the retailer, would buy the products of the manufacturing companies. So, the clothing, printed matter and electrical goods produced by the manufacturers would be the materials of the retailer and wholesaler.

All businesses will buy some sort of goods for consumption, which are generally classified as indirect materials and included in overheads. In a manufacturing business, machine spares and lubricants would be production overheads, whilst office stationery would be a non-production overhead.

Activity 1

List the raw materials that would be used to make a pair of shoes.

BUYING MATERIALS

Buying materials is the job of the buying, or purchasing, department of a business, but other departments will also become involved. The decision to buy materials will set in motion a chain of events with an accompanying trail of documentation that enables the transaction to be recorded and controlled. Each document will be raised in one department and sent to another one to inform them that a certain stage in the purchasing process has been reached and to set the next event in motion. Copies of the documents will also be kept for reference and as evidence of that particular event. All the documents in the chain may be produced by computer, and the records updated at the same time, but to explain what is happening, we will look at a manual system.

Purchase requisition

The initial decision that an item needs to be bought is often made by the stores department where the materials are kept. The storekeeper will notice that the stock of that particular item has gone down and needs replenishing. Alternatively, if stores of the item are not kept, the user department would make the decision. A PURCHASE REQUISITION will be raised and sent to the purchasing department.

PURCHASE REQUISITION				
Department: _Stores_		**No: S433**		
Requested by: _J Askey_		**Date:** _4.5.06_		
Date required: _13.5.06_				
Quantity	Description		Estimated cost	
			Unit	£
200 metres	Blue plastic-coated fabric (width 1.8 metres)		£1.20	240.00
Authorised by: _V Rainsford_				

The important details on this form are:

- sequential number: as with all documents, if they are pre-numbered in sequence it is easy to spot if there is one missing

- date

- date the items are needed: this is relevant if the items are needed for a particular job

- details of the materials required: quantity, description and estimated cost (some purchase requisitions may make no reference to cost depending upon the organisation)

- who and which department needs the material

- authorisation by a senior person in the department: this acts as a control to prevent purchasing of excessive quantities or of unneeded items

Purchase order

The job of the purchasing department is to source the required materials. They will aim to get materials of the right quality at the lowest price and which can be delivered at the right time. When they receive a purchase requisition they will contact their usual supplier or a number of suppliers to find out who can deliver the materials requested on time and for the best price. Details may be agreed over the phone or by email, but the purchasing department will still raise a purchase order. This is sent to the supplier as confirmation that it is a legitimate order and to ensure that the supplier is prompted into action!

CASTLE TOYS LTD
New Horizon Business Park
Stoneylow Middletown MD4 5BS

Purchase Order

No: PO 1232

Our ref: S433

Delivery address: As above

Date of order: 4.5.06

Delivery by: 11.5.06

Ordered by: JBL

To: Fashion Fabrics
Sunshine Trading Estate
Calfield
Middletown MD5 2PP

Passed by:

A R Hopkinson

Quantity	Description	Cost	
		Unit	£
200 metres	Blue plastic-coated fabric (width 1.8 metres)	£1.24	248.00
		Net total	248.00
		VAT @ 17.5%	43.40
		Invoice total	291.40

The important details on a purchase order are:

- sequential number
- date of the order
- delivery date required: usually already agreed over the phone
- reference: to the purchase requisition
- name and address of the supplier
- delivery address: this is sometimes different from the address on the letterhead of the business
- details of the materials required: quantity, description and cost

The purchasing department will file their copy of the order. Copies of the purchase order are also sent to:

- the supplier (obviously)
- the stores department (or other department who requisitioned the goods) so that they know that their requisition is being acted upon
- the accounts department who will match the order and the requisition and file them together
- the goods inwards department who will be alerted to expect the delivery on the required date

Goods received note

The goods inwards department will receive and check all goods that are delivered to a business. When the goods arrive, they will be accompanied by the supplier's document called a delivery note or advice note. A checker will count the goods and make sure that they are not damaged, and then will sign the delivery note which is returned to the supplier as their evidence that the goods have been delivered in a good condition. The goods inwards department then raises a goods received note (GRN).

GOODS RECEIVED NOTE

Date: 11.5.06   **No:** GRN0067

Time: 9.15

Order No: PO 1232

Supplier's advice No: 8662

Quantity	Description
200 metres	Blue plastic-coated fabric (1.8 metres wide)

Received in good condition: _R Parkin_ ....

The GRN will record the:

- sequential number

- date and time of receipt of the goods

- quantity and description of the goods (the cost is not important to the checking process)

- name of the checker in case there are any queries later on

- purchase order number

- supplier's delivery note number

A copy of the GRN will be sent to:

- stores with the materials: stores can then match the GRN with the purchase requisition and purchase order, and will use this bunch of documents as its source documents for updating the records of how much stock is held;

- the purchasing department so that they can follow up any discrepancies with the supplier

- the accounts department as advance warning that an invoice is to be expected

Invoice

The invoice will be sent by the supplier, and will give the full details of the transaction.

Fashion Fabrics
Sunshine Trading Estate
Calfield
Middletown MD5 2PP

INVOICE
VAT number: 984281572

To: Castle Toys Ltd
New Horizon Business Park
Stoneylow
Middletown MD4 5BS

No: 03969
Date: 11 May 2006

Quantity	Description	Cost	
		Unit	£
200 metres	Blue plastic-coated fabric (width 1.8 metres)	£1.24	248.00
		Net total	248.00
		VAT @ 17.5%	43.40
		Invoice total	291.40

As soon as the invoice is received, it will be stamped with a grid to be completed to ensure its efficient processing. The grid will have spaces for:

- the purchase order number
- the GRN number
- a signature of authorisation for payment
- the main ledger codes to which the main ledger postings will be made

The invoice will only be passed for payment when the details have been checked to the purchase order and GRN. The invoice is then used as the posting medium to update the main ledger and the stores ledger accounts.

STOCKS

STOCK is a collective term used to describe goods held by the business, and which (for our purposes) can be included in one of the following categories:

- **Raw materials** and components for incorporation into products, and consumable stores

- **Finished goods** ready for sale and goods purchased for resale

- **Work in progress (WIP)** which are goods (and services) that are only partially completed

WIP arises as an inevitable consequence of certain businesses. If your business is making spoons, for example, there may be several stages in the production process: stamping out the shape, removing the rough edges, polishing and packaging. At any point along the way, an unfinished spoon will be described as WIP until it is finished. Some businesses will keep WIP for a considerable time, such as makers of whisky which needs to be matured over a number of years. We will refer to WIP again in a later chapter, but for the time being we are more concerned with the other categories of stock.

Most businesses will choose to keep stocks of materials and finished goods ready for when they are needed.

- Raw materials stocks will be kept by a manufacturer so that materials are available for transfer to the production line when they are needed. Production would have to stop if there were no raw materials, with several serious knock-on effects, such as labour being unable to work but still being paid, delay in producing the products and consequent dissatisfaction of customers. This would make the products more expensive for the business to make. Goodwill might also be lost, meaning that customers would consider other suppliers in future.

- Finished products will be kept in stock by a manufacturer so that demand from customers can be met and to avoid problems such as loss of goodwill.

- Goods for resale, which are the finished goods of manufacturers that have been bought for selling by retailers and wholesalers, are stocked so that changes in demand from day to day can be catered for. A shop would not be the same without a stock of goods for the customer to look at and choose from!

- Consumable stores are needed, again so that there is no disruption of production or the administrative function of the business. For example, a stock of printer cartridges is needed so that printing of plans and diagrams (a production use of the printer), quotes for customers (sales), letters and reports (administration) would have to wait until more cartridges could be obtained.

Stock records

Most businesses will keep track of the quantities of materials that they have in stock by maintaining a stock record for each type of material held. This will be updated each time material is received into, or issued from, stores, and a new balance of stock held can be calculated. This is known as a PERPETUAL INVENTORY system, and it can be manual or computerised. There are two types of stock record which may be kept, and sometimes they will both be used. These are stock cards and stores ledger accounts.

Stock cards

STOCK CARDS (also known as bin cards) are manual records that are written up and kept in the stores department. An example is shown here.

STOCK CARD

Description: Blue plastic-coated fabric (1.8m wide)

Code No: B6309582

Stock units: metres

Stock No: 582

Maximum: 250

Minimum: 20

Reorder level: 40

Reorder quantity: 200

Receipts			Issues			Balance
Date	Reference	Quantity	Date	Reference	Quantity	Quantity
2006			2006			
1 May						40
11 May	GRN 0067	200				240
			12 May	MR 296	30	210
			14 May	MR 304	20	190
			15 May	MR 309	50	140
13 May	MRN 127	10				150

The information on the stock card gives all the details the storekeeper needs to know.

- Description: of the stock item for which this is a record

- Stock code: for unambiguous identification

- Stock units: the units in which the material is measured e.g. metres, kilograms, boxes etc

- Stock number: the location of the items in the store

- Stock control information: maximum and minimum stock levels, the level at which stock needs reordering and the quantity to order. These details help the storekeeper to monitor the stock levels and ensure they are maintained within required levels

- Issues to production: date, quantity and a reference to the materials requisition (MR), the document which the production department use to request material from stores

- Receipts: date, quantity and details of the GRN for goods delivered to the business or materials returned note (MRN) for goods returned to stock when they have not been used in production

- Balance: the quantity of stock on hand after each stock movement

Stores ledger accounts

The STORES LEDGER ACCOUNTS (or stock record cards) are very similar to stock cards. They carry all the information that a stock card does, and they are updated from the same sources: GRNs, MRs and MRNs. But there are two important differences.

1) Cost details are recorded in the stores ledger account, so that the unit cost and total cost of each issue and receipt is shown. The balance of stock after each stock movement is also valued. The value is recorded as these accounts form part of the cost accounting system.

2) The stores ledger accounts are written up and kept in the costing department, or in a stores office separate from the stores, by a clerk experienced in costing bookkeeping.

Because stock cards and stores ledger accounts are independent, they can be used as a control to check the accuracy of the records. Theoretically, the quantities of stock recorded should be the same; if they are not, this would have to be investigated and the appropriate adjustment made. An example of a stores ledger account is given further on in this chapter where you can have a go at completing the details.

Materials requisitions

A MATERIALS REQUISITION will be completed when materials are needed from stores by the production department. An official from production will sign the form to authorise it, and stores will issue the materials when the form is given to them. It is then used as a source document for:

- updating the stock card in stores
- updating the stores ledger account in the costing department
- charging the job, overhead or department that is using the materials

The originating department will fill in the requisition as shown below

---

MATERIALS REQUISITION

Material required for: _Job 3965_   **No: 296**
(job)

Department: _Toy production_   **Date:** _12 May 2006_

Quantity	Description	Code No	Price per unit	£
30	Blue plastic-coated fabric (1.8m wide)	B6309582		

Authorised by: ...... _J. Daniels_ ....

The price details and value will be filled in by the cost department prior to updating the stores ledger accounts and charging the relevant job/overhead/department.

A materials returned note will accompany any unused material back to stores. This will contain the same details as the materials requisition, and will be used as the source document to update the same records. This time, though, the material will be a receipt into stock and a deduction from the job originally charged with the material issued.

Activity 2

Explain the differences between a purchase requisition and a materials requisition.

STOCK VALUATION

The stores ledger accounts or cards record the value of materials purchased, and this information can be obtained from the purchase order and invoice. When goods are issued from stores, a value will need to be recorded on the stores ledger cards and on the costing details for the job or department that are going to bear that cost. The question is how do we value these issues if prices are changing regularly? Furthermore, how are the remaining stocks on hand valued? This is not just a costing problem; it is also something which is needed for the preparation of the financial accounts.

Some items can be specifically priced from an invoice as they are individual items, but for most materials that are bought in quantity and added to an existing stock, this is not possible, so one of the following methods can be used to estimate the cost.

FIFO (first in, first out)

This method assumes that the first items bought will be the first items issued. So, as items are issued, the earliest invoice prices are used up first, working forwards through to the latest prices. The stock on hand will always represent the later prices. This method is most appropriate in businesses where the oldest items are actually issued first, which is the case with perishable goods such as food. Even so, this is a very popular method in many types of business.

LIFO (last in, first out)

This method assumes that the most recent purchases are issued first, as might be the case if new deliveries were piled on top of existing stocks, and goods issued were picked from the top of the pile. Issues are valued at the latest prices, working back through the records. This will tend to value stock on hand at earlier prices.

AVCO (average cost)

With this method, a weighted average cost is calculated each time a new delivery is received. The weighting is provided by the number of units at each price brought into the calculation. The general formula is

$$\text{Average price per unit} = \frac{\substack{\text{Total value of} \\ \text{existing stock}} + \substack{\text{Total value of goods} \\ \text{added to stock}}}{\text{Units of existing stock + units added to stock}}$$

AVCO would be most appropriate if the stocks were to be mixed when they are stored, for example chemicals stored in a vat.

HOW IT WORKS: FIFO, LIFO and AVCO

Peregrine Pet Supplies sells doggy beds. The following transactions were recorded in September 2006.

Date	Transaction type	Quantity	Unit purchase/ selling price £
1 September	balance	50	10
3 September	purchase	100	12
6 September	sell	110	28
9 September	purchase	100	13
15 September	sell	80	29
21 September	purchase	100	14

What would be the

a)   cost of issues

b)   value of closing stock

c)   profit

in the month of September using FIFO, LIFO, and AVCO methods of valuation?

FIFO

Each time there is an issue of stock, in this case in order to sell it, we must calculate the cost of those items based upon the First In, First out assumption.

6 September sale   110 units

These will be valued as 50 @ £10 and the remaining 60 @ £12

Total =   £1,220

15 September sale   80 units

Of the £12 purchases there are still 40 left. Therefore the 80 units sold will be valued as 40 @ £12 and the remaining 40 @ £13.

Total =   £1,000

This can then all be recorded on the Stores Ledger Account as follows.

		Quantity (units)	Cost per unit	Value £
1 Sept	Opening balance	50	£10	500
3 Sept	Purchase	100	£12	1,200
Balance		150		1,700
6 Sept	Sell	110	50 @ £10 + 60 @ £12	(1,220)
Balance		40		480
9 Sept	Purchase	100	£13	1,300
Balance		140		1,780
15 Sept	Sell	80	40 @ £12 + 40 @ £13	(1,000)
Balance		60		780
21 Sept	Purchase	100	£14	1,400
Balance		160		2,180

a)   Cost of issues: in this case the goods are issued to be sold

= £1,220 + £1,000
= £2,220

b)   Value of closing stock. This is the value of the balance on hand at the bottom of the calculation = £2,180. Note that this represents the latest items to be bought, 100 @ £14 + 60 @ £13.

c)   Profit:

	£
Sales (110 @ £28 + 80 @ £29)	5,400
Less: cost of sales	(2,220)
Profit	3,180

Alternatively it can be calculated like this:

	£	£
Sales		5,400
Less: Cost of sales		
Opening stock	500	
Add: Purchases (1,200 + 1,300 + 1,400)	3,900	
	4,400	
Less: Closing stock	(2,180)	
		(2,220)
Profit		3,180

39

Given that we have already calculated the cost of the goods sold in part (a), it is less long winded to use the top method of calculating profit.

In the exam, the format for the FIFO Stores ledger account or Stock record card is as follows.

Stock Record Card								
	Purchases			Sales			Balance	
Date	Quantity	Cost £	Total cost £	Quantity	Cost £	Total cost £	Quantity	Total cost £
Balance at 1 Sept							50	500
3 Sept	100	12.00	1,200				150	1,700
6 Sept				50 60	10.00 12.00	500 720	40	480
9 Sept	100	13.00	1,300				140	1,780
15 Sept				40 40	12.00 13.00	480 520	60	780
21 Sept	100	14.00	1,400				160	2,180

LIFO

This time the cost of the goods that are sold on each occasion will be determined under the Last In, First Out assumption.

6 September sale   110 units

These will be valued as 100 units @ £12 and the remaining 10 units @ £10.

Total =   £1,300

15 September sale   80 units

Using the latest purchase price from the 9 September purchase these will all be valued at £13.

Total =   £1,040

Again this can be recorded as follows:

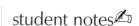

	Quantity (units)	Cost per unit	Value £
1 Sept Opening balance	50	£10	500
3 Sept Purchase	100	£12	1,200
Balance	150		1,700
6 Sept **Sell**	110	100 @ £12 + 10 @ £10	(1,300)
Balance	40		400
9 Sept Purchase	100	£13	1,300
Balance	140		1,700
15 Sept **Sell**	80	80 @ £13	(1,040)
Balance	60		660
21 Sept Purchase	100	£14	1,400
Balance	160		2,060

a) Cost of issues   = £1,300 + £1,040
             = £2,340

b) Value of closing stock = £2,060

Note that this is **not** the same as valuing at the earliest prices (50 @ £10 + 100 @ £12 + 10 @ £13 = £1,830). This is because we have already used up some of those earlier prices in costing the earlier issues.

c) Profit

	£
Sales (110 @ £28 + 80 @ £29)	5,400
Less: cost of sales	(2,340)
Profit	3,060

In the exam, the format of the LIFO Stores ledger account or Stock record card is as follows:

Stock Record Card								
	Purchases			Sales			Balance	
Date	Quantity	Cost £	Total cost £	Quantity	Cost £	Total cost £	Quantity	Total cost £
Balance at 1 Sept							50	500
3 Sept	100	12.00	1,200				150	1,700
6 Sept				100 10	12.00 10.00	1,200 100	40	400
9 Sept	100	13.00	1,300				140	1,700
15 Sept				80	13.00	1,040	60	660
21 Sept	100	14.00	1,400				160	2,060

AVCO

Under the AVCO method a weighted average price must be calculated after each purchase. This average price is then used to value the next issue or sale.

		Quantity (units)	Cost per unit	Value £
1 Sept	Opening balance	50	£10	500.00
3 Sept	Purchase	100	£12	1,200.00
Balance		150	£1,700/150 = £11.333	1,700.00
6 Sept	**Sell**	110	£11.333	**(1,246.63)**
Balance		40		453.37
9 Sept	Purchase	100	£13	1,300.00
Balance		140	£1,753.37/140=£12.524	1,753.37
15 Sept	**Sell**	80	£12.524	**(1,001.92)**
Balance		60		751.45
21 Sept	Purchase	100	£14	1,400.00
Balance		160		2,151.45

a) Cost of issues = £1,246.63 + £1,001.92
                    = £2,248.55

b) Value of closing stock = £2,151.45

c) Profit

	£
Sales (110 @ £28 + 80 @ £29)	5,400.00
Less: cost of sales	(2,248.55)
Profit	3,151.45

In the exam, the format of the AVCO Stores ledger acocunt or stock record card is as follows:

	Purchases			Sales			Balance	
Date	Quantity	Cost £	Total cost £	Quantity	Cost £	Total cost £	Quantity	Total cost £
Balance at 1 Sept							50	500
3 Sept	100	12.00	1,200				150	1,700
6 Sept				110	11.33	1,246	40	454
9 Sept	100	13.00	1,300				140	1,754
15 Sept				80	12.53	1,002	60	752
21 Sept	100	14.00	1,400				160	2,152

Stock Record Card

Activity 3

Complete the stores ledger account below using the figures calculated in the FIFO example above. (You can invent GRN and Requisition Note numbers.)

STORES LEDGER ACCOUNT

Stock item ___Doggy bed___   Maximum ___200___

Code ___D49802___   Minimum ___20___

Date	Receipts				Issues				Balance		
	GRN	Qty	Unit price £	£	Req No	Qty	Unit price £	£	Qty	Unit price £	£

Which valuation method should be used?

Reviewing the results obtained from each of the three methods used in the example above, we can compare the different answers.

	FIFO £	LIFO £	AVCO £
Issues	2,220	2,340	2,248.55
Closing stock	2,180	2,060	2,151.45
Profit	3,180	3,060	3,151.45

If costs are increasing, FIFO will give a higher profit than LIFO as issues, which form cost of sales, are at the earlier, lower prices. Closing stocks are higher under FIFO. AVCO, as you might imagine, falls somewhere between the other two methods. In the long term, over the life of the business, any such differences will disappear. all costs will eventually be charged against profit.

The choice of method is left to the management of the business, and this method should be used consistently from period to period. The advantages and disadvantages of each method should be taken into account, and these are summarised below.

FIFO

Advantages	Disadvantages
Reflects the usual usage pattern of stock: oldest items used/sold first	Managers may find it difficult to make comparisons and base decisions on prices that are constantly changing
Easy to calculate and understand	In times of rising prices, profits, and therefore the amount of tax payable, will be higher
Closing stock is valued at up-to-date prices	Issues are at out-of-date prices

LIFO

Advantages	Disadvantages
Issues are generally at up-to-date prices	As with FIFO, managers may find it difficult to make comparisons and base decisions on prices that are constantly changing
Managers are more aware of current prices as these are the ones charged to their department	The actual physical flow of goods is often the opposite of what is assumed in the LIFO calculations
Easy to calculate and understand	Some difficulties arise, as part-used batches at old costs will need to be carried in the stock records. These will result in issues at out-of-date prices when they are eventually used in calculations (when stocks fall to low levels)
	HMRC may not accept this method for tax computation as it tends to understate profit. The relevant accounting standard (SSAP 9) does not allow its use for reporting purposes as it bears little relationship to recent costs

AVCO

Advantages	Disadvantages
Fluctuations in prices are smoothed out, so that decision–making is easier	Calculations need to be to several decimal places
It is easier to use as there is no need to identify different batches separately	The resulting issue and stock values are rarely prices that actually existed
	If prices are rising, average prices tend to lag behind current prices

COST BOOKKEEPING FOR MATERIALS

We must now consider how the materials movements that have been recorded in the stores ledger account or stock record card are recorded in the costing bookkeeping accounts.

HOW IT WORKS

Given below is the stores ledger account for stock item BB24 which is a material used in the manufacture of a number of products made by Gilchrist Chemicals:

student notes✍️

STORES LEDGER ACCOUNT

Stock item _____BB24_____   Maximum _____400_____

Code _____BB2416C_____   Minimum _____50_____

Date	Receipts				Issues				Balance		
	GRN	Qty	Unit price £	£	Req No	Qty	Unit price £	£	Qty	Unit price £	£
1 May									100	4.00	400
5 May	6612	200	4.20	840					200	4.20	840
10 May					4172	100	4.00	400	300		1,240
						40	4.20	168			
						140		568	140		568
									160		672
15 May					4181	100	4.20	420	100		420
									60		252
21 May	6629	300	4.50	1,350					300		1,350
28 May									360		1,602
					4195	60	4.20	252	60		252
31 May									300		1,350

The materials movements are recorded in the MATERIALS CONTROL ACCOUNT at their valuation from the stores ledger account. We will start with the opening balance, a debit entry in the account, as it is an asset, the opening stock.

Materials control account

	£		£
1 May Opening balance	400		

Next each of the purchases in the period are entered as debits in the materials control account with the credit entry being to cash or creditors depending upon whether the purchase was on credit or not.

Materials control account

	£		£
1 May Opening balance	400		
5 May Bank/creditors	840		
21 May Bank/creditors	1,350		

Then the issues to production should be recorded. They are entered as a credit entry in the materials control account and a debit entry in the WORK IN PROGRESS CONTROL ACCOUNT. The work in progress control account is the account in which we are going to gather together all of the direct costs of production during the period, starting here with the materials cost.

Materials control account

		£			£
1 May	Opening balance	400	10 May	WIP	568
5 May	Bank/creditors	840	15 May	WIP	420
21 May	Bank/creditors	1,350	28 May	WIP	252

Work in progress control account

		£		£
10 May	Materials control	568		
15 May	Materials control	420		
28 May	Materials control	252		

Finally the materials control account can be balanced to show the closing balance at 31 May.

Materials control account

		£			£
1 May	Opening balance	400	10 May	WIP	568
5 May	Bank/creditors	840	15 May	WIP	420
21 May	Bank/creditors	1,350	28 May	WIP	252
			31 May	Closing balance	1,350
		2,590			2,590

Coding entries

One technique that is often used in the exam for Unit 6 is the requirement for students to code the accounting entries to be made for purchases of stock and issues of stock from the stores ledger account.

HOW IT WORKS

Using the stores ledger accounts from the previous example for stock item BB24 for Gilchrist Chemicals we will now **code** the ledger account entries to be made, rather than actually enter them into the ledger accounts. The codes for the cost ledger accounts are as follows:

1003	Materials control account
2005	Work in progress control account
3001	Creditors control account

We will assume that all purchases are made on credit.

The first purchase was made on 5 May - the entries for this purchase would be coded as follows:

		Dr £	Cr £
5 May	1003	840	
5 May	3001		840

This is a debit in the materials control account and a credit to the creditors control account.

The first issue is on 10 May:

		Dr £	Cr £
10 May	2005	568	
10 May	1003		568

A debit to work in progress and a credit to the materials control account.

The entries continue for the rest of the month:

		Dr £	Cr £
15 May	2005	420	
15 May	1003		420
21 May	1003	1,350	
21 May	3001		1,350
28 May	2005	252	
28 May	1003		252

This is a good method of testing your knowledge of the accounting entries for materials purchases and issues without the need for writing up ledger accounts.

Activity 4

Shrier Ltd receives £1,250 of raw materials on credit from its supplier. It issues £750 to production. The relevant codes are as follows:

Raw materials   500
Work in progress   600
Creditors   700
Cash   800

Complete the journal below to record these transactions.

JOURNAL

Code	DR (£)	CR (£)
1		
2		

Direct materials and indirect materials

We saw in the first chapter that materials, labour and expenses can be classified as either direct or indirect depending upon whether or not they relate to a specific unit of product or service. The importance of this distinction is that the direct materials are part of the cost of the units produced which is being gathered together in the work in progress control account, whereas the indirect materials are overheads which must be recorded separately in a PRODUCTION OVERHEAD CONTROL ACCOUNT.

HOW IT WORKS

During the month of June Gilchrist Chemicals made total purchases of materials of £71,400. Direct materials valued at £69,200 were issued to the factory for production and indirect materials for machine maintenance during the month were £3,600. At the beginning of June the total stock valuation was £7,300.

The materials control account is initially debited with the opening stock valuation and the purchases for the month.

Materials control account

		£		£
1 Jun	Opening balance	7,300		
30 Jun	Purchases	71,400		

The issues from stores must now be entered on the credit side of the materials control account. The direct materials are debited to the work in progress control account whilst the indirect materials are debited to the production overhead control account.

Materials control account

		£			£
1 June	Opening balance	7,300	30 June	Direct materials	
30 June	Purchases	71,400		– WIP	69,200
			30 June	Indirect materials	
				– Production o/h Control	3,600

Work in progress control account

		£		£
30 June	Materials control	69,200		

Production overhead control

		£		£
30 June	Materials control	3,600		

Finally the materials control account can be balanced to find the closing stock value. However we will not balance the other two accounts yet as there are more entries to be made to them in the next two chapters.

Materials control account

		£			£
1 June	Opening balance	7,300	30 June	Direct materials	
30 June	Purchases	71,400		–WIP	69,200
			30 June	Indirect materials	
				–Production o/h Control	3,600
			30 June	Closing balance	5,900
		78,700			78,700

Again in the exam this could be tested by requiring the entries to be coded rather than the accounts to be written up.

STOCK CONTROL

There are many different costs that can occur if a business keeps stock. These need to be controlled and kept to a minimum.

Holding costs

Costs associated with high stock levels. Examples of these are given below.

- Storage costs such as warehouse rent, storekeeper's wages, depreciation and other costs of storage equipment

- Cost of capital tied up: the price paid to buy or make the stock stored cannot be used for alternative purposes such as earning interest in a deposit account. This opportunity to invest is being lost and the interest thus foregone is therefore a cost to be brought into consideration

- Insurance

- Obsolescence and deterioration: if stock is kept for some time it may become out-of-date or damaged. These stocks may need to be sold at a reduced price or scrapped, and there may also be costs involved in disposing of them

- Security

Ordering costs

Ordering costs are more significant if stock levels are kept low and more orders have to be placed. Examples include the following.

- Administrative costs of placing an order: involving the purchasing department, accounts and goods receiving

- Transport inwards

Stock control

STOCK CONTROL is the regulation of stock levels so that the costs associated with stock are kept to a minimum. There are two main aspects to this.

1) Minimisation of the amount of stock held whilst still being able to deliver the goods on time to the user department or customer and subject to avoiding excessive ordering costs. This requires regular measurement of the amount of stock held in relation to the level of stock needed before an order needs to be placed. The minimum stock level is called 'buffer stock', as it acts as the buffer for the time between placing an order and receiving the stock (the **lead time**). Control limits of maximum and minimum stock levels will be set and

an optimal amount to order when stocks need replenishing will be calculated for each stock line

2) Minimisation of stock losses and discrepancies. This involves counting the stock on a regular basis and comparing the physical quantities with the stock records – stock cards and/or stores ledger accounts. Discrepancies revealed by this exercise would then be investigated and action taken where necessary to prevent further problems. Security is an important aspect of safeguarding stock.

Reordering stock

Small businesses may be able to review their stock levels on an informal basis and order what they judge to be the right quantity at the right time. Slightly more sophisticated than this is the **two-bin system**. This works on the basis that two bins are kept for each stock line. Stock is used from bin 1 until it is empty. At this point an order is placed for more stock and stock is now taken from bin 2. The new delivery, which should arrive just before bin 2 is empty, is placed in bin 1. An order is placed for more stock for bin 2 when that is empty, and then the process begins again.

More sophisticated methods rely on a manual or computerised **perpetual inventory system**. Earlier on we looked at stock ledger accounts and bin cards which are used in such a system. These records noted various details which would be used in deciding when stock should be ordered, and the appropriate quantity. Various formulae exist to help the business arrive at these figures.

REORDER LEVEL is the stock level that should trigger the placing of an order:

Reorder level = buffer stock + (budgeted usage × maximum lead time)

The rationale behind this formula is that an order will be placed as the amount in stock falls to the quantity that is expected to be used in the time between placing the order and receiving the goods (buffer stock). By basing the calculation on budgeted usage and maximum lead time, stock should never fall to zero.

HOW IT WORKS

Kite & Co sell 2,000 of their best selling stock line, the 'Aerobat', each year. They buy them in from a supplier at a cost of £13 each, and the costs of placing the order, delivery and receiving the goods into stock has been calculated as £250 per order. Kite & Co have also calculated that it costs £4 to hold one unit in stock for one year. Details of usage and lead time are tabulated below.

	Lead time (days)	Usage (sales per day)
Minimum	1	2
Average	3	8
Maximum	6	12

For Kite & Co the reorder level is 6 x 12 = 72 'Aerobats'. As soon as the stock of Aerobats falls to 72 units, more will need to be ordered, but how many should be ordered?

Activity 5

Burrows Ltd keeps stock of a fast-moving item, the mand. There is a time lag of 3 weeks whenever an order for mand is placed. The company plans to use 5,000 mands per week, and keeps a buffer stock of 2 weeks budgeted usage.

At what level of stock should mands be reordered?

ECONOMIC ORDER QUANTITY (EOQ) is the amount to order each time which will minimise total stockholding costs.

$$EOQ = \sqrt{\frac{2cd}{h}}$$

where c is the cost of placing an order
       d is the annual demand
       h is the cost of holding one unit in stock for one year

This formula aims to keep the costs to a minimum by finding the balance between order costs and the holding costs. If relatively few orders are placed each year, the ordering costs will be low, but this means holding larger quantities of goods and holding costs will be high. If more orders are placed for a smaller quantity of goods each time, ordering costs would rise, but holding costs would fall.

For Kite & Co the economic order quantity is:

$$EOQ = \sqrt{\frac{2 \times £250 \times 2,000}{£4}} = \sqrt{250,000} = 500 \text{ units}$$

So, each time stock is needed, 500 units will be ordered. This means that 4 orders will be placed each year to satisfy annual demand of 2,000 units.

Practical issues when ordering stock

In theory, the reorder level and EOQ should govern the ordering of stock. However, for practical reasons, other information often has to be taken into account.

We have seen that MINIMUM STOCK LEVEL or BUFFER STOCK is the level below which stock should not be allowed to fall as a general rule. It gives a buffer against unexpected demand or a problem with receiving an order in time, and aims to prevent stock-outs (running out of stock). One way of calculating this is given below.

> Buffer stock = reorder level – (average usage x average lead time)

For Kite & Co:

Minimum stock level $\ = 72 - (8 \times 3)$
$= 48$

Kite & Co hold a buffer stock of 48 units.

MAXIMUM STOCK LEVEL is the level above which stock cannot be allowed to rise. This is often due to a lack of storage space, so the space available will determine the maximum stock level. Alternatively, a formula can be used which assumes that the maximum amount that will be held in stock will arise when the minimum demand occurs in the minimum possible lead time. This will mean that when a new delivery is received there will still be a relatively large quantity of unused stock remaining.

> Maximum stock level = Reorder level + reorder quantity –
> (minimum usage x minimum lead time)

For Kite & Co:

Maximum stock level $= 72 + 500 - (2 \times 1)$
$= 570$

The maximum stock Kite & Co should need to accommodate is 570. If their storage space cannot hold this quantity they may need to adjust their reorder policy.

Activity 6

Kite & Co only have room for 520 'Aerobats' in stock at any particular time. Use the formula for maximum stock above to calculate a reorder quantity that would ensure this.

Just in time (JIT)

One way of avoiding stock holding costs and large areas of a business being given over to the storage of stock, is to adopt a JUST IN TIME STOCK POLICY. This requires materials to be delivered to the shop or production line just when they are needed so that no stock needs to be kept. It can also help in costing because a manufacturer can identify a specific batch of material or components delivered for a particular production run, eliminating the problems of FIFO, LIFO etc.

JIT does require a lot of investment in co-ordinating the supplies with manufacturing production schedules or sales in a shop, and it is very susceptible to supply problems such as might be experienced in bad weather. The correct type and quantity of materials have to be delivered; if the quantity and quality are inadequate there will be a breakdown in the system. Reliable suppliers of top quality goods located nearby are therefore an advantage.

STOCKTAKING

The second aspect of stock control is the minimisation of stock discrepancies. A major part of this is **stocktaking:** the counting of physical quantities of stock.

Periodic stocktaking is usually carried out once per year with all stock being counted on a particular day. Many businesses will use this method to actually establish a stock figure for their annual accounts as they do not keep a perpetual inventory.

Continuous stocktaking occurs on a year-round basis. A number of items are checked each week so that each stock line will have been checked over the period of one year, whilst valuable or high-turnover items are checked more often. This method is run alongside a perpetual inventory system as updated stock records are needed for checking. It also means that the stock value shown in the records can be used in the financial accounts without the disruption that is often caused by a periodic stocktake.

Stock discrepancies

A stock list will be completed by a stock checker, detailing the items checked and the quantities found in the stores. This is then compared with the bin card and stores ledger account. Differences may be due to a number of factors, but all of these should be investigated and the system tightened up where necessary, as suggested in the examples below.

- Clerical errors on the stock records. Regular stock checks by someone independent of the record-keeping department will help to prevent this. The error in the records will need rectifying

- Theft. Only authorised members of the stores department should be allowed in the stores. Stock numbers should be amended on the records to take account of the missing items

- Breakages. Correct storage and handling can reduce this. Again, the stock records should be amended

- Documentation incorrectly completed. If GRNs or materials requisitions etc have the wrong figures on them, the accounting records will be wrong. More careful counting of the stock involved and its recording on the document is required. The supervisor of the relevant department should check these amounts also

student notes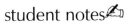

A stores credit note will be used to update the accounting records for a reduction in stock following the investigation of a stock discrepancy. A stores debit note is used for an increase in stock. An example of a stores credit note is shown below.

STORES CREDIT NOTE

Quantity	Stock code	Description	£

Date: ....

Authorised by: ....

Activity 7

Distinguish between perpetual inventory and continuous stocktaking.

CHAPTER OVERVIEW

- when materials are purchased by a business a number of documents are issued and processed:
  - purchase requisition identifying the need for the materials
  - purchase order sent from the purchaser to the supplier
  - delivery note or advice note accompanying the delivery of the materials
  - goods received note completed by the purchaser on delivery
  - invoice sent to the purchaser by the supplier

- materials can be made up of raw materials for use in production, work in progress and finished goods

- the quantity of each line of stock will often be recorded on a bin card – a stores ledger card is similar but this also includes the value of the stock held

- when materials are required from stores by a production or other department the user department will normally issue a materials requisition detailing the goods required

- the valuation of stock normally requires an assumption to be made regarding the valuation method – this will be FIFO, LIFO or AVCO

- stock movements are recorded in the materials control account

- direct materials issued to production are debited to the work in progress control account and indirect materials issued are debited to the production overhead control account

- when a business holds stocks it will incur two main types of costs – the holding costs of that stock and the ordering costs -- the purpose of stock control is to balance these two costs in order to minimise the overall cost of holding the stock

KEY WORDS

Purchase requisition a document raised by stores or a department which uses materials requesting a purchase of materials

Purchase order a document raised by the purchasing department and sent to a supplier to order the required materials

Delivery note or advice note a document raised by the supplier, accompanying the goods when they are delivered, which is signed by the goods inwards department for the supplier's records

Goods received note (GRN) a document raised in the goods inwards department to confirm the quantity and type of goods received and checked by them for the business's own records

Stock Goods held by the business as a current asset made up of raw materials, work in progress and finished goods

Perpetual inventory a continuously updated stock record system showing receipts, issues and the resulting balances of individual stock lines: **Bin cards** are usually maintained in the stores department and are in terms of quantity; **Stores ledger** cards are kept in the costing department and show values as well

Materials requisition a request for materials by the production department sent to the stores

FIFO (First in, first out) assumes that the earliest purchases or production is used first. Stock on hand is valued at the latest prices, issues at earlier prices

LIFO (last in, first out) assumes that the latest purchases are used first. Stock on hand is valued at earlier prices and issues are at the latest prices at the time of the issue

CHAPTER OVERVIEW cont.

- the reorder level for stock is calculated to ensure that the stock levels should never fall below zero during the lead time

- the economic order quantity is the amount that should be ordered when each order is placed to ensure the minimisation of the overall cost of holding stock

- often a business will set a minimum stock level or buffer stock level below which the stock level should not be allowed to fall

- a just in time stock policy is one favoured by some manufacturing businesses which ensures that the minimum stock levels are held by ensuring the correct quantity and quality of stocks are delivered at precisely the time that they are needed

- in order to control the stock that is held, businesses will regularly count their stocks and compare the physical quantity with the stock records – any discrepancies should be investigated and corrected

AVCO (average cost) a weighted average cost is calculated each time a delivery is received. Subsequent issues and stock on hand are valued at this cost

Holding costs costs of holding stock, such as storage costs, cost of capital tied up, insurance, obsolescence and security

Ordering costs costs of ordering materials, such as administrative costs and transport inwards

Stock control the regulation of stock levels so that the costs associated with stock are kept to a minimum

Reorder level the stock level that triggers the placing of an order

Lead time time taken from an order being placed to the goods arriving

Economic order quantity (EOQ) the amount to order each time in order to minimise stock holding costs

Minimum stock level or buffer stock the level below which stock should not be allowed to fall as a general rule

Maximum stock level the level above which stock cannot be allowed to rise

Just in time stock policy stock is received just when it is needed so that no stocks need to be held

Material control account cost ledger account where stock movements are recorded

Work in progress control account cost ledger account where all the direct costs of production are gathered

Production overhead control account cost ledger account for all production overheads

HOW MUCH HAVE YOU LEARNED?

1 List the details that would be found on a purchase order and explain their relevance.

2 Classify the following items as raw materials, work in progress or finished goods. (Tick the appropriate box.)

	Raw materials	WIP	Finished goods
Bricks at a brick-making factory	....	....	....
Bricks in stores at a building company	....	....	....
The ingredients for making bricks	....	....	....
A brick that has been moulded but not fired in the kiln	....	....	....

3 What is the materials requisition note used for?

4 Using the:

a) FIFO
b) LIFO
c) AVCO methods

calculate the cost of materials issues and the value of closing stock using the information below.

January 3	Balance	100 kg	Valued @ £8.80 per kg
January 16	GRN 423	400 kg	Invoiced @ £9 per kg
January 27	Materials requisition 577	250 kg	
February 5	Materials requisition 582	180 kg	
February 9	GRN 439	400 kg	Invoiced @ £9.30 per kg
February 17	Materials requisition 589	420 kg	
February 25	GRN 446	500 kg	Invoiced @ £9.35 per kg

5 What are the advantages and disadvantages of the LIFO method of valuing materials?

6 On 1 March a business has £12,400 of materials stocks. During March there were £167,200 of purchases and issues to production totalling £160,400. There were also £8,300 of indirect materials issued to the factory.

Write up the cost ledger accounts to reflect the month's transactions.

7 Give three examples each of holding costs and ordering costs. Explain what would happen to these costs if stock usage remained the same, but the reorder quantity increased.

8 Eagle Printing Company Limited print posters for which they buy paper on rolls. Each roll costs £12. Each week, 15 rolls are used; the company operates every week of the year. Each time an order for more rolls of paper is placed, it costs the company £50, and the estimated cost of storing one roll is £19.65 per annum.

You are required to calculate the economic order quantity.

9   Kestrel limited experiences a lead time of 4-8 days for orders of paint. Paint usage is between 150 and 200 litres per day. What would be a suitable reorder level?

chapter 3:
LABOUR COSTS AND EXPENSES

— chapter coverage 📖 —

This chapter looks at two other major costs: labour and expenses. In particular, how labour costs are calculated and documented. The topics to be covered are:

✍ the different ways employees can be paid

✍ the calculation of the gross pay of workers on different methods of remuneration

✍ how the hours each employee works is recorded

✍ recording payroll costs in the wages control account

✍ the various causes of expenses in a business

✍ how invoices for expenses are recorded to cost units

✍ depreciation

✍ accounting for direct and indirect expenses

Unit 6

knowledge and understanding – the business environment

3   maintaining an appropriate cost accounting system

knowledge and understanding – accounting techniques

4   recording of cost and revenue data in the accounting records

6   methods for and calculation of payments for labour

7   procedures and documentation relating to expenses

knowledge and understanding – accounting principles and theory

20   relationship between the labour costing system and the payroll accounting system

21   relationship between the accounting system and the expenses costing system

knowledge and understanding – the organisation

27   the sources of information for revenue and costing data

Performance criteria – element 6.1

A   identify direct costs in accordance with the organisation's costing procedures

B   record and analyse information relating to direct costs

C   calculate direct costs in accordance with the organisation's policies and procedures

E   resolve or refer queries to the appropriate person

LABOUR COSTS

Labour costs are amounts paid in respect of employees. We will mainly be talking about the gross pay of the employee, but don't forget that there are other costs which could be considered to be labour costs, such as employer's national insurance, training costs and benefits such as company cars. All employees will give rise to labour costs; office workers in administration departments, canteen staff, maintenance staff and supervisory staff are examples of **indirect labour** which is dealt with in detail in the next chapter. **Direct labour** costs arise from the employees that work directly on the goods produced by a manufacturing business, or employees that provide the service in a service business.

REMUNERATION METHODS

A number of different remuneration methods exist, the bases of which are given below. These are the simplest situations; combinations of these methods and variations on the basic ideas can lead to more complicated methods of remuneration.

Time rate (or day rate)

A time rate means that a basic amount is paid per hour worked.

> Wages = hours worked x basic rate of pay per hour

This method of remuneration is fairly simple to understand, and does not lead to complicated negotiations when rates of pay are being revised. It is appropriate if the quality of the output is more important than the quantity but it gives no incentive to improve performance. This is because workers will be paid so much per hour no matter how many they produce. A plus point for a time rate system is that workers will not feel that they have to rush, so quality can take priority.

If the hours worked exceed a pre-set maximum, OVERTIME is often paid at a higher rate. You may have heard the expression 'time and a half', which refers to overtime being paid at 1 ½ x basic rate.

In the Unit 6 exam, you may well be asked to calculate the total cost for labour, separating out the cost of hours at the basic rate from the hours of overtime premium paid. The overtime premium is simply the amount paid for an hours work less the basic rate for that hour.

HOW IT WORKS

Finch Limited pays overtime at time and a third for all complete hours worked over 35 hours per week. Peter is paid a basic wage of £6 per hour. During the week ending 24 March he worked a total of 39 hours. Work out Peter's total pay for the week.

	£
Basic (35 x £6)	210
Overtime (4 x £6 x 1 1/3)	32
Total pay for the week	242

The overtime pay in this illustration is £32. This comprises two elements.

a) The basic element is the basic pay rate x additional hours worked, in this case 4 hours x £6 = £24.

b) The OVERTIME PREMIUM is the extra paid on top of the basic rate for the additional hours worked. In this case the hourly premium is £6 x 1/3 = £2. The total overtime premium is therefore 4 hours x £2 = £8

In the exam the layout you should use is as follows:

	£
Pay at basic rate: 39 hours @ £6	234
Overtime premium: 4 hours @ £6/3	8
	242

This analysis is necessary as most (but not all) businesses treat the basic pay as a direct cost, but the overtime premium as an indirect cost for costing purposes. This way, all units produced are costed at the basic labour cost, irrespective of whether they were produced during normal working hours or at the weekend, for example, when overtime was being paid. There are, however, three situations where overtime premiums are included in the direct cost.

■ If the overtime is worked at the request of the customer so that his order can be completed within a certain time, the overtime premium will be a direct cost of that particular order

■ If overtime is normally worked in the production department, an average direct labour hourly rate can be calculated which will include the overtime premium which is generally incurred

■ If the examiner directs they should be included (as is normally the case in the exam)

Activity 1

Pauline is paid £10 per hour for a 37-hour week as an assembly worker. She is paid overtime at time and a half. Calculate the direct and indirect labour cost incurred if Pauline works for 41 hours in a particular week.

Piecework

With PIECEWORK, an amount is paid for each unit or task successfully completed, acting as an INCENTIVE to produce more. This method of remuneration can only be used in certain situations i.e. when there are specific, measurable tasks to be done which are not affected by other employees' performances.

DIFFERENTIAL PIECEWORK offers higher rates as production increases. For example, 5p per unit is paid for production of up to 2,000 units per week, rising to 7p per unit for 2001 to 3000 units, and so on.

Activity 2

Simon sews pockets in a tailoring factory. He is paid 10p for every pocket sewn up to a total of 4,000 in one week. Thereafter, he receives an extra 2p per pocket for every extra 500 he sews. One week he sews 4,730 pockets. What will his gross pay be in that week? What are the disadvantages of this type of piecework remuneration system?

Bonus systems

A BONUS SYSTEM involves the payment of a bonus if output is better than expected. This will be in addition to the normal time rate. The trigger for the payment of a bonus depends on the type of system that operates.

- A time-saved bonus is paid if the employee performs a task in a shorter time than the standard time allowed

- A discretionary bonus is paid if the employer judges that the employee deserves one

- A group bonus scheme pays a bonus to all workers who contributed to a successful job

- A profit-sharing scheme involves the payment of a proportion of the business's profits to employees, the size of the proportion paid often reflecting level of responsibility

This system can operate at all levels in any business, and can give an incentive for workers to produce more with the security of their basic time rate. As with piecework, though, a bonus system can be complex to calculate and will need quality control checks.

Salary

Employees on a monthly SALARY are paid one twelfth of their agreed annual salary each month. Overtime, bonuses and commissions on sales, for example, can be paid on top of this. Salaries tend to relate to indirect labour, such as office staff and supervisors. In the service sector, though, many salaried staff are a direct cost of providing the service, such as solicitors and accountants.

HOW IT WORKS

Osprey Fish Co. buys fresh fish, prepares the fish for sale in supermarkets and distributes its products throughout the UK using its own fleet of delivery vehicles.

Steven fillets the fish and is paid on the following basis:

	£ per fish
Trout	0.20
Haddock	0.24
Salmon	0.30

In the week ending 24 November, Steven filleted 290 trout, 480 haddock and 395 salmon.

Shirley is a mechanic for the delivery vehicles, who earns £9 per hour for a 40-hour week. She is paid overtime at time and a quarter, and earns a bonus of £5 for each job on which she makes a time saving of 5% or more on the standard time. In the week-ending 24 November she works a total of 43 hours and qualifies for bonus payments in respect of five jobs performed.

Patrick works in the sales office. His contract of employment specifies a 35-hour week and an annual salary of £15,000 per year. Any hours worked in excess of the contractual weekly amount are paid at Patrick's basic rate. In the month of November he works a total of 15 hours overtime.

The gross pay of each employee for the appropriate period is calculated as follows.

Steven: piecework

Week ending 24 November

Gross pay $= (290 \times £0.20) + (480 \times £0.24) + (395 \times £0.30)$
$= £291.70$

Shirley: time rate with overtime and time-saved bonus

Week ending 24 November

	£
Basic pay (40 hours x £9)	360.00
Overtime premium (3 hours x £9 x 1.25)	33.75
Bonus (5 jobs x £5)	25.00
Gross pay	418.75

Patrick: salary with overtime

November

	£
Basic salary (£15,000 / 12)	1,250.00
Overtime $\dfrac{£15,000}{35\,\text{hours} \times 52\,\text{weeks}}$ x 15 hours	123.63
Gross pay	1,373.63

In this case, we had to work out a basic hourly rate by dividing the annual salary by the total number of hours worked in a year under the contract. This was then used to work out how much Patrick could be paid for overtime.

Activity 3

For each of the statements in the table overleaf, one of the highlighted words will relate to time rates and the other to piecework rates. Write the appropriate word in the appropriate box.

	Time rate	Piecework rate
Easy/complicated to calculate an employee's pay	....	....
Can/can't be used for all direct labour employees	....	....
More efficient workers are paid **more than/the same as** less efficient workers	....	....
The quality of the goods produced **is/is not** affected by workers being tempted to rush a job so that they earn more	....	....
The employees' pay **fluctuates/remains the same** if output fluctuates	....	....
More supervisors/more inspectors may be needed for this system	....	....
Production problems **can/cannot** lead to a cut in pay	....	....
Systems **do/do not** need to be set up to check the amount of work produced by each employee	....	....

RECORDING LABOUR COSTS

Information on labour hours worked and rates of pay is needed by two departments. The payroll department needs to know so that the amount that each employee has earned can be worked out. The costing department needs to know so that the labour cost of each task or unit of product can be calculated.

The **personnel department** will maintain records of each employee's contract of employment and basic rate of pay. They will issue the payroll department with a list of employees and rates of pay. Computerised payroll systems will often have access to a database containing pay rates, piecework rates etc.

The time worked by each employee is recorded on various types of document, depending upon the nature of the job.

Attendance time records

Sometimes, all that needs to be recorded is the attendance of the employee at the place of work. This can be achieved by using one of the following.

- **Attendance record.** Essentially a calendar for an individual; a tick in the box recording the presence of the employee at work on that day. If absent, the reason (sickness, holiday etc) can be indicated.

- **Signing-in book.** This book will have a page for each employee, and is signed by the employee when entering or leaving the building, or when a break is taken. This allows a more accurate calculation of time worked.

- **Clock cards**. Each employee has a card which is entered in a time recording clock as work is commenced and finished. The time is recorded on the clock card which is then used for pay calculations. Computerised systems perform the same function by means of a plastic swipe card. The time is recorded by the computer rather than on the card.

A typical clock card would look like this:

Name		Week ending				
	Hours	**Rate £**	**Amount £**	**Deductions**		**£**
Basic				Income tax NI Other		
Overtime				Total deductions		
Total						
Less: deductions						
Net pay due						
Time	**Day**			**Basic time**		**Overtime**
Signature						

The time recording clock will stamp this part of the card

Payroll clerks will work out the hours worked and then the pay due

student notes ✍

Job costing

Where an employee works on more than one job in a day or a week, more detailed analysis of time worked needs to be recorded so that the jobs can be costed. Note that attendance time records will also, generally, be kept for payroll purposes.

- TIMESHEETS are used to record the time spent by an employee on each job that they have worked on. Timesheets are passed to the costing department daily (**daily timesheets**), or weekly if there are few job changes in a week (**weekly timesheets**). Timesheets are often used in the service sector, for example accountants will fill in a weekly timesheet showing the number of hours and the clients for whom they have performed accounting services during that week.

- JOB CARDS are prepared for each job or an operation on a larger job. The job card will describe the task to be performed. The employee will fill in the start and finish times of the job, and time out for any breaks. The card will be completed in the accounting department where the cost of that job can be calculated.

JOB CARD

Job No   824

Date

Time allowed   2 hours   **Start time**

Finish time

Job description	Hours	Rate	Cost £
Apply dark oak varnish to the exterior surfaces			

Employee number   ....

Employee signature   ....

Supervisor's signature ....

- **Route cards** are similar to job cards, but they detail all the operations to be carried out on a job, rather than just one, and will follow the job through to completion. As each operation is completed, the relevant employee will enter the time spent on it. The full cost of the job will gradually build up on the route card.

Job costing systems will be considered in more detail in Chapter 6.

Piecework

A **piecework ticket (or operation card)** is used to record the number of units produced in a piecework system. Piecework tickets are very similar to job cards, and are used for each operation to be performed on a batch of units. The worker will record the number of units completed, the number of rejects, and the number of good units; they will only be paid for good production. A supervisor and an inspector will be required to sign the ticket to validate the quantities.

THE WAGES CONTROL ACCOUNT

The source documents above will be used to compile the **payroll.** This is a record showing each employee's gross pay, net pay and deductions such as PAYE, National Insurance and pensions. There is also usually an analysis, which is used for cost accounting purposes. The payroll analysis can analyse gross pay by department, class of labour, product, and be broken down into various constituents such as direct, indirect and idle time. Idle time is time when employees are at work and being paid but they are not producing goods or services. This is normally treated as an indirect labour cost.

A wages control account is used to record the payroll costs. Obviously, the amount debited as the wages expense will be the gross pay, as this will be the cost to the business and the cost which needs to be used for costing purposes. However, the constituents of gross pay will be posted separately to the wages control account.

- Net pay is posted from the cash book.

- Deductions are debited with the credit entries being recorded in creditor accounts until the amounts are due to be paid to the Inland Revenue / pension scheme etc.

The credits to the wages control account are:

- direct labour (debited to WIP)

- indirect production labour (debited to a production overheads account)

- administration labour (debited to a non-production overheads account)

HOW IT WORKS

Returning to Gilchrist Chemicals from the previous chapter, the payroll records the following details for the month of June.

	£
Net pay	100,000
PAYE and NIC deductions	25,000
Contributions to company welfare scheme	15,000
Gross pay	140,000

The payroll analysis shows that £110,000 relates to direct labour, and £30,000 is for indirect labour.

These details are recorded in the wages control account as follows.

Wages control account

	£		£
Bank	100,000	WIP	110,000
HM Revenue & Customs	25,000	Production overheads	30,000
Welfare scheme			
contributions	15,000		
	140,000		140,000

The other sides of the entries are added to the materials entries in the work in progress control account and the production overheads control account.

Work in progress control account

		£		£
30 Jun	Materials control	69,200		
30 Jun	Wages control	110,000		

Production overhead control

		£		£
30 June	Materials control	3,600		
30 June	Wages control	30,000		

You will notice that the wages control account has no balance carried down on it as it simply shares out the total gross wage cost between direct and indirect labour costs. Again we will not yet balance the other two accounts as there is more to enter.

EXPENSES

Apart from materials and labour costs, all other costs are generally called expenses. To recap on what was covered in Chapter 1, expenses fall into different categories:

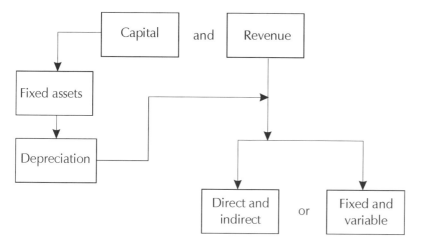

These classifications are important in costing as we deal with them in different ways when we calculate the cost of a product or predict how costs in general will change as output changes.

Activity 4

Briefly write down the meaning of the following terms, referring to Chapter 1 if necessary.

Capital expenditure _____

_____

Revenue expenditure _____

_____

Direct costs _____

_____

Indirect costs _____

_____

Variable costs _____

_____

Fixed costs _____

Types of expense

A business can have many different costs in addition to labour and materials. Various aspects of business operations cause these costs.

Buildings costs

- Rent, usually payable in advance according to a tenancy agreement

- Business rates, which are charges payable to the local authority, usually in April and October

- Buildings insurance, premiums being paid annually

- Depreciation of owned buildings

Buildings services

- Gas and electricity, payable quarterly and comprising a fixed or standing charge, and a variable charge based on energy consumption in the period

- Water rates

- Cleaning

- Repairs and maintenance

People-related costs

- Canteen costs
- Training
- Uniforms
- Health and safety

Machinery services

- Insurance
- Depreciation of owned machinery
- Hire of machinery
- Maintenance
- Fuel or power
- Cleaning

Communication and data processing

- Telephone bills: quarterly, with fixed rental and variable charge costs
- Internet charges
- Computer depreciation, insurance and maintenance
- Postage
- Stationery, including CDs and printer cartridges
- Annual subscriptions to trade or professional journals

Professional fees

- Audit and tax fees, paid annually
- Solicitors
- Market research
- Surveyors

Finance costs

- Interest and bank charges in respect of loans
- Finance charges on lease agreements for leased assets

Selling and distribution costs

- Advertising
- Salesmen's salaries and commission
- Cost of delivering goods to customers (Carriage outwards)
- Warehouse and storage costs of finished goods
- Running costs, depreciation etc of delivery vehicles

Initial recording

Expenses are generally billed by means of an invoice. When an invoice is received, it will be checked to any relevant purchase order or service contract and then coded. Direct expenses are coded to the product, job or contract to which they relate, for example subcontractors costs and plant hire relating to a particular job. In this way they are charged directly to cost units and are included in their cost. However direct expenses are relatively rare.

Most expenses are indirect and, together with indirect labour and materials, indirect costs form the group of costs that are referred to as **overheads**. Overheads may be essential for production, such as machine maintenance costs, but they cannot be coded in the same way as direct costs as they are not incurred in respect of products. They tend to be incurred in respect of a department, a group of machines or a group of people that perform a particular function within the business, and so indirect costs are coded to these. The collective term for sections of the business to which costs are charged is cost centres. The costs of the cost centres are then shared amongst the products that pass through that cost centre so that indirect costs are eventually included in the cost of making the products. This process warrants a more detailed explanation, and this is given in the next chapter.

Depreciation

Depreciation is an expense that is calculated internally so as to make a charge for the part of the cost of the fixed asset that has been used up in the period. It is usually an indirect expense, although if an asset is bought specifically for a particular job, the depreciation on that asset would be a direct cost of that job.

There are several ways of calculating depreciation, bearing in mind that the aim is to use an appropriate method to spread the cost of the asset over the periods benefiting from its use.

- The STRAIGHT-LINE METHOD charges the same amount for depreciation in each year of the asset's life. The formula for calculating the annual charge is:

$$\text{Annual charge} = \frac{\text{Cost} - \text{residual value}}{\text{Useful life (in years)}}$$

    The residual value of the asset is an estimate of the amount for which the asset can be sold at the end of its useful life. This represents part of the cost that is not used up and it should not be part of the charge. Obviously, the useful life is also an estimate.

- The REDUCING BALANCE METHOD charges more depreciation in the early years of an asset's life, and less in the later years. The idea is that more use is made of an asset in its earlier years when it is more efficient and has less "down time", and the amount charged will reflect the amount of use. The calculation requires a fixed percentage rate being applied to the net book value (cost − accumulated depreciation) of the fixed asset:

    Charge for the year = X% × (cost − accumulated depreciation)

    The business will choose the appropriate percentage.

- The MACHINE-HOUR METHOD aims to charge depreciation in proportion to the amount of use the asset has.

Charge for the year =

$$\frac{\text{Cost} - \text{residual value}}{\text{Total estimated hours of use}} \times \text{number of hours used in the year}$$

HOW IT WORKS

Owl Limited owns three fixed assets:

1) A freehold factory bought for £100,000, including land which accounted for £20,000 of this cost. The company plans to move to new premises in ten years' time, and estimates that the land will still be worth £20,000, but the factory building will only sell for £10,000. The company does not depreciate land, but uses the straight-line method for depreciating buildings.

2) Computer equipment which originally cost £12,000. The balance on the accumulated depreciation account at the beginning of the current year was £3,000. The reducing balance method of depreciation is used for this equipment, using a rate of 25%.

3) A production line which cost £180,000. The makers of this machinery estimate its useful life at 500,000 hours. During the year, the production line was used for 4,000 hours. The machinery can be sold for scrap at the end of its useful life for an estimated £10,000.

Calculation of the current year's depreciation on the three assets would be as follows.

Straight line method

Annual charge = $\dfrac{£80,000 - £10,000}{10}$

= £7,000

Reducing balance method

Charge for the year = 25% x (£12,000 – £3,000) = £2,250

Machine-hour method

Charge for the year $= \dfrac{£180,000 - £10,000}{500,000} \times 4,000$

$= £1,360$

ACCOUNTING FOR DIRECT AND INDIRECT EXPENSES

As was discussed earlier in this chapter most expenses incurred will be indirect expenses as they cannot be directly linked to a unit of production or service. Such indirect expenses related to production will be charged to the production overheads control account and the indirect expenses not related to production will be charged to a non-production overheads account.

However some expenses, such as hire of an item of machinery for a batch of production, or patent costs due for each unit of production, are direct expenses. These will be charged directly to the work in progress control account.

HOW IT WORKS

Gilchrist Chemicals have paid patent royalties for the month of June for the right to produce its products of £16,500. The business has also incurred £38,900 of indirect production expenses in the month. The patent expense is debited to the work in progress control account whereas the indirect expenses are debited to the production overheads control account.

Work in progress control account

		£		£
30 June	Materials control	69,200		
30 June	Wages control	111,000		
30 June	Bank	16,500		

Production overhead control

		£		£
30 June	Materials control	3,600		
30 June	Wages control	30,000		
30 June	Bank/creditors	38,900		

The final treatment of these accounts will be considered in the next chapter.

CHAPTER OVERVIEW

- remuneration methods generally fall into one of the following categories:

  - time rate
  - piecework
  - bonus system
  - salary

- employees record their attendance times on attendance records, signing-in books or clock cards

- job costing requires more detailed records of time spent on each job, and this is recorded on a timesheet, a job card or a route card

- piecework is recorded on a piecework ticket (or operation card)

- direct expenses are charged to the cost units i.e. product, job, process or contract in respect of which they are incurred. Indirect expenses are charged to cost centres

- The objectives of depreciation accounting are:

  - to make a charge for the cost of the fixed asset used in the period

  - to spread the capital cost of the asset over the periods in which the asset is used

- acceptable methods of depreciation are:

  - the straight line method
  - the reducing balance method
  - the machine-hour method

- direct expenses are charged to the work in progress control account

- indirect production expenses are charged to the production overheads control account

KEY WORDS

Time rate a basic amount per hour is paid

Overtime a higher rate of pay if hours worked in a week exceed a pre-set limit

Overtime premium the additional cost of overtime hours above the basic rate

Piecework an amount is paid for each unit or task successfully completed

Differential piecework the piecework rate increases for additional units over and above a pre-set quantity

Idle time when work cannot be done because of problems with machinery breakdown or shortage of materials, for example

Bonus system the payment of an amount in addition to the time rate or salary if a target is exceeded

Salary the payment of a set amount at agreed intervals, usually weekly or monthly

Clock card a card for each employee that records the start and finish times of periods of work

Timesheet a form completed by an employee detailing the time spent on each client's work each day, or week

Job card details the task to be performed on a particular job, and follows the job round; each employee records the time spent on their operation on the job

Cost centre a section of the business to which overheads can be charged

Straight-line method a method of depreciation that charges the same amount each period

Reducing balance method a method of depreciation which charges more depreciation in the earlier years of a fixed asset's life

Machine-hour method a method of depreciation that charges depreciation in proportion to the amount of use the asset has in the period

HOW MUCH HAVE YOU LEARNED?

1   The piecework rate for milling each unit is 14p. Calculate Mary Dunnock's gross pay for the
    week ended 7 July 2006 by completing her operation card.

OPERATION CARD

Operator	Mary Dunnock	**Works order No**	1492
Clock No	16	**Part No**	233
Week ending	7.7.06	**Description**	Wooden lids

Operation Sanding top and bottom surface using grade 2 sandpaper

Quantity produced	Quantity rejected	Good production	Rate £	£
Monday 350	12			
Tuesday 428	21			
Wednesday 483	2			
Thursday 376	14			
Friday 295	18			

Employee number ....LGS................   Date ...7.7.06.............

Employee signature ....PGL..................

Supervisor's signature ....M Dunnock.....

2 Cockerel Breakfast Cereals Limited pays a time rate of £7 per hour for a 35 hour week. Overtime is paid at time and a half for time worked in excess of 7 hours on weekdays, and double time for any work done at the weekend.

Calculate the gross pay of the employees whose clock card information is summarised below.

	Hours worked			
	J Sparrow	K Finch	M Swallow	B Cuckoo
Monday	7	7	7.25	7
Tuesday	7	8	7	7
Wednesday	7.5	7	7.5	7
Thursday	8	8	7.5	7.5
Friday	7	7.5	7.5	7
Saturday	3		2	2

3 Norman Gander is a direct worker who operates a lathe. During one week he works 40 hours, 35 of which are paid at a time rate of £10 per hour, the remainder being overtime which is paid at a premium of £4 per hour. Calculate the direct and indirect labour cost.

4 Explain how a business can remunerate employees so as to give them an incentive to produce more. What are the drawbacks of such schemes?

5 Heron Limited has bought a new machine costing £20,000. It should give 40,000 hours of use and is expected to be useful for eight years, after which it could be scrapped for £1,000. In its first year in the business it is used for 8,000 hours.

Heron Limited is trying to decide upon an appropriate method of depreciation. It uses the 20% reducing balance method for some of its machinery, and the straight-line method for the rest. For the first time the company is considering the machine-hour method. Calculate the first year's depreciation using the three methods under consideration and suggest which is the best for costing purposes if the use of the machine tends to reduce as it begins to break down more.

chapter 4:
OVERHEADS

chapter coverage 📖

Finding the indirect cost of output is not as straightforward as the direct cost. This chapter examines ways in which this can be done. The topics that are to be covered are:

✍ the approach used in absorption costing: allocation, apportionment and absorption of overheads

✍ how service cost centre overheads are dealt with

✍ the treatment of under- and over- absorbed overheads

✍ accounting for absorption of overheads

✍ non-production overheads

Unit 6

knowledge and understanding – the business environment

3   maintaining an appropriate cost accounting system

knowledge and understanding – accounting techniques

4   recording of cost and revenue data in the accounting records

8   bases of allocating and apportioning indirect costs to responsibility centres: direct and step down methods

10   the arbitrary nature of overhead apportionments

11   bases of absorption

Performance criteria – element 6.2

A   identify overhead costs in accordance with the organisation's procedures

B   attribute overhead costs to production and service cost centres in accordance with agreed bases of allocation and apportionment

C   calculate overhead absorption rates in accordance with agreed bases of absorption

D   record and analyse information relating to overhead costs in accordance with the organisation's procedures

E   make adjustments for under and over recovered overhead costs in accordance with established procedures

F   review methods of allocation, apportionment and absorption at regular intervals in discussions with senior staff and ensure agreed changes to methods are implemented

G   consult staff working in operational departments to resolve any queries in overhead cost data

ABSORPTION COSTING

From previous chapters, we know that OVERHEADS is the collective term for indirect materials, indirect labour and indirect expenses. Overheads tend to be grouped as to their function.

- **Production (or factory) overheads** include indirect materials, indirect factory wages, factory rent and rates, and power and light used in the factory

- **Non-production overheads:**

  - **Administration overheads** include office rent and rates, office salaries, indirect office materials and depreciation of office equipment that is used for administration (rather than the main activity of the business)

  - **Selling and distribution overheads** include delivery costs, salaries of sales staff and depreciation of delivery vehicles

  - **Finance overheads** are bank interest and charges

In most cost accounting systems the aim will be to find the full production cost of the cost units. This means that a method has to be found of including the **production overheads** in the cost of each cost unit. Be clear that we are only dealing with production overheads at this stage. Non-production overheads will be dealt with later in the chapter.

If you study the examples of production overheads above, you will appreciate the problem that the cost accountant has. None of these costs is directly attributable to a cost unit, but unless they are included in the cost of producing cost units production costs will be underestimated which may lead, for example, to selling prices being set too low.

ABSORPTION COSTING(sometimes called full costing) is one way of finding an appropriate amount of overhead per cost unit so that the total cost of producing a product or job can be found.

The first stage in the process is that all of the production overheads must be shared out amongst the relevant cost centres. Some cost centres will be PRODUCTION COST CENTRES such as the assembly department or finishing department where the cost units are actually produced. However, production overheads will also be incurred by SERVICE COST CENTRES which are areas of the business which support the production of the cost units such as stores, canteen maintenance etc.

Once all of the overheads have been allocated or apportioned to each of the relevant production and service cost centres **the next stage** is to take the service cost centre overhead totals and share these amongst the production cost centres in some fair manner. Now all of the production overheads are included in the production cost centres.

The final stage is to absorb the production cost centre overheads into the units produced during the period.

This process is summarised in the diagram below.

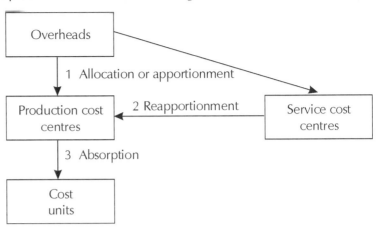

Stage 1: allocation and apportionment

ALLOCATION of overheads is the charging of an overhead to a single cost centre that has incurred the whole of that overhead. For example, the cost of a supervisor could be allocated to the department supervised and the depreciation of the warehouse could be allocated to the warehouse directly.

APPORTIONMENT of overheads is the charging of a proportion of an overhead to each cost centre that incurs part of the overhead. Rent of a business premises might need to be shared between the various departments making up the business, for example. Apportionment should be done so that the share charged to a cost centre reflects its usage of that overhead. This means that each type of overhead needs to be considered separately to find a suitable basis. Examples of commonly used methods are given in the table below.

Overhead	Suitable basis for apportionment
Buildings costs such as rent, rates, repairs, insurance, heating, lighting and depreciation	Floor area or volume of space occupied by the cost centre
Canteen costs	Number of employees using the cost centre
Equipment costs such as insurance and depreciation	Cost or net book value of equipment
Maintenance costs	Amount of usage of maintenance department

In the exam, there are usually costs to be allocated directly as well as costs to be apportioned across departments in line with usage, calculated on a 'suitable basis' as set out above.

Activity 1

Rose Ceramics Limited rents office premises and owns a factory and a warehouse. There are four cost centres in the factory, the factory offices are the fifth cost centre, and the warehouse forms a sixth.

On 25 January, several invoices were received for overheads. For each of these decide:

a) whether the cost would be allocated or apportioned
b) the cost centre(s) to be charged
c) a suitable basis if apportionment is required

Overhead	a) **Allocate or apportion?**	b) **Cost centre(s) charged?**	c) **Basis of apportionment?**
Factory light & heat	....	....	....
		....	....
Rent	....	....	....
		....	....
Factory rates	....	....	....
		....	....
Office stationery	....	....	....
		....	....
Cleaning of workers' overalls	....	....	....
		....	....
Roof repair to warehouse	....	....	....
		....	....

HOW IT WORKS: overhead apportionment

Bluebell Electronics Limited produces electronic equipment for the broadcasting industry. Certain components are made in the components shop; others are bought-in and are kept in the Stores, along with various raw materials; the equipment is assembled in the Assembly department. The Maintenance department is responsible for the upkeep of the machines. The company is preparing its budget for the forthcoming period and forecasts overheads of £51,950 as follows.

	Total £	Components shop £	Assembly depth £	Stores £	Maintenance £
Indirect wages	19,050	4,700	10,300	1,900	2,150
Indirect materials	15,400	9,400	2,500	3,500	
Supervisor's wages	2,500				
Rent and rates	6,300				
Heat and light	3,200				
Buildings insurance	500				
Depreciation of machinery	5,000				
	51,950				

Additional information:

Floor area (sq metres)	500	250	150	50	50
Net book value of machinery	£50,000	£40,000	£5,000	£2,000	£3,000
Supervisor's time in the department (hours per week)	40	30	10		
Number of employees	17	9	4	2	2

How are these costs distributed to the four cost centres?

- Indirect wages and indirect materials have been incurred by each department individually, and have already been allocated. Bluebell Electronics will have been able to identify these costs separately from clock cards and materials requisitions.

- Supervisor's wages can be apportioned on the basis of the time spent in each cost centre, a 30:10 split between components shop and assembly.

- Rent and rates, heat and light and buildings insurance can be apportioned on the basis of floor area as details of volume occupied is not available; we can assume that all departments are housed in the same building and that the ceiling is at a uniform height. The split will be 250:150:50:50. You can apportion each cost given separately, or save time by doing all three costs together, as shown below.

- Depreciation of machinery will be based on the net book value of the machinery, giving a 40:5:2:3 split.

The final overhead apportionments for each cost centre can now be built up.

	Total	Components shop	Assembly depth	Stores	Maintenance
	£	£	£	£	£
Indirect wages	19,050	4,700	10,300	1,900	2,150
Indirect materials	15,400	9,400	2,500		3,500
Supervisor's wages **30:10**	2,500				
30/40 x 2,500		1,875			
10/40 x 2,500			625		
Rent and rates	6,300				
Heat and light	3,200				
Buildings insurance.	500				
250:150:50:50					
250/500 x £10,000		5,000			
150/500 x £10,000			3,000		
50/500 x £10,000				1,000	
50/500 x £10,000					1,000
Depreciation of machinery					
40:5:2:3	5,000				
40/50 x £5,000		4,000			
5/50 x £5,000			500		
2/50 x £5,000				200	
3/50 x £5,000					300
Total	51,950	24,975	16,925	3,100	6,950

Stage 2: reapportionment

The initial allocation or apportionment will be to production and service cost centres. The next step is to reapportion the overheads of the service cost centres to production cost centres. This is achieved by considering the relative amount of use made of the service department by the production departments. So, if production department A (PA) has twice as many workers using the canteen as production department B (PB), canteen costs could be split between PA and PB in the ratio 2:1. The only complication that can arise is when service cost centres reciprocate, i.e. they perform services for other service cost centres as well as production cost centres. Thus, when reapportionment is carried out more costs will be given to the service departments that we are trying to empty of their costs.

There are various methods which can be used for the reallocation of service department costs; the two required for Unit 6 are:

- **direct apportionment** is suitable if the service cost centres only provide services for production cost centres. Service cost centre costs are only reapportioned to production cost centres. (This is the method that has most recently appeared in the exam.)

- **the step-down method** is appropriate if there is some reciprocation. Reapportionment is performed in a particular order so that, once the costs of a service cost centre have been reapportioned, no further costs are allocated to it.

HOW IT WORKS: reapportionment

If we continue with the example of Bluebell Electronics Limited, we can look at each method individually and see how the reapportionment is achieved.

Direct reapportionment

Suppose the Maintenance and Stores departments do no work for each other. This enables us to use the direct method as all the service department costs are incurred in servicing the production departments. All we have to do is find a suitable basis for reapportioning each service cost centre's costs. For Stores, the number or value of materials requisitions could be used. For Maintenance, we could use the number of hours worked or the value of machinery.

Budgeted use of service cost centres.

	By the Component shop	By the Assembly department
Number of materials requisitions from Stores	750	200
Maintenance hours required	300	120

The final apportionment to production cost centres will be as follows.

	Total £	Components shop £	Assembly depth £	Stores £	Maintenance £
Overheads	51,950	24,975	16,925	3,100	6,950
Reapportion maintenance 300 : 120		**4,964**	**1,986**		**(6,950)**
					–
Reapportion stores 750 : 200		**2,447**	**653**	**(3,100)**	
				–	
	51,950	32,386	19,564		

The total overheads of £51,950 have been apportioned to the two production cost centres, and the figures are now ready for the third stage of the process of finding the overhead cost per unit.

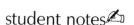

Activity 2

Jaques Ltd has three cost centres, A, B and C (which is a service centre, providing equal services to A and B). Overheads incurred in May are as follows:

		To be apportioned
Electricity	£15,000	3:2:1
Rent	£12,000	6:3:1
Supervision	£5,000	1:1:0
Licence for Service Centre C	£2,000	n/a

Using direct reapportionment calculate the total overheads for A and B.

Cost centre	Basis used	A £	B £	C £	Total £
Electricity					15,000
Rent					12,000
Supervision					5,000
Licence		___	___	___	2,000
Reapportion C		___	___	( )	
Total		═══	═══	0	34,000

The step-down method

This time, let's assume that Maintenance makes use of Stores by requisitioning spare parts for machinery and other materials, but Stores does not use the services of Maintenance at all.

Budgeted use of service cost centres.

	By the Component shop	By the Assembly department	By maintenance
Number of materials requisitions from Stores	750	200	50
Maintenance hours required	300	120	

The step-down method is appropriate in this case, which means that we must give some thought to which department is reapportioned first. If we empty Maintenance first, when we reapportion Stores' costs we will put some costs back into Maintenance, as a charge for the services provided by Stores. Therefore, it is more efficient to do Stores first, and then Maintenance, as no further reapportionment will be necessary.

	Total	Components shop	Assembly depth	Stores	Maintenance
	£	£	£	£	£
Overheads	51,950	24,975	16,925	3,100	6,950
Reapportion stores 750 : 200 : 50		2,325	620	(3,100)	155
				–	7,105
Reapportion maintenance 300 : 120		5,075	2,030		(7,105)
					–
	51,950	32,375	19,575		

Stage 3: Absorption

Overhead absorption is the way that overheads are charged to output. This is also known as **overhead recovery.** An OVERHEAD ABSORPTION RATE or **overhead recovery rate** is calculated so that each time a cost unit passes through the production cost centre, it is charged with a certain amount of overheads. The aim is for all the overheads incurred over a particular time to be absorbed into cost units made in that period.

The overhead absorption rate is calculated in advance based on the budgeted overheads and the budgeted level of activity. Activity can be expressed in a number of ways: hours worked, machine hours used, costs incurred or units produced, and any of these can be used to calculate the absorption rate. This will have an effect on how the overheads are charged to output. If hours worked is used, then each time an hour is worked, production will be charged with a portion of the overheads; if machine hours is the basis, then for each hour a machine is used, production will be charged with a portion of overheads. For Unit 6 the bases of absorption to be considered are labour hours and machine hours.

Rate per direct labour hour $\dfrac{\text{Overheads}}{\text{Direct labour hours}}$

Rate per machine hour $\dfrac{\text{Overheads}}{\text{Machine hours}}$

HOW IT WORKS: absorption

Bluebell Electronics makes two products, the Videobooster and the Blastbox. It is trying to decide on an appropriate basis for the absorption of overheads. The following budgeted information is provided.

Production units	Videobooster 4,000		Blastbox 6,000	
	Components shop £	Assembly £	Components shop £	Assembly £
Direct labour:				
hours per unit	1.25	0.5	2	1
total hours	5,000	2,000	12,000	6,000
Machine hours				
per unit	2	1	0.3	0.2
total hours	8,000	4,000	1,800	1,200

Calculate:

a) separate departmental overhead absorption rates using first labour hours and then machine hours as the absorption basis

b) the overhead absorbed by each product under each of the overhead absorption bases.

Note. The final apportionment of overheads to the two production cost centres was: Components shop, £32,375; and Assembly, £19,575.

a) Departmental absorption rates

	Components	Assembly

Rate per direct labour hour

$$\frac{\text{Overheads}}{\text{Direct labour hours}} = \qquad \frac{£32,375}{5,000 + 12,000} \qquad \frac{£19,575}{2,000 + 6,000}$$

$$= \qquad £1.90 \text{ per direct labour hour} \qquad £2.45 \text{ per direct labour hour}$$

Rate per machine hour

$$\frac{\text{Overheads}}{\text{Machine hours}} = \qquad \frac{£32,375}{8,000 + 1,800} \qquad \frac{£19,575}{4,000 + 1,200}$$

$$= \qquad £3.30 \text{ per machine hour} \qquad £3.76 \text{ per machine hour}$$

b) The overhead absorbed by each product

Rate per direct labour hour

	Videobooster	£	Blastbox	£
Components shop	£1.90 x 1.25h	2.38	£1.90 x 2h	3.80
Assembly	£2.45 x 0.5h	1.23	£2.45 x 1h	2.45
Total absorbed per unit		3.61		6.25

Rate per machine hour

	Videobooster	£	Blastbox	£
Components shop	£3.30 x 2h	6.60	£3.30 x 0.3h	0.99
Assembly	£3.76 x 1h	3.76	£3.76 x 0.2h	0.75
Total absorbed per unit		10.36		1.74

Which absorption rate should you use?

As you can see from the example above, the type of absorption rate used can have a huge effect on the cost of a product; the amount of overhead absorbed into the Blastbox varied from £1.74 to £6.25! It is therefore important to consider very carefully which rate is appropriate for each department. The way in which the cost is incurred can guide us towards the best method.

- A rate per direct labour hour would be appropriate if the department is labour intensive and most of the overheads relate to labour (this may apply to Bluebell's assembly department).

- A rate per machine hour is a fair method if the department is largely mechanised, with relatively little labour input (perhaps Bluebell's component shop).

The methods chosen for each department should be reviewed on a regular basis. This is because production methods or products might change, and the existing overhead absorption method may no longer be the best one.

The examiner will give a very clear hint in the question as to whether or not the enterprise is highly mechanised (in which case a machine hour rate should be used).

HOW IT WORKS

If we use the labour hour basis for absorption of Bluebell's assembly department and the machine hour basis for the components shop the overheads charged to each product will now be

	VideoBooster	Blastbox
Components shop	6.60	0.99
Assembly	1.23	2.45
Total	£7.83	£3.44

Activity 3

Cactus Limited has 2 production departments, X and Z, which make several different products. Budgeted overheads apportioned to each department are estimated at X £20,000 and Z £40,000. Total labour hours for the budgeted period are expected to be X 4,000 and Z 16,000. Budgeted machine hours are X 12,000 and Z 100

Calculate:

a)   separate departmental absorption rates based on labour hours
b)   separate departmental absorption rates based on machine hours
c)   comment on your results

The arbitrary nature of overhead apportionment

One of the major criticisms of absorption costing is the difficulty of achieving a totally fair overhead cost in each cost unit. Even if the bases for apportionment and absorption are carefully considered, a precise result is not possible.

UNDER- AND OVER-ABSORPTION OF OVERHEADS

The overhead cost of output is found using the budgeted overhead costs for the period and the budgeted activity level. The calculations are performed in advance of the costs actually being incurred, partly because of the nature of overheads: they are often incurred in relation to time periods and there are often agreements and contracts entered into in advance. Predicting overhead costs is also needed so that selling prices can be set in advance and to enable control of costs by investigating variances between actual overheads and budgeted figures.

But using budgeted figures means that the actual overhead cost is unlikely to be the same as the overheads absorbed into production, as we are relying on two estimates:

- overhead costs
- activity levels

These will inevitably differ from the actual values that are experienced during the period. Consequently, at the end of the period when the profit and loss account is drawn up, the profit figure will be wrong as the overhead charge will be the absorbed amount rather than the actual amount. The error in the profit figure results from one of two possibilities.

1) If more overheads are absorbed than have actually been incurred, this is known as OVER-ABSORPTION.

2) If fewer overheads are absorbed than have actually been incurred, this is known as UNDER-ABSORPTION.

The amount over- or under- absorbed is adjusted for in the profit and loss account after the production cost has been charged. Under-absorption means that too little overhead has been charged in the production cost, so a deduction is made from profit. Over-absorption means that too much overhead has been charged, so there is a compensating addition to profit..

HOW IT WORKS

Cowslip Limited budget to make and sell 10,000 units of their product in each of the next three months. They will be sold for £20 each and direct costs per unit are £6. Budgeted overheads are £15,000 per month, which is recovered using a rate per machine hour basis. Each unit requires 3 hours of machine time, the budgeted machine hours being 30,000. Actual overheads over the next three months are:

	£
February	15,000
March	14,000
April	16,000

All other actual costs, revenues and quantities are as budgeted (i.e. only the overheads incurred differ from budget).

$$\text{The overhead absorption rate will be} = \frac{\text{Overheads}}{\text{Machine hours}}$$

$$= \frac{£15,000}{10,000 \text{ units} \times 3\text{h per unit}}$$

$$= £0.50 \text{ per machine hour}$$

Firstly, **in February**, the actual and budgeted overheads are the same at £15,000.

Profit and loss account for February

	£
Sales (10,000 x £20)	200,000
Less production cost of sales	
direct costs (10,000 x £6)	(60,000)
overheads (30,000 h x £0.50)	(15,000)
Profit	125,000

A comparison of actual overheads and absorbed overheads will show that the two are the same:

	£
Actual overheads	15,000
Absorbed overheads (10,000 units x £1.50)	15,000
Under/over absorption	Nil

In March, however, actual overheads are lower than budget, at £14,000. The production cost charged in the profit and loss account will still be the same, as the same number of machine hours have been used. But we can't leave profit at the same level as before: the overheads are £1,000 less than were budgeted for, so we should have a profit of £1,000 more. By including 30,000 machine hours at a cost of £0.50 per hour in the profit and loss account, we have absorbed more overheads than were actually incurred, which is an over absorption.

	£
Actual overheads	14,000
Absorbed overheads (30,000h x £0.50)	15,000
Over absorption	1,000

This is credited to the profit and loss account.

Profit and loss account for March

	£
Sales (10,000 x £20)	200,000
Less production cost of sales	
direct costs	(60,000)
overheads	(15,000)
	125,000
Add over absorption of overheads	1,000
Profit	126,000

In April actual overheads are £16,000

	£
Actual overheads	16,000
Absorbed overheads (30,000h x £0.50)	15,000
Under absorption	1,000

The under-absorbed overheads will be debited to the profit and loss account. Under-absorption means that not enough overheads have been charged against profits, so we deduct the under absorption from profit to make up for this.

Profit and loss account for April

	£
Sales	200,000
Less: production cost of sales	
direct costs	(60,000)
overheads	(15,000)
	125,000
Less: under absorption of overheads	(1,000)
Profit	124,000

Note be very careful to calculate the under or over absorption based on actual v absorbed costs; budgeted costs are not brought in to this calculation. This is particularly relevant when the actual amounts of both overheads and activity are different from budget.

Let's say that **in May**, the number of units produced and sold by Cowslip Limited is 12,000, machine hours amounted to 38,000 and overheads actually incurred amount to £16,500. So this time both overheads and activity level are different from budget.

Calculate the overhead under- or over-absorbed as before, being careful to pick up the correct figures (highlighted).

	£
Actual overheads	**16,500**
Absorbed overheads (**38,000**h x £0.50)	19,000
Over absorption	2,500

The profit calculation will take account of the over absorption.

Profit and loss account for May

	£
Sales (12,000 x £20)	240,000
Less: production cost of sales	
direct costs (12,000 x £6)	(72,000)
overheads absorbed (38,000h x £0.50)	(19,000)
	149,000
Add: over absorption of overheads	2,500
Profit	151,500

Activity 4

Tulip Limited planned to make 30,000 units, each of which was expected to require 2 hours of direct labour. Budgeted overheads were £54,000. Actual production was 28,000 units, requiring a total of 55,000 direct labour hours. Actual overheads were £47,000.

Calculate:

a) The overhead absorption rate based on direct labour hours; and

b) The under- or over-absorption, stating whether this would be an addition to, or a deduction from, profit.

ACCOUNTING FOR OVERHEAD ABSORPTION

We have now seen the process necessary to calculate the Overhead Absorption Rate based upon budgeted overheads and budgeted activity levels. We have also seen how the profit and loss account is adjusted for any eventual under or over absorption.

Now we must take a step back and see how the amount of overhead to be absorbed is actually included in the cost ledger accounts. The accounting is straightforward and logical. The absorbed overhead is part of the production cost of the cost units and therefore it is **debited** to the work in progress control account together with the direct materials, direct labour and any direct expenses incurred, to give the total production cost for the period. The **credit entry** is to the production overhead control account which will have been debited with the actual overhead incurred. Any balance on the production overhead control account is the transfer to the profit and loss account as under or over absorbed overhead.

HOW IT WORKS

We will return to the cost ledger accounts of Gilchrist Chemicals where both the work in progress control account and production overhead control account were not yet completed for the month of June.

Work in progress control account

	£		£
30 June Materials control	69,200		
30 June Wages control	110,000		
30 June Bank	16,500		

Production overhead control

	£		£
30 June Materials control	3,600		
30 June Wages control	30,000		
30 June Bank	38,900		

The debits in the production overhead control account are the actual overheads incurred during the month. You are now told that the amount of overhead to be absorbed into production based upon the overhead absorption rate is £75,000.

This must be debited to the work in progress control account and credited to the production overhead control account.

Work in progress control account

	£		£
30 June Materials control	69,200		
30 June Wages control	110,000		
30 June Bank	16,500		
30 June Production o/h	75,000		

Production overhead control

	£		£
30 June Materials control	3,600	30 June WIP	75,000
30 June Wages control	30,000		
30 June Bank	38,900		

If we balance the production overhead control account we will find any under or over absorbed overhead to transfer to the profit and loss account.

Production overhead control

	£		£
30 June Materials control	3,600	30 June WIP	75,000
30 June Wages control	30,000		
30 June Bank	38,900		
30 June Profit and loss	2,500		
	75,000		75,000

The overheads actually incurred total £72,500 (£3,600 + £30,000 + £38,900) whereas the overhead absorbed was £75,000. This is an over absorption of overhead, which is debited in the production overhead control account and credited to the profit and loss account, thereby increasing profit. If the balance had been on the credit side of the production overhead control account this would have been an under absorption which would then have been debited or charged to the profit and loss account.

We will now finish the cost accounting process by considering the work in progress control account. The total on this account of £270,700 is the total production cost for the period. We are now told that during the period finished products with a production cost of £250,000 have been transferred to the warehouse ready for sale. The accounting entries reflect this with £250,000 being credited to work in progress and debited to a finished goods account.

Work in progress control account

		£			£
30 June	Materials control	69,200	30 June	Finished goods	250,000
30 June	Wages control	110,000			
30 June	Bank	16,500			
30 June	Production o/h	75,000	30 June	Closing balance	20,700
		270,700			270,700

Finished goods account

		£		£
30 June	WIP	250,000		

The closing balance on the work in progress control account is the amount of work in progress at the end of the month, cost units which have been started but not yet completed in the month.

NON-PRODUCTION OVERHEADS

So far we have concentrated on how we find the production cost of output, and how production overheads are incorporated into that cost. As far as financial accounting is concerned, this is where the cost of the product should stop. In the financial statements, other overheads will be charged as expenses in the profit and loss account. But for internal purposes, the business will need to know the full cost of producing each unit, including selling and distribution, administration, finance and research and development costs etc. They need to know if each product is making a profit and some businesses, such as solicitors and builders, set their prices by adding a certain percentage to full cost.

Some non-production overheads can be specifically allocated to a particular product, for example advertising for one type of product, and refrigerated distribution which is required only for one product. Sales value is a reasonable basis for the absorption of selling, distribution and marketing costs. It is difficult to find a reasonable basis for the absorption of other non-production overheads, so a percentage of production cost is used as the basis, which can be represented by the formula below.

$$\text{Percentage of production cost} = \frac{\text{Non-production overheads}}{\text{Production cost of output}} \times 100\%$$

Of course, this calculation will use budgeted figures, as with all overhead absorption.

HOW IT WORKS

Non-production overheads are expected to be £4,000. The production cost of the budgeted 24,000 units is £32,000. What is the overhead absorption rate for non-production overheads?

$$\text{Overhead absorption rate} = \frac{£4,000}{£32,000} \times 100\%$$

$$= 12.5\% \text{ of production cost}$$

CHAPTER OVERVIEW

- absorption costing is a method used to charge an appropriate amount of production overheads to cost units

- some overheads can be allocated to a cost centre, others have to be apportioned or split between a number of cost centres

- a fair basis for the apportionment of each type of overhead has to be found

- service cost centre overheads must be reapportioned to the production cost centres – reapportionment of service cost centre costs is achieved using an appropriate method depending upon whether one service cost centre provides services for another cost centre

- the production cost centre costs must then be absorbed into the cost of units of production

- a fair basis for the absorption of production cost centre overheads must be used – this is usually based upon direct labour hours or machine hours

- overhead absorption rates are based on budgeted values for activity levels and overheads incurred. This results in under- and over-absorption of overheads which is adjusted for in the profit and loss account
  - under-absorption is a deduction in the profit and loss account
  - over-absorption is an addition in the profit and loss account

- non-production overheads are charged to cost units to help with price-setting purposes

KEY WORDS

Overheads indirect labour, indirect materials and indirect expenses

Absorption costing a way of finding an appropriate amount of overhead per cost unit so that the total cost of producing a product or job can be found

Production cost centres a cost centre that actually produces cost units

Service cost centres a cost centre that is not directly involved with production, but with supporting production by providing a service, eg maintenance and stores

Allocation where the whole of an overhead has been incurred by one cost centre, so it is charged in full to that cost centre

Apportionment where overheads are shared, on a fair basis amongst the cost centres that jointly incurred the cost

Reapportionment apportionment of service cost centre costs to the production cost centres that use their service

Overhead absorption rate the rate at which overheads are charged to cost units calculated by dividing overheads by the level of activity

Over-absorption more overheads are absorbed into production than have actually been incurred

Under-absorption less overheads are absorbed into production than were actually incurred

HOW MUCH HAVE YOU LEARNED?

1   Bramble Fabrications Limited has three production departments: the machine shop, assembly and painting. There is one service department which usually spends 40% of its time servicing the machine shop, and the rest of the time equally in the other two production departments. Budgeted overheads to be apportioned between the departments are:

	£
Factory rent, rates and insurance	9,000
Depreciation of machinery	4,000
Supervisor's salary	8,000
Heat and light	2,000

Information for apportionment purposes:

	Machine shop	Assembly	Painting	Services
Floor area (square metres)	500	200	300	200
Value of machinery	£12,000	£4,000	£3,000	£1,000
Number of employees	8	9	5	2

You are required to calculate the final apportionment of budgeted overheads to the three production departments by:

a)   apportioning the budgeted overheads to the four departments

b)   reapportioning the service department overheads

2   Vine Limited has two production departments, V and W. There are two service departments, S1 and S2. The budgeted costs of each department, along with overheads that have yet to be allocated or apportioned are listed below, along with details which can be used for allocation and apportionment.

	Total £	V £	W £	S1 £	S2 £
Indirect materials	310,000	160,000	120,000	10,000	20,000
Indirect labour	1,125,000	400,000	650,000	40,000	35,000
Buildings depreciation and insurance	100,000				
Cleaning	25,000				
Machinery depreciation and insurance	1,500,000				
Supervision of production	70,000				
Power	250,000				
Heat and light	20,000				

	Total	V	W	S1	S2
Volume occupied					
(cubic metres)	10,000	6,000	3,000	800	200
% of power usage		25%	45%	20%	10%
Supervisor hours					
worked per week		15	20		
Value of machinery	£1,000,000	£380,000	£600,000		£20,000
% use of department S1		40%	60%		
% use of department S2		40%	50%	10%	
Direct labour hours worked		200,000	500,000		

You are required to calculate:

a)   the total overheads for each department after allocation and apportionment

b)   the overheads in departments V and W after reapportionment of the service departments using the step-down method

c)   overhead absorption rates based on direct labour hours

3   Overheads apportioned to two production departments have been worked out, along with estimates for labour hours and machine hours expected in the coming budget period. P1 is a labour intensive department, whilst P2 is highly mechanised with relatively few machine operatives. The budgeted figures are as follows.

	P1	P2
Overheads apportioned	£50,000	£60,000
Machine hours	900	4,000
Labour hours	2,500	650

You are required to calculate separate departmental overhead absorption rates for production departments P1 and P2 using an appropriate basis, and explain your choice of basis.

4   Calculate the under- or over-absorption of overheads in each of the three cases below, and state how this would be adjusted for in the profit and loss account.

a)   An overhead absorption rate of £3 per unit, based on expected production levels of 500 units. Actual overheads turn out to be £1,600, and actual production is 650 units.

b)   The budget is set at 1,000 units, with £9,000 overheads recovered on the basis of 600 direct labour hours. At the end of the period, overheads amounted to £8,600, production achieved was only 950 units and 590 direct labour hours had been worked.

c)   3,000 units of product X are to be made. Overheads are to be absorbed at a rate of £5 per machine hour. Actual production was the same as planned in the budget, incurring overheads of £3,500, and using 552 machine hours.

chapter 5:
ABSORPTION COSTING AND
MARGINAL COSTING

— chapter coverage 📖 —

In this chapter we will consider two alternative costing methods that are available to management - absorption costing and marginal costing - and their effects for costing and reporting purposes. The topics that are covered are:

✎ methods of costing

✎ the effect on profit of the two costing methods

✎ the choice between absorption and marginal costing

KNOWLEDGE AND UNDERSTANDING AND PERFORMANCE CRITERIA COVERAGE

Unit 6

knowledge and understanding – accounting techniques

9 marginal versus absorption costing for costing and reporting purposes

12 calculation of product and service cost

15 the identification of fixed, variable and semi-variable costs and their use in cost recording, cost reporting and cost analysis

knowledge and understanding – accounting principles and theory

22 marginal costing
23 absorption costing
24 cost behaviour

Performance criteria - element 6.2

D record and analyse information relating to overhead costs in accordance with the organisation's procedures

METHODS OF COSTING

In the previous chapter we saw how all of the production overheads were allocated, apportioned and then absorbed into the cost of the product given a total production cost for each cost unit. This is known as ABSORPTION COSTING (or full costing). However there is a different method of costing known as MARGINAL COSTING (or variable costing), which may be preferred by some organisations and can be more useful for some reporting purposes.

Under a marginal costing system the cost unit is valued at just the variable (or marginal) cost of production. The fixed production costs for the period are charged to the profit and loss account as an expense for the period rather than being included as part of the cost of the cost unit.

HOW IT WORKS

Graham Associates produce just one product in their factory. The factory has two production departments, assembly and packaging. The anticipated production for the next month, March, is 50,000 units and the expected costs are as follows:

Direct materials	£20 per unit
Direct labour	3 hours assembly at £8 per hour
	1 hour packaging at £6 per hour
Assembly variable overheads	£240,000
Assembly fixed overheads	£120,000
Packaging variable overheads	£100,000
Packaging fixed overheads	£40,000

Overheads are absorbed on the basis of labour hours.

We will start by calculating the cost of each cost unit using absorption costing.

Absorption costing

	Assembly	Packaging
Total overhead (variable + fixed)	£360,000	£140,000
Total labour hours 50,000 x 3	150,000	
50,000 x 1		50,000
Overhead absorption rate	$\dfrac{£360,000}{150,000}$	$\dfrac{£140,000}{50,000}$
=	£2.40 per labour hour	£2.80 per labour hour

Unit cost

		£
Direct materials		20.00
Direct labour	assembly 3 hours x £8	24.00
	packaging 1 hour x £6	6.00
Overheads	assembly 3 hours x £2.40	7.20
	packaging 1 hour x £2.80	2.80
Total unit cost		60.00

Marginal costing

Now we will calculate the same unit cost using marginal costing and therefore only including the variable costs which are direct materials, direct labour and variable overheads.

	Assembly	Packaging
Variable overhead	£240,000	£100,000
Total labour hours	150,000	50,000
Overhead absorption rate	$\dfrac{£240,000}{150,000}$	$\dfrac{£100,000}{50,000}$
=	£1.60 per labour hour	£2.00 per labour hour

Unit cost

		£
Direct materials		20.00
Direct labour	assembly	24.00
	packaging	6.00
Variable overhead	assembly 3 hours x £1.60	4.80
	packaging 1 hour x £2.00	2.00
Prime cost		56.80

Activity 1

A factory produces a single product with the following budgeted costs:

Direct materials	£3.40
Direct labour	£6.80
Variable overheads	£1.20
Fixed overheads	£340,000

Overheads are absorbed on the machine hour basis and it is estimated that in the next accounting period machine hours will total 100,000. Each unit requires 2 hours of machine time.

What is the cost per unit using:

a)   absorption costing
b)   marginal costing?

ABSORPTION VERSUS MARGINAL COSTING - EFFECT ON PROFIT

We can now have a look at what effect the two different accounting methods have on the profits that are reported. Under absorption costing the full production cost of the units actually sold in the period is charged as part of cost of sales. The only other entry may be some adjustment for under or over absorption of overheads.

However under marginal costing the lower, variable, cost per unit is charged as part of cost of sales and deducted from sales. This resulting figure is called contribution - it is sales minus variable costs of production and is the contribution towards the fixed costs and any profit. The fixed overheads are then charged to the profit and loss account as a period cost.

HOW IT WORKS

Returning to Graham Associates the budgeted sales and production for each of the next three months, March, April and May are 50,000 units. The budgeted cost figures for each month remain the same at:

Direct materials	£20 per unit
Direct labour	3 hours assembly at £8 per hour
	1 hour packaging at £6 per hour
Assembly variable overheads	£240,000
Assembly fixed overheads	£120,000
Packaging variable overheads	£100,000
Packaging fixed overheads	£40,000

The actual production and sales for each of the three months turned out to be:

	March	April	May
Sales	50,000	45,000	52,000
Production	50,000	50,000	50,000

There were no stocks of the product at the beginning of March. In each month both variable and fixed overheads were exactly as budgeted. Sales were at a selling price of £70 per unit.

Remember that the cost per unit for absorption costing is £60.00 and for marginal costing is £56.80.

March - profit and loss account

Absorption costing

	£'000	£'000
Sales (50,000 x £70)		3,500
Less: cost of sales		
Opening stock	-	
Cost of production (50,000 x £60)	3,000	
	3,000	
Less: closing stock	-	
		3,000
Profit		500

Marginal costing

Sales		3,500
Less: cost of sales		
Opening stock	-	
Cost of production (50,000 x 56.80)	2,840	
	2,840	
Less: closing stock	-	
		2,840
Contribution		660
Less: fixed costs (120,000 + 40,000)		160
Profit		500

In this month the profits under absorption costing and under marginal costin~ are exactly the same. The reason for this is that there has been no change i stock levels. There were no opening stocks and as production and sales wer for equal amounts there is also no closing stock. **When opening and closin~ stock amounts are equal then absorption costing profit and margina~ costing profit will be equal.**

April - profit and loss account

In April sales were 45,000 units and production was 50,000 units leavin~ closing stocks of 5,000 units.

Absorption costing

	£'000	£'000
Sales (45,000 x £70)		3,150
Less: cost of sales		
Opening stock	-	
Cost of production (50,000 x £60)	3,000	
	3,000	
Less: closing stock (5,000 x £60)	300	
		2,700
Profit		450

Marginal costing

	£'000	£'000
Sales		3,150
Less: cost of sales		
Opening stock	-	
Cost of production (50,000 x 56.80)	2,840	
	2,840	
Less: closing stock (5,000 x 56.80)	284	
		2,556
Contribution		594
Less: fixed costs (120,000 + 40,000)		160
Profit		434

In this month there is a difference in profit:

	£'000
Absorption costing profit	450
Marginal costing profit	434
Difference	16

The difference in reported profit under the two costing methods is due to the fixed overheads absorbed into stock. Under marginal costing the entire fixec overhead for the month is charged to the profit and loss account. However, under absorption costing the fixed overhead is included in the cost per uni~ and therefore any fixed overhead in the closing stock is carried forward to the next period rather than being charged in this period.

As stock levels have risen from zero opening stock to 5,000 units of closing stock this means that the fixed overhead amount included in the stock valuation for those 5,000 units has been deducted from this month's cost o~

ales and carried forward to the next month. This has not happened under marginal costing therefore the absorption costing profit is higher.

he two profit figures can be reconciled as **the difference is due solely to the increase in stocks and the fixed overhead included in that stock valuation.**

ixed overheads per unit $= \dfrac{£120,000 + £40,000}{50,000} = £3.20$

Remember that the difference in profit was £16,000 - this has been caused by:

ixed overhead included in increase in stock
(5,000 units x £3.20)   £16,000

May - profit and loss account

Absorption costing

	£	£
Sales (52,000 x £70)		3,640,000
Less: cost of sales		
Opening stock (5,000 x £60)	300,000	
Cost of production (50,000 x £60)	3,000,000	
	3,300,000	
Less: closing stock (3,000 x £60)	180,000	
		3,120,000
Profit		520,000

Marginal costing

	£	£
Sales		3,640,000
Less: cost of sales		
Opening stock (5,000 x 56.80)	284,000	
Cost of production (50,000 x 56.80)	2,840,000	
	3,124,000	
Less: closing stock (3,000 x 56.80)	170,400	
		2,953,600
Contribution		686,400
Less: fixed costs (120,000 + 40,000)		160,000
Profit		526,400

In May the marginal cost profit is £6,400 higher than the absorption cost profit as in this month stock levels have decreased from 5,000 units to 3,000 units. Therefore under absorption costing more of the brought forward fixed costs have been charged to the profit and loss account in the month than have been carried forward to the following month in closing stock.

The difference is made up of:

Fixed overhead in stock decrease 2,000 x £3.20 = £6,400

Should we use absorption or marginal costing?

Absorption costing has the advantage of allowing managers to see whether the sales of their products are covering all of the production costs of those products. However, owing to the different nature of fixed costs from that of variable costs it is argued that CONTRIBUTION is a much more useful figure for management than a profit figure after production overheads have been apportioned. We will see later in this text that for decision making purposes contribution is certainly the figure that must be used.

A further argument for the use of marginal costing rather than absorption costing for cost reporting purposes is to do with the profit differences and stock levels. Under absorption costing we have seen that it is possible to report a higher profit figure by increasing the closing stock levels. If a manager is assessed and possibly remunerated on the basis of the figure that he reports for profit then the profit can be manipulated by over producing and building up stock levels. Although this will increase absorption costing profit it may not be in the best interests of the organisation. This type of manipulation of profit cannot take place if marginal costing is used.

Activity 2

Given below is budgeted information about the production of a factory's single product for the month of October.

Opening stock	1,400 units
Production	12,000 units
Sales	11,600 units
Direct materials	£6.40 per unit
Direct labour	2 hours per unit @ £7.50 per hour
Variable overheads	£120,000
Fixed overheads	£360,000

Overheads are absorbed on the basis of labour hours. The selling price of the product is £65 per unit.

Prepare the budgeted profit and loss account for October using:

a)   absorption costing
b)   marginal costing

CHAPTER OVERVIEW

- under absorption costing all production overheads are allocated and apportioned to production cost centres and then absorbed into the cost of the products on some suitable basis

- under marginal costing the cost of the products is the variable cost of production with all fixed production costs being charged to the profit and loss account as a period charge

> **KEY WORDS**
>
> **Absorption (full) costing** both variable and fixed production overheads are included in unit cost
>
> **Marginal (variable) costing** unit cost includes only variable production costs
>
> **Contribution** sales value less variable cost of the goods sold

- if stock levels are constant then both absorption costing and marginal costing will report the same profit figure

- if stock levels are increasing absorption costing profit will be higher as **more** fixed overheads are carried forward to the following period in closing stock than those brought forward in opening stock

- if stock levels are falling marginal costing profit will be higher as **less** fixed overheads are carried forward under absorption costing in the closing stock figure than those brought forward in opening stock

- the difference in profit will be the fixed production overhead included in the increase/decrease in stock levels under absorption costing

- the contribution figure shown in marginal costing can be argued to be more use to management than the full absorption costing profit figure

- it is possible to manipulate profit reporting under absorption costing by increasing stock levels and thereby increasing reported profit

HOW MUCH HAVE YOU LEARNED?

1 Explain how fixed production overheads are treated in an absorption costing system and in a marginal costing system.

2 Given below is the budgeted information about the production of 60,000 units of a single product in a factory for the following quarter:

Direct materials	£12.50 per unit
Direct labour - assembly	4 hours @ £8.40 per hour
- finishing	1 hour @ £6.60 per hour
Assembly production overheads	£336,000
Finishing production overheads	£84,000

It is estimated that 60% of the assembly overhead is variable and that 75% of the finishing overhead is variable.

What is the budgeted cost of the product using:

a) absorption costing
b) marginal costing?

3 Given below are the budgeted figures for production and sales of a factory's single product fo the months of November and December:

	November	December
Production	15,000 units	15,000 units
Sales	12,500 units	18,000 units
Direct materials	£12.00 per unit	£12.00 per unit
Direct labour	£8.00 per unit	£8.00 per unit
Variable production cost	£237,000	£237,000
Fixed production cost	£390,000	£390,000

Overheads are absorbed on the basis of the budgeted production and the selling price of the product is £75.

There were 2,000 units of the product in stock at the start of November.

a) Prepare the budgeted profit and loss accounts for each of the two months using:

i) absorption costing

ii) marginal costing

b) Prepare a reconciliation explaining any difference in the two profit figures in each of the two months.

chapter 6:
COSTING SYSTEMS

chapter coverage 📖

So far we have concentrated on gathering together the costs for individual cost units – the products that a business makes. However there are other costing systems depending upon the type of product or service that a business provides. In this chapter we shall consider costing systems other than those which gather costs into the cost of a single cost unit. The topics to be covered are:

✎   costing systems

✎   job costing

✎   batch costing

✎   process costing

Unit 6

knowledge and understanding - the business environment

1   the nature and purpose of internal reporting

3   maintaining an appropriate cost accounting system

knowledge and understanding - accounting techniques

12   calculation of product and service cost

knowledge and understanding - the organisation

26   costing systems appropriate to the organisation: job, batch, unit and process costing systems

Performance criteria – element 6.1

A   identify direct costs in accordance with the organisation's costing procedures

B   record and analyse information relating to direct costs

C   calculate direct costs in accordance with the organisation's policies and procedures

Performance criteria – element 6.2

A   identify overhead costs in accordance with the organisation's procedures

C   calculate overhead absorption rates in accordance with agreed bases of absorption

D   record and analyse information relating to overhead costs in accordance with the organisation's procedures

COSTING SYSTEMS

For many organisations the basic system of costing is that which we have considered so far – the collection of direct costs and overheads into the production cost centres in order eventually to absorb these costs into each individual cost unit or product that the business makes.

However there are three other types of costing system that are mentioned in the knowledge and understanding for Unit 6 – job costing, batch costing and process costing. Each of these will be considered in this chapter.

JOB COSTING

JOB COSTING is used in types of business where the product that is produced is a "one-off" job for a customer which is different for each individual customer. Typical types of business where job costing is used are engineering, building, painting and decorating, printing etc. These are businesses where there is no previously produced product to sell. What is being done for the customer is entirely to the customer's specification.

There are three main areas of job costing that are of concern to the accountant:

- the setting of the price for the job

- the gathering of actual costs for the job

- the control of the job by the monitoring of variances between the expected cost and the actual cost of the job.

Setting the price

The problem with jobbing businesses is that there is no price list as such as there is no standard product. Each individual job will be different with different costs.

When a customer approaches the business requesting a quote for a price for the job they will provide details of the precise requirements they have for this particular job. The business must then decide how much the job is going to cost and how much profit it is to earn on the job and then come up with a price that satisfies this.

It is important to realise that not only must the price of the job cover the direct costs of materials, labour and any direct expenses but it must also cover a portion of the overheads, so that all of the overheads for a period are covered by the prices of the jobs done in that period.

Activity 1

What are the three main tasks of the accounting function in a job costing business?

HOW IT WORKS

Brecon Builders have been approached by a potential customer, Petra Jones, who wishes to have a loft conversion. The engineer has visited the site and inspected the loft and taken detailed measurements and drawings. From his estimates the accountant then draws up the following set of estimates for the job on a standard job quote card:

JOB NUMBER 03677
PETRA JONES LOFT CONVERSION

	£
Direct materials	
Plasterboard	1,800.00
Wood and door frames	740.00
Insulation	1,250.00
Electrical fittings	320.00
Staircase	840.00
Windows	720.00
Paint	270.00
Direct labour	
Construction 45 hours @ £13.20	594.00
Electrical 8 hours @ £15.50	124.00
Plastering 16 hours @ £16.00	256.00
Decorating 15 hours @ £11.00	165.00
Direct expenses	
Hire of specialist lathe	240.00
Overheads (based upon direct labour hours)	
84 hours @ £15.00	1,260.00
Total cost	8,579.00
Profit (20% of total cost)	1,715.80
Net price	10,294.80
VAT at 17.5%	1,801.59
Total price	12,096.39

The important points to note about this job quotation are:

- each job will be assigned an individual number which will be used when any materials, labour or expense are incurred by the job

- the costs of the direct materials will have come from the stores ledger records for any materials that are already in stock and from the purchasing department for any additional materials that are required

- the direct labour costs will be an estimate of the number of hours required for each task and the labour hour rate for each type of employee

- the direct expenses are any specific items of expense that relate to this job only

- the overheads are to be absorbed on a direct labour hour basis. The overhead absorption rate will have been calculated (as we have seen in an earlier chapter) by gathering together all of the budgeted overheads for the period and then dividing by the budgeted number of labour hours for the period

- once all of the costs of the job have been gathered together, including the absorption of the overheads, then the profit percentage that the business wishes to make over and above the costs is added – this is the net price to the customer

- finally the VAT must be added in at 17.5%, if the business is registered for VAT (see Unit 7) to give the final total price for the job to the customer.

If the customer accepts this price quotation then Brecon Builders will go ahead with the job.

Activity 2

Why is it important that overheads are included in the price quoted to a customer for a job?

Actual costs of the job

The next problem with job costing is to ensure that all of the costs of the job are accurately gathered together. This means ensuring that all materials issued to the job are coded and recorded as relating to that particular job and that all of the time of employees who work on that job is coded and recorded as relating to it. Any direct expenses of that job, such as hire of a piece of machinery for the job, must also be recorded.

Finally a portion of the overheads of the business must be apportioned to the job, normally on a basis similar to that used for unit costing such as direct labour hours or direct machine hours.

HOW IT WORKS

Brecon Builders now start work on Petra Jones' loft extension.

Each time that materials are requisitioned from the stores department for this job a materials requisition form must be completed showing clearly that the materials are required for job number 03677.

For example three wooden doors are required for the entrance to the loft and the wardrobes that are being fitted. The materials requisition must be filled out as follows:

MATERIALS REQUISITION

Material required for: Job 03677   No.   44285

Date.   4 July

Quantity	Description	Code no.	Price per unit	£
3	Imperial doors	DI2553	64.00	192.00

Authorised by: K Finch

Each materials requisition is passed to the accounts department and they will gather together the cost of the total materials that have been used on Job 03677.

When each employee works on the loft extension they will complete a job card showing the number of hours worked on the job as follows:

JOB CARD

Job No   03677

Date 7 July

Time allowed 7 hours   **Start time** 9.00 am

                                 Finish time 4.00 pm

Job description	Hours	Rate	Cost £
Plastering wall surfaces	7		

Employee name   *Melvin Hurd*

Employee signature   *Melvin Hurd*

Supervisor's signature   *John Hunt*

Again each employee's JOB CARD will be sent to the accounts department who will record the correct hourly rate for this employee and gather together all of the labour costs for Job 03677.

When the invoice is received for the hire of the special lathe for the loft conversion this will again be coded for Job 03677 and incorporated into the accounts department's total costs for the job.

Finally, when the job is completed, the number of direct labour hours will be totalled and the overhead absorption rate of £15.00 per hour added to the direct costs. In this case the number of hours finally totalled 90 direct labour hours and therefore the overheads absorbed into Job 03677 are £1,350.00 (90 hours x £15.00 per hour).

Monitoring of variances

Once the job has been completed and all of the costs have been gathered together, the actual costs must be compared to the original costs used to price the job and variances will be calculated. This serves as a control over the costs of the actual job itself and over the initial pricing process.

HOW IT WORKS

Petra Jones' loft conversion was completed in early August 2006 and by 15 August the accounts department had gathered together all of the costs of the job and produced the following variance schedule (FAV = favourable variance ie actual cost was lower than budget; ADV = adverse variance ie actual cost was higher than budget).

JOB NUMBER 03677
PETRA JONES LOFT CONVERSION

	Budget £	Actual £	Variance £
Direct materials			
Plasterboard	1,800.00	1,750.00	50.00 FAV
Wood & door frames	740.00	800.00	60.00 ADV
Insulation	1,250.00	1,340.00	90.00 ADV
Electrical fittings	320.00	300.00	20.00 FAV
Staircase	840.00	840.00	–
Windows	720.00	760.00	40.00 ADV
Paint	270.00	250.00	20.00 FAV
Direct labour			
Construction	594.00	641.00	47.00 ADV
Electrical	124.00	160.00	36.00 ADV
Plastering	256.00	250.00	6.00 FAV
Decorating	165.00	205.00	40.00 ADV
Direct expenses			
Hire of specialist lathe	240.00	240.00	–
Overheads (based upon direct labour hours)			
90 hours @ £15.00	1,260.00	1,350.00	90.00 ADV
Total cost	8,579.00	8,886.00	307.00 ADV
Profit	1,715.80	1,408.80	
Net price	10,294.80	10,294.80	
VAT at 17.5%	1,801.59	1,801.59	
Total price	12,096.39	12,096.39	

In total this shows that the business has made £307.00 less profit on the job than expected as the net variances total an adverse variance of £307.00 and the price of the job is fixed.

This shows the importance of ensuring that the very best estimates are made when the initial price is quoted to the customer.

BATCH COSTING

BATCH COSTING is used in manufacturing businesses which make batches of different products rather than single products. For example a shoe manufacturer may make a batch of 400 shoes of one style in size 4 and then a batch of 300 shoes of a different style in size 7. Similarly a food manufacturer may make a batch of 500 portions of chicken tikka followed by a batch of 200 portions of prawn korma.

Batch costing is a costing system whereby all of the costs of making the entire batch are gathered together. This will be the direct materials, direct labour and any direct expenses, together with the overheads that are absorbed into that batch. We have already seen how overheads are absorbed into individual units.

Once all of the costs of the batch have been determined the cost of each individual unit of product in that batch can be found as follows:

$$\text{Cost per unit} = \frac{\text{Cost of the batch}}{\text{Number of units in the batch}}$$

Activity 3

The costs to a clothing manufacturer of producing a batch of 450 men's leather jackets was £38,925. What is the cost of each jacket?

PROCESS COSTING

In many manufacturing businesses the product is made in a process whereby materials are input to the process, work is carried out on the materials, overheads are incurred by the process and finally a number of completed, identical products appear out of the process. Examples include the brewing industry, oil refining and paint manufacture.

A specific type of costing system is needed in order to cost the final product in such circumstances, known as PROCESS COSTING. The aim of process costing is to gather together all of the costs incurred in a process in a period and divide these costs by the number of units produced in the period. As each of the units is identical what we are effectively doing is finding the average cost for each unit produced in the period.

HOW IT WORKS

Nuneaton Enterprises is a food processing manufacturer which makes a
number of different types of product in a number of different processes. The
following information is available for Process VF1 for the month of May:

Materials input into the process 120,000 kg	£38,000
Labour hours spent on the process	1,200 @ £9 per hour
Overheads to be absorbed into the process	£11,200
Units produced from the process	120,000 kg

The costs of the process are first totalled:

	£
Direct materials	38,000
Direct labour (1,200 x £9)	10,800
Overheads absorbed	11,200
Total process cost	60,000

The cost per unit produced is the total process cost divided by the number
of units produced:

$$\text{Cost per unit} = \frac{£60,000}{120,000\,\text{kg}}$$

$$= 50 \text{ pence per kg}$$

The costs and the production are normally shown in a process account. The
process account for process VF1 for May would be made up as follows:

- the materials input into the process in both kilograms and value
  are debited to the process account.

Process VF1

	kg	£		£
Materials	120,000	38,000		

- the labour and overhead costs are also debited to the account
  (sometimes these two costs are given together and called the
  conversion costs).

Process VF1

	kg	£		£
Materials	120,000	38,000		
Labour		10,800		
Overheads		11,200		

■ the output is shown on the credit side as 120,000 kgs each valued at 50pence therefore totalling £60,000 and the process account is balanced.

	kg	£		kg	£
		Process VF1			
Materials	120,000	38,000			
Labour		10,800			
Overheads		11,200	Output	120,000	60,000
	120,000	60,000		120,000	60,000

NORMAL PROCESS LOSSES

In many processes the quantity of material put into the process is not the same as the quantity that is produced from the process as the process has losses during the processing time, for example due to evaporation or defective units. Over time an organisation will be able to judge what is the normal level of loss from a process. The normal loss is the amount of loss that is expected from a process. This is normally expressed as a percentage of the materials input to the process.

As the normal loss is part of the normal manufacturing process no value is given to the normal loss units; instead the process costs are averaged out over the good units of production.

HOW IT WORKS

Another of Nuneaton's processes is the GS3. There is a normal loss of 10% of materials input into this process. The costs incurred in this process and the output achieved for the month of May are:

Direct materials	50,000 kg	£22,500
Direct labour		£16,500
Overheads		£ 6,000
Output		45,000 kg

The steps to follow are:

Step 1   Calculate the number of normal loss units:

50,000 kg x 10% = 5,000 kg

Step 2   Calculate the expected output from the process:

50,000 kg - 5,000 kg = 45,000 kg

Step 3   Total the process costs:

£22,500 | £16,500 + £6,000 = £45,000

Step 4   Calculate the cost per unit of expected output

$$\frac{£45,000}{45,000\,kg} = £1 \text{ per kg}$$

This can then all be written up in the process account:

Process GS3

	kg	£		kg	£
Materials	50,000	22,500	Normal loss	5,000	-
Labour		16,500	Output	45,000	45,000
Overheads		6,000			
	50,000	45,000		50,000	45,000

Both the kgs and the value columns must balance. No value has been assigned to the normal loss units, all of the process costs have been shared between the expected output units.

Activity 4

During week 26 16,000 litres of material costing £108,000 were added to a process. The process has a normal loss of 5%. The conversion costs for the process were £22,720 for the week. Output from the process during the week was 15,200 litres.

a)   What is the cost per litre of good output?
b)   Write up the process account.

ABNORMAL LOSSES AND GAINS

In many processes the **actual** process loss will differ from the **expected** or normal loss. If the actual loss is greater than the expected loss the difference is known as an ABNORMAL LOSS. If the actual loss is less than the expected loss the difference is known as an ABNORMAL GAIN.

Whereas the normal loss units are expected and unavoidable any abnormal losses or gains are not expected and are considered avoidable therefore the accounting treatment of abnormal losses and gains is different from that of the normal loss. The normal loss units were assigned no value; however, any abnormal loss units are valued in the same way as the good output.

HOW IT WORKS

The normal loss for another of Nuneaton's processes PE7 is 5%. The inputs, costs and output of this process in May are given below.

Direct materials	20,000 kg	£15,400
Direct labour		£ 6,200
Overheads		£ 1,200
Output		18,400 kg

Step 1 Calculate the number of normal loss units:

20,000 kg x 5% = 1,000 kg

Step 2 Calculate the expected output from the process:

20,000 kg - 1,000 kg = 19,000 kg

Step 3 Total the process costs:

£15,400 + £6,200 + £1,200 = £22,800

Step 4 Calculate the cost per unit of expected output

$$\frac{£22,800}{19,000\,kg} = £1.20\ per\ kg$$

The process account is now written up - this is where the units column becomes important. Our expected output was 19,000 kg but in fact only 18,400 kg were produced so there is an abnormal loss of 600 kg which are valued at the same value as the good output, £1.20 per kg, so £720 in total. The good output of 18,400 kg is also valued at £1.20 per kg totalling £22,080 and both the unit columns and value columns balance.

Process PE7

	kg	£		kg	£
Materials	20,000	15,400	Normal loss	1,000	-
Labour		6,200	Abnormal loss	600	720
Overheads		1,200	Output	18,400	22,080
	20,000	22,800		20,000	22,800

The abnormal loss has been credited to the process account and must be debited to an abnormal loss account:

Abnormal loss account

	kg	£		kg	£
Process PE7	600	720			

At the period end, the abnormal loss account is cleared to the profit and loss account. In this case it will be an expense of £720.

Activity 5

During the month of March 110,000 kgs of materials with a cost of £526,000 were entered into a process which has a normal loss of 6%. Labour costs for the month for the process were £128,300 and overheads were £110,860. The actual output for the period was 100,400 kgs.

a)   What is the cost per kg?
b)   Write up the process account for the month.

Abnormal gain

The treatment of an abnormal gain is exactly the same as an abnormal loss but the double entry is the other way around.

HOW IT WORKS

Process RD4 in Nuneaton Enterprises has a normal loss of 10%. The inputs, costs and outputs for the month of May are given below:

Direct materials	10,000 kg	£11,200
Direct labour		£9,400
Overheads		£6,400
Output		9,350 kg

Step 1   Calculate the number of normal loss units:

10,000 kg x 10% = 1,000 kg

Step 2   Calculate the expected output from the process:

10,000 kg - 1,000 kg = 9,000 kg

Step 3   Total the process costs:

£11,200 + £9,400 + £6,400 = £27,000

Step 4   Calculate the cost per unit of expected output

$$\frac{£27,000}{9,000 \text{ kg}} = £3 \text{ per kg}$$

Now we can write up the ledger accounts. In this case there is an abnormal gain as actual output is 350 kg more than the expected output. The abnormal gain units are debited to the process account and valued at the cost per unit of £3. The normal loss as usual has no value assigned to it and the output of 9,350 kg is also valued at £3.

Process RD4

	kg	£		kg	£
Materials	10,000	11,200	Normal loss	1,000	-
Labour		9,400			
Overheads		6,400			
Abnormal gain	350	1,050	Output	9,350	28,050
	10,350	28,050		10,350	28,050

The abnormal gain has been debited in the process account and therefore must be credited in an abnormal gain account.

Abnormal gain

	kg	£		kg	£
			Process RD4	350	1,050

This amount is then credited to the profit and loss account as an abnormal gain.

Activity 6

48,000 litres of material were input to a process at the start of the week at a cost of £164,200. Conversion costs for the week were £56,120. The process has a normal loss of 10% and the output for the week was 44,000 litres.

a) What is the cost per litre?
b) Write up the ledger accounts to record this.

Losses with a scrap value

In some instances the loss units are defective units or waste materials which can be sold for a scrap value. This has a number of effects on our calculations and accounting entries:

- the most common treatment for the normal loss units is to treat their scrap value as a deduction from the process costs

- in the process account the normal loss is then valued at its scrap value

- the abnormal loss is still valued at its full process cost and transferred to the abnormal loss account at that value

- the scrap value is then credited to the abnormal loss account to reduce the charge to the profit and loss account.

student notes✍

HOW IT WORKS

We will return to Nuneaton's Process PE7 with normal loss of 5%. This time however all loss units can be sold for 38 pence per kg. The inputs, costs and output of this process in May are given below.

Direct materials	20,000 kg	£15,400
Direct labour		£ 6,200
Overheads		£ 1,200
Output		18,400 kg

Step 1   Calculate the number of normal loss units:

20,000 kg x 5% = 1,000 kg

Step 2   Calculate the expected output from the process:

20,000 kg - 1,000 kg   =   19,000 kg

Step 3   Total the process costs but deduct the scrap value of the normal loss:

(£15,400 + £6,200 + £1,200) - (1,000 x £0.38) = £22,420

Step 4   Calculate the cost per unit of expected output

$$\frac{£22,420}{19,000\,kg} = £1.18 \text{ per kg}$$

Now we will write up the process account:

■   the normal loss will be given a value of £380 (1,000 x £0.38)

■   the output and abnormal loss will be valued at the process cost of £1.18 per kg

Process PE7

	kg	£		kg	£
Materials	20,000	15,400	Normal loss	1,000	380
Labour		6,200	Abnormal loss	600	708
Overheads		1,200	Output	18,400	21,712
	20,000	22,800		20,000	22,800

Finally the abnormal loss account. The account is debited with the abnormal loss value of £708 and then credited with the scrap value of these 600 kg (600 x £0.38) = £228.

Abnormal loss						
	kg	£			kg	£
Process PE7	600	708	Scrap value		600	228
			Profit and loss			
			account			480
	600	708			600	708

The charge to the profit and loss account for the abnormal loss has now been reduced from £708 to £480 due to the scrap value of the units.

Activity 7

During the month of April 10,000 kg of material were input to a process at a cost of £98,000. The process has a normal loss of 5% and any loss units can be sold for £1.40 per kg. Labour costs were £36,000 for the month and overheads totalled £9,200. Output for the month of April was 9,100 kg.

a) What is the cost per kg?

b) Write up the ledger accounts to record the process for the month.

Work in progress

At the end of a period in which a process has been carried out it is entirely possible that not only has there been a number of units completed in the process, but there are also a number of partially completed units remaining within the process. These partially completed units are known as CLOSING WORK IN PROGRESS.

As some work has been carried out on these units they must have some cost assigned to them. However as they are not complete they cannot be given the same cost value as the completed units of output from the process. The method that is used to cost this closing work in progress is to use EQUIVALENT UNITS. For example, suppose that there are 100 units of work in progress at the end of a period which are judged to be half complete. These units are treated as equivalent to 50 completed units.

HOW IT WORKS

Nuneaton Enterprises has another process, SL4. During the month of May the costs of that process were £21,000 and the output was 10,000 completed units and 1,000 units that were half completed. How do we value each of the units of completed output and work in progress? We use equivalent units.

	Equivalent units
Completed production	10,000
Work in progress (1,000 x 1/2)	500
	10,500

Therefore during the period the equivalent of 10,500 completed units have passed through the process. The cost per equivalent unit (EU) can now be found.

$$\text{Cost per equivalent unit} = \frac{£21,000}{10,500 \text{ EU}}$$

$$= £2 \text{ per equivalent unit}$$

In the process account the completed production will be valued at:

Completed production 10,000 x £2   =   £20,000

The closing work in progress will be valued at £2 for each equivalent unit:

Closing work in progress 500 x £2   =   £1,000

The process account will appear as follows:

Process account			
	£		£
Input costs	21,000	Completed production	20,000
		Closing work in progress	1,000
	21,000		21,000

Different stages of completion

Remember that in a process we not only have materials input to the process, but also labour costs and overheads. In practice it is common for the materials, labour and overheads to be incurred at different stages of the process. Therefore at the end of the period the closing work in progress may have had all of its material input but only half of the labour input. The method of dealing with this is to split out the costs into their different categories, materials and labour/overheads, and to calculate equivalent units of completion for each category of cost.

HOW IT WORKS

Another of Nuneaton Enterprises processes is the KS2. The costs incurred in this process for the month of May are as follows:

Materials	£23,760
Labour and overheads	£10,200

At the end of the period there were 8,000 units of completed output and ,000 units of closing work in progress. The work in progress has had 80% of s material input and 50% of the labour and overheads input.

We must now calculate the cost per equivalent unit for materials and abour/overheads.

	Units	Materials		Labour/overheads	
		Proportion complete	Equivalent units	Proportion complete	Equivalent units
Completed	8,000	100%	8,000	100%	8,000
Work in progress	1,000	80%	800	50%	500
Total equivalent units			8,800		8,500
Cost per equivalent unit			$\frac{£23,760}{8,800}$		$\frac{£10,200}{8,500}$
			= £2.70 per EU		= £1.20 per EU

Finally we can find values for the completed output and the closing work in progress.

	£
Completed output	
Materials (8,000 x £2.70)	21,600
Labour/overhead (8,000 x £1.20)	9,600
	31,200
Work in progress	
Materials (800 x £2.70)	2,160
Labour/overhead (500 x £1.20)	600
	2,760

This can all then be entered into the process account.

Process account

	£		£
Materials	23,760	Completed output	31,200
Labour/overhead	10,200	Closing work in progress	2,760
	33,960		33,960

Activity 8

During the month of June the following inputs were made to a process:

	£
Materials	15,575
Labour and overheads	8,480

The output from the process for the month consisted of 4,000 completed units and 600 units of closing work in progress. The closing work in progress was 75% complete as to material input but only 40% complete as to labour and overheads.

What is the value of the completed units and the closing work in progress?

Tutor's Note

For Unit 6 you do not have to deal with opening work in progress nor will you have to deal with a combination of closing work in progress and process losses.

CHAPTER OVERVIEW

- job costing is a costing system that is used in a business that provides individual "one-off" products for customers

- in a job costing system the accounting function must first produce a schedule of the expected costs of the product that the customer wants – this schedule must include not only the direct costs of producing the product but also any overheads that need to be absorbed into the job to ensure that all of the overheads of the business for the period are eventually covered by the prices set for the jobs done

- the price of the job must also include the profit element for the business and the VAT if the business is registered for VAT

- once the price has been agreed and the job is started all of the costs of the job must be gathered together by the accounting function – any materials requisitions must quote the job number and all job cards for employees' hours must also show which job was worked on

- the accounting function will then absorb overheads into the job according to the organisation's policies

- once the job has been completed the accounting function will prepare a comparison of the actual costs of the job with those quoted initially to the customer – showing any variances from the original estimated costs

- batch costing is used in businesses where instead of there being production runs of identical products there are a number of production runs of batches of different products

- the purpose of batch costing is to find the cost of an entire batch of a product and then to divide that cost by the number of units produced in the batch – this will then give the unit cost of each unit of that product

- where identical products are produced in a continuous process then a process costing system will be in operation

- the costs of the process are divided by the expected output from the process to find the cost per unit of the good output – any normal losses are not assigned any value

- abnormal losses or gains are also valued at the full process cost per unit

- any scrap value for normal loss units is deducted from the process cost – the normal loss units are valued at that scrap value – the abnormal losses, gains and good output are valued at the full process unit cost

---

KEY WORDS

Job costing costing system which allocates costs to individual "one-off" jobs for customers

Job card an individual employee's record of the time spent on each job

Batch costing a costing system which gathers together the costs of production of an entire batch of a similar product in order to find the cost of each individual item in that batch

Process costing a costing system where the unit cost is determined by averaging the periodic costs of the process over the expected good output from the process

Conversion costs labour and overhead costs of the process

Normal loss the expected loss from the process

Abnormal loss any actual loss units in excess of the normal loss units

Abnormal gain any actual loss units that are less than the normal loss units

Closing work in progress partially completed units from a process at the end of the period

Equivalent units the number of complete units that the work in progress is equivalent to

---

CHAPTER OVERVIEW

- at the end of the period there may be some partially completed units, or closing work in progress

- in order to value the completed units and the closing work in progress the total number of equivalent units must be calculated and the cost per unit determined

- if the closing work in progress has different stages of completion for the different elements of input, materials and labour/overheads, then a cost per equivalent unit must be calculated for each element of the input

HOW MUCH HAVE YOU LEARNED?

1   A curtain manufacturer has been asked to give a quote for the making of a set of curtains for a large, square bay window. It is estimated that the cost of the curtain fabric will be £590 and the lining materials £175. The job is estimated to take 27 hours at a rate of £7.70 per hour. The business absorbs overheads at the rate of £8.70 per hour.

   a)   What is the estimated cost of the production of these curtains?

   b)   If the business aims to achieve a profit of 15% per job and is also registered for VAT, what is the final quote to the customer?

2   A kitchen manufacturer has been asked to supply a kitchen to a customer. The estimates of costs are given below:

   Materials for manufacturing the units – £12,500
   Direct labour for fitting the units – 23 hours @ £8.60 per hour
   Direct labour for redecorating – 5 hours @ £6.50 per hour
   Overheads are absorbed on the basis of £12.40 per direct labour hour.
   Profit on each job is taken at 25% of total costs
   VAT is charged at 17.5%

   Prepare a job costing schedule showing how much the kitchen will cost the customer.

3   A pie factory operates on a batch of production system. The latest batch to have been produced is 1,200 cheese and mushroom pies. The costs of this batch are:

Ingredients	£840.00
Labour 7 hours @ £6.50	£ 45.50

   Overheads are absorbed on the basis of £1.20 per labour hour.

   What is the cost of each pie?

4   Given below are the details for a process for the month of January:

Direct materials	50,000 kg	£350,000
Direct labour		£125,000
Overheads		£ 57,000
Normal loss		5%
Output		46,000 kg

   Write up the ledger accounts to record the process results for the month.

5   Given below are the details for a process for week 18:

Direct materials	6,000 litres	£14,300
Direct labour		£ 7,200
Overheads		£11,980

   The normal loss from the process is 10% and the output for the week was 5,600 litres.

   Write up the ledger accounts to reflect the process costs for the week.

6   Given below are the details of a process for the month of March. Any loss units can be sold fo‌ scrap for £1.00 per kg.

Direct materials	40,000 kgs	£158,200
Direct labour		£ 63,500
Overheads		£ 31,740
Normal loss		8%
Output		35,000 kg

Write up the ledger accounts to reflect the process results for the month.

7   A process has the following inputs for the month of July:

	£
Materials	8,960
Labour/overheads	4,290

The output from the process consists of 2,000 completed units and 400 units of closing worl‌ in progress. The work in progress is 60% complete as to materials but only 50% complete fo‌ labour and overheads.

Calculate the value of the completed output and the closing work in progress, and prepare the process account for the month.

chapter 7:
COST BOOKKEEPING

---

chapter coverage 📖

In the previous chapters we have looked at the bookkeeping for each aspect of costing, materials, labour and overheads. In this chapter we will bring it all together with a reminder of how the individual elements of the bookkeeping work and then a comprehensive example of how it all ties in together. The topics covered are:

✎ control accounts used in bookkeeping

✎ an integrated bookkeeping system

✎ a worked example of the cost bookkeeping for all aspects

KNOWLEDGE AND UNDERSTANDING AND PERFORMANCE CRITERIA COVERAGE

Unit 6

knowledge and understanding - the business environment

3 maintaining an appropriate cost accounting system

knowledge and understanding - accounting techniques

4 recording of cost and revenue data in the accounting records

knowledge and understanding - accounting principles and theory

19 relationship between the materials costing system and the stock control system
20 relationship between the labour costing system and the payroll accounting system
21 relationship between the accounting system and the expenses costing system

Performance criteria – element 6.1

B   record and analyse information relating to direct costs

Performance criteria – element 6.2

D   record and analyse information relating to overhead costs in accordance with the organisation's procedures

E   make adjustments for under and over recovered overhead costs in accordance with established procedures

THE BASIC REQUIREMENTS FOR COST BOOKKEEPING

The preceding chapters have described the basic information that is needed for cost accounting. It is plain, therefore, that a cost bookkeeping system will need to be able to cope with a great deal of detail. For example, it will be insufficient to record all items purchased as 'purchases'; there will need to be distinctions made between direct and indirect items, and each type of material will need its own record. Similarly, each product, batch, job or process will need its own account to record the materials, labour and production overheads incurred on it. To help organise the information into a manageable system there are two important techniques with which you must be familiar:

- use of control accounts
- use of an integrated bookkeeping system

Control accounts

You will be familiar with the idea of a cash control account in the main ledger that summarises the detail recorded in the cash book, and the debtors and creditors control accounts that summarise the total of transactions in the individual debtor and creditor accounts in the debtors' and creditors' ledgers. In a cost bookkeeping system, control accounts can be used to summarise the information in separately maintained detailed accounts, for example

- MATERIALS OR STORES CONTROL ACCOUNT will record the total purchases of materials and issues to WIP, summarising the individual materials or stores ledger accounts;

- WAGES CONTROL ACCOUNT will record the total payroll costs, and the total direct labour charged to each individual product, job, batch or process in WIP, and indirect labour charged to appropriate cost centres;

- PRODUCTION OVERHEAD CONTROL ACCOUNT will record the total production overheads incurred by different cost centres, and the total charged to each individual product, job, batch or process in WIP; and

- WORK IN PROGRESS CONTROL ACCOUNT will summarise each individual product, job, batch or process in WIP, recording the total costs of direct materials, direct labour and production overheads that have been charged and the transfer of items to finished goods.

As with the debtors' and creditors' control accounts, these control accounts will need to be reconciled with the more detailed, individual accounts to help to ensure that the information recorded is accurate.

THE INTEGRATED BOOKKEEPING SYSTEM

There are two main systems of cost bookkeeping.

- The INTEGRATED SYSTEM combines the cost accounting ar financial accounting functions into one system of ledger account This gives a saving in terms of time and cost. However, it has th disadvantage of trying to fulfil two purposes with one set of account and in chapter 1 we looked at the different needs of cost ar financial accounting.

- The INTERLOCKING SYSTEM keeps separate ledgers for the co accounting function (the cost ledger) and the financial accountir function (the financial ledger). The cost ledger will include a co ledger control account which is essentially there to provide a plac for items of a financial nature. For example, when an invoice received for materials, the materials account is debited, and as th cost ledger does not record creditors, the cost ledger control accou is credited. A financial ledger control account is used to maintain th integrity of the double entry system in the financial ledger. These tw ledgers will need reconciling on a regular basis to ensure that they a in agreement.

The integrated system is much more common, especially in computerise systems, and this is the system which we are going to concentrate on. In th system, the main ledger will contain the cost ledger accounts as well as th usual ledger accounts for cash, capital, fixed assets etc. The double entries ar performed as usual; this system must balance to produce a set of financi. statements as well as costing information. The table and the diagram belo take a general look at how the double entries are recorded, and how th profit and loss account is built up. Note that absorption costing is used.

Activity 1

How does an integrated system of cost bookkeeping work?

Summary of cost bookkeeping double entries in an integrated system
(read in conjunction with the diagram on the next page)

1	Production costs are recorded	Debit: Materials Debit: Wages Debit: Production ohds	Credit: Cash/creditors Credit: Cash/HMRC Credit: Cash/creditors
2	Direct costs issued to production	Debit: WIP Debit: WIP	Credit: Materials Credit: Wages
3	Indirect labour transferred to production overheads	Debit: Production ohds	Credit: Wages
4	Production overheads absorbed into production	Debit: WIP	Credit: Production ohds
5	Completed WIP transferred to finished goods	Debit: Finished goods	Credit: WIP
6	Finished goods are sold	Debit: Cost of sales Debit: Cash/debtors Debit: Sales	Credit: Finished goods Credit: Sales Credit: Profit and loss

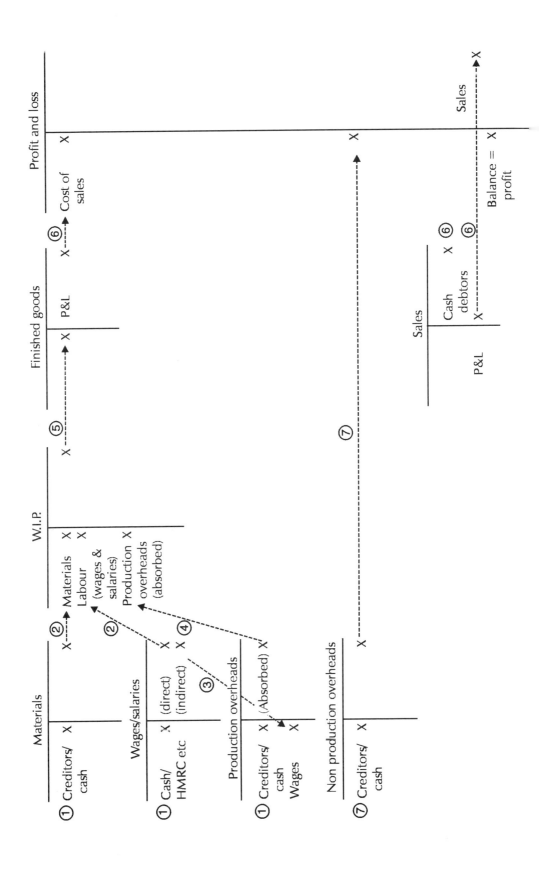

Activity 2

What would be the double entry in an integrated system of cost accounting for materials purchased on credit for the production process?

Under- and over- absorption of overheads

The production overheads account is debited with overhead costs incurred, and if absorption costing is used, credited with the amount of overheads absorbed into production based on a pre-determined absorption rate. As we stressed in a previous chapter, the absorption rate is calculated in advance of the accounting period and is based on estimates of the level of activity and the overhead cost; the estimates are likely to be inaccurate such that the amount absorbed into production will not be the same as the actual cost incurred. The overheads under- or over- absorbed will appear as a balance on the account, and will be transferred to the profit and loss account.

Over-absorbed   Absorbed > incurred   Debit: production overheads
                                          Credit: profit and loss
Under-absorbed Incurred > absorbed   Debit: profit and loss
                                          Credit: production overheads

Illustration

Cranefly Limited absorbs production overheads at a rate of £2.40 per direct labour hour. During June, 690 labour hours are worked in Department X, and actual overheads incurred were £1,530.

There is an over-absorption of overheads here:

	£
Actual overheads	1,530
Absorbed overheads (690 x £2.40)	1,656
Over-absorbed	126

The production overheads account would show this, and calculate it automatically, as long as all the other entries are correct.

Production overheads account

	£		£
Cash/creditors	1,530	WIP	1,656
Over-absorption	126		
	1,656		1,656

Activity 3

The overhead absorption rate for a factory is £3.24 per direct labour hour. During the month of July 20X1 the number of direct labour hours worked was 1,050 and the overheads incurred were £3,690.

Write up the production overheads account and explain the accounting treatment of any under or over absorption.

HOW IT WORKS: integrated accounts

The information below relates to Shieldbug Limited for the month of Apri 2006. (Note that VAT has been ignored for the purpose of this example.)

OPENING TRIAL BALANCE AT 1 APRIL 2006

Account	Debit £	Credit £
Stock:		
Raw materials	150	
Work in progress	380	
Finished goods	600	
Debtors	937	
Creditors		502
HMRC (PAYE and NIC owing)		250
Cash at bank	1,634	
Plant and equipment	3,000	
Provision for depreciation of plant and equipment		500
Share capital		2,000
Profit and loss		3,449
	6,701	6,701

Transactions in April

Summary of bank transactions

	Debit £	Credit £
Debtors cheques received	3,000	
Cheques paid to creditors		1,900
Wages paid		810
Inland revenue		250
Pension scheme		50
Production overheads		660
Administration overheads		140
Selling overheads		120
Total	3,000	3,930

Other information

	£	£
Invoices for materials received		1,840
Materials requisitions:		
Production		1,790
Administration		95
Payroll:		
Net	810	
PAYE & NIC	186	
Pension scheme contributions	50	
Total		1,046
Payroll analysis:		
Direct labour (100 hours)	920	
Indirect: production salaries	100	
Indirect: admin salaries	26	
		1,046
Sales invoices issued		3,170
Production transferred to finished goods in the period		2,100
Value of closing stock of finished goods		200
Overhead absorption rate per direct labour hour		10.50
Depreciation of plant and equipment for the month		
(factory plant: £80, office equipment: £25)		

Record the above information in appropriate T-accounts, closing the profit and loss items to a trading and profit and loss account, and prepare an opening trial balance at 1 May.

Solution

Work through the accounts below, checking that you understand each double entry. You may find it useful to begin by checking the opening balances from the trial balance, and then working down the transactions as listed. Finally, follow the amounts transferred to the trading and profit and loss account, and any balances left on accounts should appear in the opening trial balance for May.

Raw materials account

	£		£
Balance b/d	150	WIP (direct materials)	1,790
Creditors	1,840	Administration overheads	95
		Balance c/d	105
	1,990		1,990

Wages and salaries account

	£		f
Cash at bank	810	WIP (direct labour)	920
HMRC	186	Production overheads	100
Pension scheme		Administrative overheads	26
contributions	50		
	1,046		1,046

Production overheads account

	£		£
Wages and salaries	100	WIP (absorbed:	
Plant depreciation	80	100 h @ £10.50)	1,050
Cash at bank	660		
Profit and loss			
(over-absorbed)	210		
	1,050		1,050

WIP account

	£		£
Balance b/d	380	Finished goods	2,100
Raw materials	1,790		
Wages and salaries	920		
Production overheads	1,050	Balance c/d	2,040
	4,140		4,140

Finished goods account

	£		£
Balance b/d	600	Profit and loss:	
WIP	2,100	cost of sales	2,500
		Balance c/d	200
	2,700		2,700

Administration overheads account

	£		£
Materials	95		
Wages and salaries	26		
Equipment depreciation	25		
Cash at bank	140	Profit and loss	286
	286		286

Selling overheads account

	£		£
Cash at bank	120		
		Profit and loss	120
	120		120

Sales account

	£		£
Profit and loss	3,170	Debtors	3,170
	3,170		3,170

Trading and profit and loss account for April

	£		£
Cost of sales	2,500	Sales	3,170
Administration overheads	286	Over-absorbed overheads	210
Selling overheads	120		
Net profit (transfer to			
profit and loss reserve)	474		
	3,380		3,380

Cash at bank account

	£		£
Balance b/d	1,634	Creditors	1,900
Debtors	3,000	Wages and salaries	810
		HMRC	250
		Pension scheme	50
		Production overheads	660
		Administration overheads	140
		Selling overheads	120
		Balance c/d	704
	4,634		4,634
Balance b/d	704		

Debtors account

	£		£
Balance b/d	937	Cash at bank	3,000
Sales	3,170	Balance c/d	1,107
	4,107		4,107
Balance b/d	1,107		

Creditors account

	£		£
Cash at bank	1,900	Balance b/d	502
Balance c/d	442	Raw materials	1,840
	2,342		2,342
		Balance b/d	442

HMRC creditor account

	£		£
Cash at bank	250	Balance b/d	250
Balance c/d	186	Wages and salaries	
		for April	186
	436		436
		Balance b/d	186

Pension scheme creditor

	£		£
Cash at bank	50	Wages and salaries	
		for April	50
	50		50

Plant and equipment account

	£		£
Balance b/d	3,000		

	£		£
		Balance b/d	500
		Production overhead	
		(plant depn)	80
		Administration overheads	
Balance c/d	605	(office equipment depn)	25
	605		605
		Balance b/d	605

Share capital account

	£		£
		Balance b/d	2,000

Profit and loss reserve account

	£		£
		Balance b/d	3,449
		Profit for April (transferred from trading and profit and loss	
Balance c/d	3,923	account for the month)	474
	3,923		3,923
		Balance b/d	3,923

OPENING TRIAL BALANCE AT 1 MAY 2006

Account	Debit £	Credit £
Stock:		
Raw materials	105	
Work in progress	2,040	
Finished goods	200	
Debtors	1,107	
Creditors		442
HMRC (PAYE and NIC owing)		186
Cash at bank	704	
Plant and equipment	3,000	
Provision for depreciation of plant and equipment		605
Share capital		2,000
Profit and loss		3,923
	7,156	7,156

The trading and profit and loss T-account could have been presented more formally, if required.

Cranefly Limited

Trading and profit and loss account for April 2006

	£
Sales	3,170
Cost of sales	(2,500)
Gross profit	670
Administration overheads	(286)
Selling overheads	(120)
Over-absorption of overheads	210
Net profit	474

Activity 4

At 1 July 2006 the Work in Progress ledger account for a business had a balance of £730. During the month of July the following transactions took place:

Materials requisitions for the factory	£2,460
Direct factory labour	£1,070
Production overheads	140 hours @ £2.10 per hour
Production transferred to finished goods	£4,100

Write up the work in progress ledger account.

CHAPTER OVERVIEW

- control accounts are used in a cost bookkeeping system in order to summarise information about the major elements of production – materials purchased and issued, wages, production overheads and work in progress

- each cost incurred must be correctly coded to ensure that it is posted to the correct account in the cost bookkeeping ledger

- an integrated cost bookkeeping system is one which combines both the entries required for the financial accounting function and the cost accounting function

- an interlocking system is one where a separate cost accounting ledger is kept – a cost ledger control account is kept for all of the entries which relate to the financial accounting function such as cash, debtors and creditors

- the production overheads account is debited with the overheads actually incurred in the period and credited with the overheads that are to be absorbed into the work in progress for the period – any balance on the account is an under or over absorption of overheads and is taken to the profit and loss account

KEY WORDS

Materials control account records all purchases of materials and issues to WIP

Wages control account records the total payroll costs and the transfers of direct labour to WIP and indirect labour to overheads

Production overhead control account records the actual overhead incurred, the amount of overhead absorbed into WIP and any under or over absorption

Work in progress control account records the total direct materials, direct labour and production overhead used in the production process in the period

Integrated system a cost bookkeeping system that combines the cost accounting and financial accounting functions

Interlocking system cost bookkeeping system where a separate ledger is kept for the cost accounting function

HOW MUCH HAVE YOU LEARNED?

1   A manufacturing business has the following transactions for the week ending 17 August 2003:

Materials purchased on credit	£4,380
Materials requisitions from the factory	£4,190
Total payroll costs – direct factory labour	£3,200
– indirect factory labour	£940
Production overheads incurred	£1,200
Production overheads to be absorbed	480 hours @ 3.10 per hour
Transfer of production to finished goods	£7,900

Write up the following ledger accounts in an integrated cost bookkeeping system to reflect these transactions, showing clearly which account the other side of the entry would be found in.

- Materials control account
- Wages control account
- Production overhead control account
- Work in Progress control account

2   A manufacturing business absorbs production overheads into work in progress at a rate of £6.80 per direct labour hour. In the month of June 2006 the overheads incurred totalled £3,800 and the direct labour hours worked were 550.

Write up the production overhead control account. Explain the accounting treatment of any balance on the account.

3   Given below are extracts from the trial balance of a business at 1 July 2006:

	Debit £	Credit £
Stock:		
Raw materials	550	
Work in Progress	680	
Finished goods	1,040	
Debtors	3,700	
Creditors		2,100
Cash at bank	2,090	

You are also given a summary of some of the transactions of the business for the month of July:

Materials purchased on credit	£5,300
Materials requisitions	
– factory	£4,670
– administration	£760
Wages cost	
– direct factory labour (360 hours)	£2,520
– indirect factory labour	£640
Sales invoices issued	£12,000
Cheques received from debtors	£11,000
Cheques paid to creditors	£5,140
Production transferred to finished goods	£10,000
Production overheads paid by cheque	£2,700
Administration overheads paid by cheque	£1,580
Closing stock of finished goods	£2,010

Production overheads are absorbed at the budgeted overhead absorption rate of £7.80 per direct labour hour.

You are required to write up the following ledger accounts to reflect these transactions and to balance each of the accounts at the end of the month:

Materials control account

£		£

Wages control account

£		£

Production overhead control account

£		£

Work in progress control account

£		£

Finished goods control account

£		£

Debtors control account

	£		£

Creditors control account

	£		£

Cash at bank account

	£		£

Administration overheads account

	£		£

Sales account

	£		£

4 Returning to the previous question, prepare the profit and loss account for the period.

chapter 8:
SHORT-TERM DECISION MAKING

chapter coverage 📖

In Chapter 1 we saw that one of the main priorities of management is decision making. In this chapter we will consider a variety of techniques and information that is useful to management in the making of short-term decisions. The topics that are covered are:

✍ contribution and profit

✍ cost-volume-profit analysis

✍ break-even point

✍ target profit

✍ margin of safety

✍ profit volume ratio

✍ break-even charts

✍ limiting factor analysis

✍ writing a report

Unit 6

knowledge and understanding – the business environment

1   the nature and purpose of internal reporting
2   management information requirements

knowledge and understanding – accounting techniques

12   calculation of product and service cost

13   analysis of the effect of changing activity levels on unit costs

14   methods of presenting information in written reports

15   the identification of fixed, variable and semi-variable costs and their use in cost recording, cost reporting and cost analysis

16   cost-volume-profit analysis

17   the identification of limiting factors

Performance criteria - element 6.3

A   identify information relevant to estimating current and future revenues and costs

B   prepare estimates of future income and costs

C   calculate the effects of variations in capacity on product costs

D   analyse critical factors affecting costs and revenues using appropriate accounting techniques and draw clear conclusions from the analysis

E   state any assumptions used when evaluating future costs and revenues

F   identify and evaluate options and solutions for their contribution to organisational goals

G   present recommendations to appropriate people in a clear and concise way and supported by a clear rationale

CONTRIBUTION AND PROFIT

In the chapter on marginal costing we defined CONTRIBUTION as sales revenue less variable costs. We can look at contribution in total, as we did in marginal costing, or at contribution per unit.

Provided that the selling price and variable costs remain constant at different levels of activity then contribution per unit will also be a constant figure at each level of activity. However, when we considered fixed costs, we saw that as activity levels increase, although the fixed costs themselves remain constant, the fixed cost per unit falls as the fixed costs are spread over more units. This means that even though contribution per unit will remain constant with increasing levels of activity, profit per unit will increase.

HOW IT WORKS

J R Grantham & Partners are considering expanding their business from its current production and sales of 100,000 units per annum. Market research suggests that it will almost certainly be possible to increase sales to 150,000 and possibly even to 180,000 units per annum.

The single product that the partnership produces sells for £20 and has variable costs of production of £15. The fixed costs are currently £400,000 per annum and are not expected to increase.

We will look at the contribution per unit, cost per unit and profit per unit at each activity level.

	100,000	150,000	180,000
	£	£	£
Sales	2,000,000	3,000,000	3,600,000
Variable costs	1,500,000	2,250,000	2,700,000
Contribution	500,000	750,000	900,000
Fixed costs	400,000	400,000	400,000
Profit	100,000	350,000	500,000
Contribution per unit	£5	£5	£5
Cost per unit (variable + fixed)			
£15 + £400,000/100,000	£19		
£15 + £400,000/150,000		£17.67	
£15 + £400,000/180,000			£17.22
Profit per unit	£1	£2.33	£2.78

As we can see there is a significant decrease in cost per unit as the activity level rises due to the fixed costs being spread over a larger number of units. This also therefore means that there is a significant increase in profit per unit as the activity level increases. However contribution per unit has remained constant.

This is one of the reasons why for decision making purposes contribution per unit is a much more meaningful figure than profit per unit, as the profit per unit figure is simply being affected by the spreading of the fixed costs.

Thus, for decision making purposes, you should always treat total profit as having two distinct elements:

1	Total contribution (= contribution/unit × units)	X
	Less:	
2	Fixed costs	(X)
		X

Element **1** (contribution) varies proportionately with volume, whilst element **2** (fixed costs) is a lump-sum period deduction.

COST-VOLUME-PROFIT ANALYSIS

COST-VOLUME-PROFIT ANALYSIS is the general term for the analysis of the relationship between activity levels, costs and profit. One of the most common areas of this analysis is BREAK-EVEN ANALYSIS whereby the break-even point for a business is determined.

The BREAK-EVEN POINT is the level of activity where the sales revenue is equal to the total costs of the business, meaning that all costs are covered by sales revenue but no profit is made. This is obviously an important point for managers of a business to be aware of; if the activity level falls below the break-even point then losses will be made.

So the break-even point activity level can be expressed as the point where:

Sales revenue = Variable costs + Fixed costs

Alternatively

Sales revenue - Variable costs = Fixed costs

Remember that sales revenue minus variable costs is equal to contribution. So the relationship is that the break-even point is where:

Contribution = Fixed costs

Contribution per unit × break-even point (units) = Fixed costs

We saw in an earlier example in this chapter that provided that selling price and variable costs remain constant at different levels of activity then contribution per unit will also remain constant. We can therefore use this to calculate the break-even point.

$$\text{Break-even point} = \frac{\text{Fixed costs}}{\text{Contribution per unit}}$$

HOW IT WORKS

Reardon Enterprises sells a single product with a selling price of £10 per unit. The variable costs of producing the product are £6 per unit and the fixed costs of the business are £200,000.

What is the break-even point in units?

$$\text{Break-even point} = \frac{£200,000}{£10 - £6}$$

$$= 50,000 \text{ units}$$

We can prove that this is the point where no profit or loss is made.

	£
Sales (50,000 x £10)	500,000
Variable costs (50,000 x £6)	300,000
Contribution	200,000
Fixed costs	200,000
Profit	-

Therefore the management of Reardon Enterprises will know that they must ensure that sales volumes exceed 50,000 units per annum in order for the business to cover its total costs and make any profit.

Activity 1

A business has a single product that it sells for £28. The variable costs of producing the product are £19 per unit and the fixed costs of the business are £360,000.

What is the break-even point in units?

Target profit

It is also possible to extend the analysis using contribution per unit in order to determine the level of sales that are necessary in order to not only cover all of the costs but also to make a particular amount of profit, the **target profit**.

Thus we want:

Contribution per unit × target activity level	X
Less: fixed costs	(X)
Target profit	X

Working back this gives us:

$$\text{Activity level} \quad = \quad \frac{\text{Fixed costs + target profit}}{\text{Contribution per unit}}$$

HOW IT WORKS

Returning to Reardon Enterprises the managing director, Anna Reardon, would like to ensure a profit of £100,000 for the coming year. What level of sales is required for this profit to be made?

$$\text{Activity level} \quad = \quad \frac{£200,000 + £100,000}{£10 - £6}$$

$$= \quad 75,000 \text{ units}$$

Therefore if the business sells 75,000 units of the product a profit of £100,000 will be made. Again we can check this:

	£
Sales (75,000 x £10)	750,000
Variable costs (75,000 x £6)	450,000
Contribution	300,000
Fixed costs	200,000
Profit	100,000

Activity 2

A business has fixed costs of £250,000. It sells just one product for a price of £80 and the variable costs of production are £60.

How many units of the product must be business sell in order to make a profit of £150,000?

Margin of safety

Another figure that management might be interested in is the MARGIN OF SAFETY. This is difference between the budgeted or forecast sales or actual current sales and the break-even sales level. This is usually expressed as a percentage of the budgeted, forecast or actual sales. (In the exam, make sure you express the margin of safety as a percentage of the budgeted, forecast or actual sales, **not** as a percentage of break-even sales.)

HOW IT WORKS

Remember that Reardon Enterprise's break-even sales volume was 50,000 units. If the budgeted sales for the forthcoming year are 70,000 units what is the margin of safety?

Margin of safety   =   70,000 units - 50,000 units
                   =   20,000 units

This can be expressed as a percentage of budgeted sales, which should be used as the denominator in calculations.

$$\text{Margin of safety} \quad = \quad \frac{20,000}{70,000} \times 100$$

                   =   28.6%

This tells management that sales can drop below the budgeted figure by 28.6% before losses start to be made.

Activity 3

A business has budgeted to sell 75,000 units of its single product in the following year. The product sells for £32 and the variable costs of production are £24. The fixed overheads of the business are £480,000.

What is the margin of safety?

Profit volume ratio

When we were calculating the break-even point above the figure that was derived using contribution per unit and fixed costs was the number of **units** that were required to be sold in order to break-even. However the break-even point can also be expressed in terms of the sales **revenue** required in order to break-even, by using the profit volume ratio (P/V) which can also be called the CONTRIBUTION OF SALES RATIO (C/S).

$$\text{Profit volume ratio} \quad = \quad \frac{\text{Contribution}}{\text{Sales}} \times 100$$

Thus the P/V ratio measures contribution **per £ sales revenue** rather than per **physical sales unit**.

Thus, at break-even sales revenue

Total contribution (PV ratio × break-even sales revenue)	X
Less: fixed costs	(X)
Profit	0

The break-even point in terms of sales revenue can then be found as:

$$\text{Break-even point (£)} \quad = \quad \frac{\text{Fixed costs}}{\text{Profit volume ratio}}$$

HOW IT WORKS

Reardon Enterprises sell their product for £10 and the variable costs are £6 per unit. Total fixed costs are £200,000.

$$\text{Profit volume ratio} \quad = \quad \frac{£10 - £6}{£10} \times 100$$

$$= \quad 40\%$$

$$\text{Break-even point (£)} \quad = \quad \frac{£200,000}{0.40}$$

$$= \quad £500,000$$

(which corresponds to a unit activity level of $\dfrac{£500,000}{£10}$ = 50,000 as before)

Activity 4

A business has a single product that it sells for £36. The variable costs of producing the product are £27 per unit and the fixed costs of the business are £360,000.

What is the break-even point in terms of sales revenue?

CHARTS

Break-even points and activity levels where target profits are made are traditionally illustrated on a number of charts. They all show basically the same information - variable costs, fixed costs, sales revenue, profit - but each one has a slightly different emphasis. The three most common are:

- the break-even chart
- the contribution break-even chart
- the profit-volume chart

HOW IT WORKS

We will use the information for Reardon Enterprises to illustrate these charts.

Selling price per unit	£10
Variable cost per unit	£6
Contribution per unit	£4
Fixed costs	£200,000
Break-even point	50,000 units or £500,000
Budgeted sales	70,000 units

Break-even chart

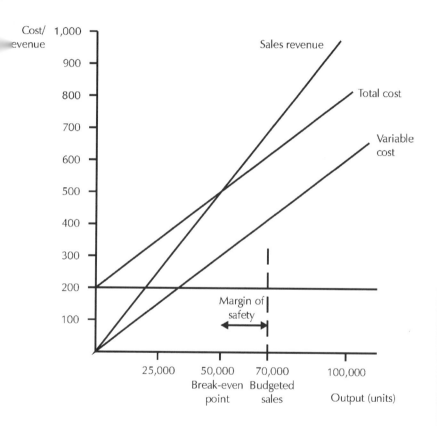

This chart shows variable costs, fixed costs, total costs and sales revenue at various different activity levels.

How to draw it up

- The fixed cost line is a horizontal line at £200,000

- Variable costs start at the origin - if there are no sales then there are no variable costs. Then plot one further point, for example variable costs at 100,000 units are £600,000 and join this to the origin

167

- The total cost line is parallel to the variable cost line but starts a £200,000, the level of the fixed costs

- Sales revenue again starts at the origin - plot another point such a revenue of £1,000,000 if sales are 100,000 units and join this with a line to the origin.

What does the chart show?

- The break-even point is the point where the sales revenue line crosses the total costs line

- The margin of safety is the horizontal distance between budgetec sales of 70,000 units and break-even sales of 50,000 units

- The amount of profit or loss at each activity level is the vertica distance between the sales revenue line and the total cost line

Contribution break-even chart

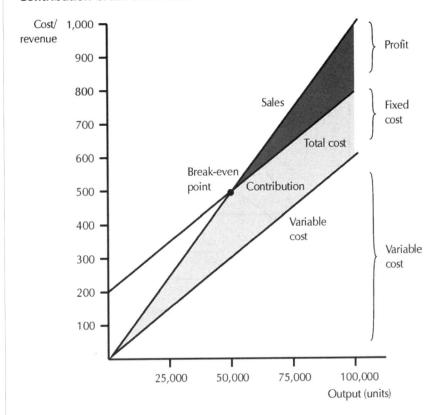

This chart again plots costs and revenue but this time no line for fixed costs.

How to draw it up

- The variable cost line and sales revenue line are drawn up as in the previous chart

- The total cost line is parallel to the variable cost line but starting at £200,000

What does the chart show?

- The break-even point is where the sales and total cost line cross

- The shaded area between the sales line and the variable cost line clearly shows the contribution at each activity level

- The area between the variable cost line and total cost line is the fixed cost

- The double-shaded area between the sales revenue line and the total cost line is the profit

The only main difference between these first two charts is that in this second one the contribution can be read off more clearly.

Profit volume chart

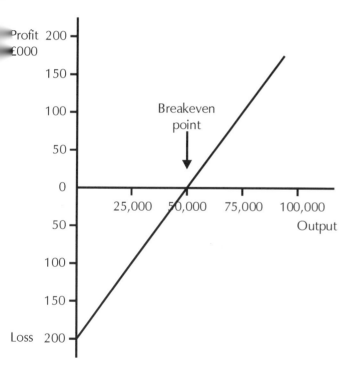

The profit-volume chart simply shows the level of profit or loss at any given level of activity.

How to draw it up

- The vertical axis must range from the profit made at the highest level of activity to the loss made when there are zero sales

- The loss when there are zero sales is equal to the fixed costs £200,000

- The profit at the 100,000 units activity level is £200,000

- Draw a line between these two points

What does the chart show?

- The profit or loss at any level of activity can be read off the chart

- The break-even point is where the profit line crosses the horizontal axis - where profit is zero

- The horizontal axis could alternatively have shown sales revenue rather than activity level

LIMITING FACTOR ANALYSIS

Obviously the managers of a business will wish to produce and sell more than the break-even number of units in order to cover fixed costs and make a profit. However, in practice, the quantity that they can produce and sell may be limited by one or more factors, the LIMITING FACTOR(S).

In many cases the limiting factor will be market demand, or the amount of units that customers are prepared to buy. However, in other instances the limiting factor might be the amount of materials that are available or the number of machine or labour hours that are available. This has been the most common recent scenario in Unit 6 exams.

HOW IT WORKS

A business sells a single product for £35. The variable costs of the product are:

Direct materials	3 kg per unit @ £3 per kg
Direct labour	2 hours per unit @ £7.50 per hour

The fixed costs of the business are £800,000.

Materials as limiting factor

If the supply of materials is limited to 360,000 kg, how many units can the business produce and how much profit will be made?

Number of units that can be produced = 360,000kg/3kg per unit
= 120,000 units

	£
Sales (120,000 x £35)	4,200,000
Variable costs (120,000 x (£9 + £15))	2,880,000
Contribution	1,320,000
Fixed costs	800,000
Profit	520,000

Labour hours as limiting factor

materials are now not restricted, but the business only has 280,000 labour hours available for production, how many units can be made and what is the profit at this production level?

$$\text{Number of units that can be produced} = 280,000 \text{ hours}/2 \text{ hours per unit}$$
$$= 140,000 \text{ units}$$

	£
Sales (140,000 x £35)	4,900,000
Variable costs (140,000 x £24)	3,360,000
Contribution	1,540,000
Fixed costs	800,000
Profit	740,000

MORE THAN ONE PRODUCT

We will now make the position a little more complicated by introducing a business that makes more than one product. If the availability of either materials or labour hours is the limiting factor then it will be necessary to determine the optimum production mix.

In order to make a decision we must determine our criterion for the decision making process. In business the overriding criterion will normally be to make as much profit as possible. As fixed costs in total are assumed to be constant whatever combination of products is made, maximisation of profit will be achieved by maximising **contribution**.

If a business has more than one product, and one limiting factor, the technique to use in order to maximise contribution is to determine the contribution per unit of the scarce resource or limiting factor and concentrate upon the production of the product with the highest contribution per limiting factor unit.

HOW IT WORKS

Farnham Engineering makes three products A, B and C. The costs and selling prices of the three products are:

	A £	B £	C £
Direct materials @ £4 per kg	8	16	12
Direct labour @ £7 per hour	7	21	14
Variable overheads	3	9	6
	18	46	32
Selling price	22	54	39
Contribution	4	8	7

Sales demand for the coming period is expected to be as follows:

Product A	3,000 units
Product B	7,000 units
Product C	5,000 units

The supply of materials is limited to 50,000 kg during the period and the labour hours available are 28,000.

We have to decide firstly if there is a limiting factor other than sales demand. Consider the materials usage for each product if the maximum sales demand is produced. (You are not given the actual usage of materials of each product but you can work it out - for example the materials cost for A is £8 and as the materials are £4 per kg, product A must use 2 kg etc.)

	A	B	C	Total
Materials	6,000 kg	28,000 kg	15,000 kg	49,000 kg
Labour	3,000 hours	21,000 hours	10,000 hours	34,000 hours

As 50,000 kg of materials are available for the period and only 49,000 kg are required for the maximum production level, materials are not a limiting factor.

However, only 28,000 labour hours are available whereas in order to produce the maximum demand 34,000 hours are required. Therefore labour hours are the limiting factor.

The next stage is to calculate the contribution per limiting factor unit - so in this case the contribution per labour hour - for each product. Then rank the products according to how high the contribution per labour hour is for each one.

	A	B	C
Contribution	£4	£8	£7
Labour hours per unit	1 hour	3 hours	2 hours

Contribution per labour hour			
£4/1	£4.00		
£8/3		£2.67	
£7/2			£3.50
Ranking	1	3	2

therefore in order to maximise contribution we must concentrate first on production of A up to the maximum sales demand, then on C, and finally, if here are any remaining hours available, on B.

he optimal production plan in order to maximise contribution is:

	Units produced	Labour hours required
A	3,000	3,000
C	5,000	10,000
B (balance)	5,000	15,000 (balancing figure)
		28,000

he contribution earned from this production plan is:

		£
A	(3,000 x £4)	12,000
B	(5,000 x £8)	40,000
C	(5,000 x £7)	35,000
Total contribution		87,000

Activity 5

A business produces four products and the details are:

	P	Q	R	S
Contribution per unit	£12	£15	£9	£14
Materials per unit	3 kg	4 kg	1 kg	2 kg
Maximum demand (units)	2,000	6,000	1,000	4,000

Fixed costs amount to £30,000 each period, and the materials supply is limited to 30,000 kg. What is the production plan that will maximise profit and what will be the profit earned by this production plan?

WRITING A REPORT

In this chapter we have looked at a number of techniques that can be used to determine unit costs, sales levels and optimal production levels. Each technique has allowed you to determine information that is of use to management, such as the break-even point for sales or the production plan that will maximise profits. In practice and in assessments and exams you may be asked to produce this information for management in the form of written report.

The Unit 6 assessor has indicated that Section 2 of the exam will include requirement for you to write a memo or a report commenting on data that you have derived in an earlier task in Section 2.

Chapter 12 of this Course Companion is a detailed chapter on report writing and you may wish to turn to this chapter now. When writing a report regarding the short-term decision making techniques covered in this chapter the main points to note are:

- show your calculations in an appendix to the report and only refer to the results of the calculations in the body of the report

- clearly show any conclusion that you reach or recommendation that you make, such as the break-even point or optimal production plan

- justify your conclusions or recommendations with reference to the calculations that you have made

CHAPTER OVERVIEW

- due to the nature of fixed costs, total unit cost will tend to decrease as activity levels increase as the fixed costs are spread over more units of production – however if selling price and variable costs remain constant then contribution per unit will remain constant as activity levels change

- the break-even point in units is found by dividing the fixed costs by the contribution per unit

- if a target profit is required the unit sales to achieve this can be found by dividing the fixed costs plus target profit by the contribution per unit

- the difference between budgeted or actual sales and the break-even point is the margin of safety, which can be expressed as a percentage of budgeted or actual sales.

- the profit volume ratio can be used to find the break-even point in terms of sales revenue

- sales revenue, costs, contribution, profit and break-even point can be illustrated by a number of different break-even charts

- normally production of products is limited by sales demand however in some instances factors such as the availability of material, labour hours or machine hours is the limiting factor

- where there is more than one product and a limiting factor, overall profit is maximised by concentrating production on the products with the highest contribution per limiting factor unit

---

KEY WORDS

Contribution sales revenue or selling price per unit less variable costs

Cost-volume-profit analysis analysis of the relationships between activity levels, costs and profits

Break-even analysis calculations to determine the break-even point

Break-even point level of sales whereby sales revenue is equal to total costs

Margin of safety excess of budgeted or actual sales over the break-even point sales

Profit volume (P/V) ratio ratio of contribution to sales

Contribution to sales (C/S) ratio alternative name for the profit volume ratio

Limiting factor a factor of production or sales that limits the amount of a product that can be produced or sold

---

HOW MUCH HAVE YOU LEARNED?

1 If selling prices and variable costs remain constant at differing levels of activity explain why unit cost will tend to fall as activity levels increase.

2 A business has budgeted sales of its single product of 38,000 units. The selling price per unit is £57 and the variable costs of production are £45. The fixed costs of the business are £360,000.

   What is the break-even point in units and the margin of safety?

3 A business has fixed costs of £910,000. It sells a single product at a selling price of £24 and the variable costs of production and sales are £17 per unit.

   How many units of the product must the business sell in order to make a profit of £500,000?

4 A business sells its single product for £40. The variable costs of this product total £32. The fixed costs of the business are £100,000.

   What is the sales revenue required in order to make a profit of £200,000?

5 A business produces three products, the production and sales details of which are given below

	Product		
	R	S	T
Direct materials @ £2 per kg	£16	£12	£10
Direct labour @ £9 per hour	£18	£36	£9
Selling price	£40	£60	£25
Machine hours per unit	6	4	3
Maximum sales demand	10,000 units	20,000 units	5,000 units

   During the next period the supply of materials is limited to 250,000 kgs, the labour hours available are 120,000 and the machine hours available are also 120,000. Fixed costs are £50,000 per period.

   What is the production plan which will maximise profit and what is the profit that will be earned under that production plan?

chapter 9:
LONG-TERM DECISION MAKING

Unit 6

knowledge and understanding – the business environment

1   the nature and purpose of internal reporting
2   management information requirements

knowledge and understanding – accounting techniques

14   methods of presenting information in written reports
18   methods of project appraisal: payback and discounted cash flow methods (NPV and IRR)

knowledge and understanding – accounting principles and theory

25   the principles of discounted cash flow

Performance criteria - element 6.3

A   identify information relevant to estimating current and future revenues and costs

B   prepare estimates of future income and costs

D   analyse critical factors affecting costs and revenues using appropriate accounting techniques and draw clear conclusions from the analysis

E   state any assumptions used when evaluating future costs and revenues

F   identify and evaluate options and solutions for their contribution to organisational goals

G   present recommendations to appropriate people in a clear and concise way and supported by a clear rationale

THE NATURE OF LONG-TERM DECISIONS

Many decisions that the managers of a business will have to make will affect the business over a fairly long time period. In particular the purchase of buildings, machinery or equipment will be expected to bring benefits to the business over a number of future years. The decision which managers will have to take is should this capital item, which is often a significant amount of expenditure, be purchased? Are the future benefits from this current expenditure enough to justify the investment?

The answers to these questions are highly subjective as managers will have to base their decision on estimates of future costs, revenues and performance. However these estimates have to be made and assessed in order to make informed decisions.

As the costs and revenues involved in these types of decisions are to be considered over a number of years into the future there are a number of techniques which can be used. For Unit 6 you need to be able to analyse a project using either the payback method or discounted cash flow techniques. We will start with the payback method.

PAYBACK PERIOD

If a large amount of money is to be spent now on a project, such as the purchase of a major fixed asset, one decision criterion that the management of the business may apply is keeping the length of time over which the benefits from this asset pay back the original cost within acceptable limits. This is what is meant by the PAYBACK PERIOD.

To find the payback period the initial cost of the project must firstly be known. Then the future cash income or cost savings must be estimated. To calculate the payback period we need to determine how long it will take for this future income or cost saving to pay back the initial expenditure.

HOW IT WORKS

Uckport Industrials is considering investment in major new plant for their factory which will cost £250,000 if purchased now, 1 January 2006. The benefit of the new plant is that it will provide major cost savings in future production. The production manager has estimated that the cost savings for each year will be:

2006	£80,000
2007	£80,000
2008	£80,000
2009	£60,000
2010	£40,000

The payback period can be calculated by considering the cumulative cost savings:

Year	Cost saving	Cumulative cost savings
	£	£
2006	80,000	80,000
2007	80,000	160,000
2008	80,000	240,000
2009	60,000	300,000

With the initial cost being £250,000 we can see that by the end of 2008 we have not quite covered that figure but by the end of 2009 the initial cost has been covered. This is where we must start making assumptions about the timing of these cost savings in order to determine the payback period. There are two options here - either we can assume that the cost savings occur at the end of each year, ie. on 31 December, or that they occur evenly throughout the year.

Assumption - cost savings occur at end of year

If we assume that the cost savings occur at the end of each year then the payback period is four years as the initial cost of £250,000 is not totally paid back until 31 December 2009.

Assumption - cost savings occur evenly throughout year

If the assumption is made that the cost savings occur evenly throughout the year then we can see that by the end of 2008 we have almost recovered the cost with cumulative savings of £240,000. In 2009 the cost savings total £60,000 but in order to payback the initial cost we only need a further £10,000 of this. Therefore the payback period can be calculated as:

Payback period   =   3 years + (£10,000/£60,000 x 12 months)
　　　　　　　　 =   3 years and 2 months

Whenever you make an assumption in your calculations it is important that you clearly state that assumption in your presentation of the information.

How is payback period used?

Once we have calculated the payback period for a project we must then consider how it is to be used in the decision making process. If payback period is used to assess projects then the management will have set a PAYBACK PERIOD LIMIT. This is the time period within which all projects must payback their initial cost if they are to be accepted. In an exam, if you are not told about the payback limit required by the business, you cannot conclude on the investment purely on the basis of payback.

HOW IT WORKS

Suppose that the management of Uckport Industrials have a payback period limit of 4 years. In this case this project (under either assumption) does have a payback period which is either four years or less and therefore the project would be accepted.

If Uckport Industrials had had a payback period limit of 3 years, however, then the project would have been rejected.

Activity 1

A business is considering investment in new machinery at a cost of £100,000 now, 1 January 2006. The machinery will be used to make a new product which will provide additional cash inflows as follows:

Year ending
31 December 2006	£30,000
31 December 2007	£40,000
31 December 2008	£40,000
31 December 2009	£20,000

The cash inflows occur evenly throughout the year. What is the payback period?

Advantages of payback period

The payback period method is one of the most widely used methods of project appraisal. It is a fairly simple calculation to make and is easily understood by management. It also appears to consider the risk of a business being parted from its money as it is considering the time period between the cash outflow for the initial cost and the cash inflow from income or cost savings.

Disadvantages of payback period

It can however be argued that the payback period method is too simple does not take account of all of the cash flows associated with the project, on those up to the end of the payback period and it does not take any accoun of how those cash flows occur over the period. For example, with Uckpo Industrials' project, if the same machinery had not had any cost savings in th first three years but £300,000 of cost savings in 2009 it would still have ha a payback period of 4 years but clearly may not have been acceptable du to the cash flow implications.

Most importantly the payback period fails to take any account of the TIM VALUE OF MONEY.

THE TIME VALUE OF MONEY

The time value of money is all to do with our preference to receive mone sooner rather than later. If we are offered £100 now or in a year's time then we would prefer to have the money now rather than wait. There are three main reasons for this:

RISK PREFERENCE — if the money is received now then i is ours and there is no risk that i might not be paid in one year's time

CONSUMPTION PREFERENCE — if the money is received now then we can spend it now rather than having to wait for a year (when i may be worth less in real terms)

INVESTMENT PREFERENCE — if the money is received now then we can invest it, and earn interest on it so that in one years time it is worth more than £100

It is the third of these, the investment preference, which concerns us here.

Present values

If we are offered £100 now or £100 in one year's time we are not comparing like with like. If interest rates are, say, 10% per annum then if the £100 were received now then it could be invested for a year at 10% interest. After one year the amount that we would have would be:

£100 x 1.10 = £110

We would therefore definitely prefer the £100 now.

We would only be indifferent if we were offered the option of £100 now or £110 in one year's time. By turning it around we can say that the **present value** of £110 in one years time is £100 now (if interest rates are 10%) - the equivalent sum now of that future income. We can calculate the present value (PV) as:

$$PV \quad = \quad \frac{£110}{1.10} \quad = \quad £100$$

Lets now suppose that if we had £100 now we were to invest it for two years at 10% interest without removing the interest - this is known as COMPOUND INTEREST.

After one year our investment would be   £100 x 1.10 =   £110
After two years our investment would be   £110 x 1.10 =   £121

This can be simplified to:

Investment after two years   £100 x 1.10 x 1.10 =   £121

OR $£100 \times 1.10^2$

We can therefore also say that the present value of £121 arising after two years is £100. This would have been calculated as:

$$\frac{£121}{1.10^2}$$

OR $£121 \quad \times \quad \dfrac{1}{1.10^2}$

The element that the cash flow is multiplied by, in this case:

$$\frac{1}{1.10^2}$$

is known as the DISCOUNT FACTOR.

In general terms, the present value of a future amount of £x can be expressed as:

$$£x \quad \times \quad \frac{1}{(1+r)^n}$$

where r = the periodic interest rate or **discount rate** (expressed as a decimal)

        n = the number of periods before payment/receipt

student notes✍

Present value tables

Fortunately you do not need to remember that formula or to make the long hand calculations as these calculations have already been made for you in present value tables (included at the end of this Course Companion).

The first page of the present value tables is printed below so that it can be explained.

Present value table

Present value of £1 ie, $\dfrac{1}{(1+r)^n} = (1+r)^{-n}$

where   r = discount rate
       n = number of periods until payment

Discount rates (r)

Periods

(n)	1%	2%	3%	4%	5%	6%	7%	8%	9%	10%
1	0.990	0.980	0.971	0.962	0.952	0.943	0.935	0.926	0.917	0.909
2	0.980	0.961	0.943	0.925	0.907	0.890	0.873	0.857	0.842	0.826
3	0.971	0.942	0.915	0.889	0.864	0.840	0.816	0.794	0.772	0.751
4	0.961	0.924	0.888	0.855	0.823	0.792	0.763	0.735	0.708	0.683
5	0.951	0.906	0.863	0.822	0.784	0.747	0.713	0.681	0.650	0.621
6	0.942	0.888	0.837	0.790	0.746	0.705	0.666	0.630	0.596	0.564
7	0.933	0.871	0.813	0.760	0.711	0.665	0.623	0.583	0.547	0.513
8	0.923	0.853	0.789	0.731	0.677	0.627	0.582	0.540	0.502	0.467
9	0.914	0.837	0.766	0.703	0.645	0.592	0.544	0.500	0.460	0.424
10	0.905	0.820	0.744	0.676	0.614	0.558	0.508	0.463	0.422	0.386
11	0.896	0.804	0.722	0.650	0.585	0.527	0.475	0.429	0.388	0.350
12	0.887	0.788	0.701	0.625	0.557	0.497	0.444	0.397	0.356	0.319
13	0.879	0.773	0.681	0.601	0.530	0.469	0.415	0.368	0.326	0.290
14	0.870	0.758	0.661	0.577	0.505	0.442	0.388	0.340	0.299	0.263
15	0.861	0.743	0.642	0.555	0.481	0.417	0.362	0.315	0.275	0.239

Periods

(n)	11%	12%	13%	14%	15%	16%	17%	18%	19%	20%
1	0.901	0.893	0.885	0.877	0.870	0.862	0.855	0.847	0.840	0.833
2	0.812	0.797	0.783	0.769	0.756	0.743	0.731	0.718	0.706	0.694
3	0.731	0.712	0.693	0.675	0.658	0.641	0.624	0.609	0.593	0.579
4	0.659	0.636	0.613	0.592	0.572	0.552	0.534	0.516	0.499	0.482
5	0.593	0.567	0.543	0.519	0.497	0.476	0.456	0.437	0.419	0.402
6	0.535	0.507	0.480	0.456	0.432	0.410	0.390	0.370	0.352	0.335
7	0.482	0.452	0.425	0.400	0.376	0.354	0.333	0.314	0.296	0.279
8	0.434	0.404	0.376	0.351	0.327	0.305	0.285	0.266	0.249	0.233
9	0.391	0.361	0.333	0.308	0.284	0.263	0.243	0.225	0.209	0.194
10	0.352	0.322	0.295	0.270	0.247	0.227	0.208	0.191	0.176	0.162
11	0.317	0.287	0.261	0.237	0.215	0.195	0.178	0.162	0.148	0.135
12	0.286	0.257	0.231	0.208	0.187	0.168	0.152	0.137	0.124	0.112
13	0.258	0.229	0.204	0.182	0.163	0.145	0.130	0.116	0.104	0.093
14	0.232	0.205	0.181	0.160	0.141	0.125	0.111	0.099	0.088	0.078
15	0.209	0.183	0.160	0.140	0.123	0.108	0.095	0.084	0.074	0.065

The column headings show that interest or discount rates from 1% to 20% are covered. The rows are for time periods from time 1 to time 15. The figures that are calculated for each time period for each interest rate are the discount factor for a cash flow at the end of that time period and at that discount rate.

For example when we were finding the present value of £121 in two years' time at an interest rate of 10% per annum the calculation that we performed was:

$$£121 \quad \times \quad \frac{1}{1.10^2}$$

Using the tables - we need to move along to the 10% column and down to the time 2 row; we can then read off the discount factor as 0.8264. Therefore the calculation of the present value of £121 in two years time becomes:

£121 x 0.8264 $=$ £99.99 (which would be rounded up to £100).

Timing of cash flows

Using the present value tables you must take care to ensure that you are quite clear which time period row you are using. Dates are very important. Today's date is time 0, time 1 is in one year's time, time 2 is in two years' time etc.

Activity 2

Calculate the present value of each of the following cash flows. Today's date is 31 March 2006.

a) Cash outflow at 31 March 2008 of £7,100 - interest rate 7%
b) Cash inflow at 31 March 2010 of £380 - interest rate 11%
c) Cash inflow at 31 March 2007 of £2,030 - interest rate 5%

Annuity factors

An ANNUITY is the same amount of cash received or paid in successive time periods, starting in one year's time. For example, if we were to receive £100 at the end of each of the next three years this would be an annuity. If interest rates are 10% per annum the present value of this annuity could be calculated as:

			Present value £
Year 1 (one year's time)	£100 x 0.9090	$=$	90.90
Year 2 (two years' time)	£100 x 0.8264	$=$	82.64
Year 3 (three years' time)	£100 x 0.7513	$-$	75.13
			248.67

Alternatively the second page of the present value tables could be used - the annuity table. This is shown below for explanation.

Annuity table

Present value of an annuity of 1 ie, $\dfrac{1-(1+r)^{-n}}{r}$ or $\dfrac{1}{r}\left(1-\dfrac{1}{(1+r)^{n}}\right)$

where r = discount rate
       n = number of periods

Periods

(n)	1%	2%	3%	4%	5%	6%	7%	8%	9%	10%
1	0.990	0.980	0.971	0.962	0.952	0.943	0.935	0.926	0.917	0.909
2	1.970	1.942	1.913	1.886	1.859	1.833	1.808	1.783	1.759	1.736
3	2.941	2.884	2.829	2.775	2.723	2.673	2.624	2.577	2.531	2.487
4	3.902	3.808	3.717	3.630	3.546	3.465	3.387	3.312	3.240	3.170
5	4.853	4.713	4.580	4.452	4.329	4.212	4.100	3.993	3.890	3.791
6	5.795	5.601	5.417	5.242	5.076	4.917	4.767	4.623	4.486	4.355
7	6.728	6.472	6.230	6.002	5.786	5.582	5.389	5.206	5.033	4.868
8	7.652	7.325	7.020	6.733	6.463	6.210	5.971	5.747	5.535	5.335
9	8.566	8.162	7.786	7.435	7.108	6.802	6.515	6.247	5.995	5.759
10	9.471	8.983	8.530	8.111	7.722	7.360	7.024	6.710	6.418	6.145
11	10.368	9.787	9.253	8.760	8.306	7.887	7.499	7.139	6.805	6.495
12	11.255	10.575	9.954	9.385	8.863	8.384	7.943	7.536	7.161	6.814
13	12.134	11.348	10.635	9.986	9.394	8.853	8.358	7.904	7.487	7.103
14	13.004	12.106	11.296	10.563	9.899	9.295	8.745	8.244	7.786	7.367
15	13.865	12.849	11.938	11.118	10.380	9.712	9.108	8.559	8.061	7.606

Periods

(n)	11%	12%	13%	14%	15%	16%	17%	18%	19%	20%
1	0.901	0.893	0.885	0.877	0.870	0.862	0.855	0.847	0.840	0.833
2	1.713	1.690	1.668	1.647	1.626	1.605	1.585	1.566	1.547	1.528
3	2.444	2.402	2.361	2.322	2.283	2.246	2.210	2.174	2.140	2.106
4	3.102	3.037	2.974	2.914	2.855	2.798	2.743	2.690	2.639	2.589
5	3.696	3.605	3.517	3.433	3.352	3.274	3.199	3.127	3.058	2.991
6	4.231	4.111	3.998	3.889	3.784	3.685	3.589	3.498	3.410	3.326
7	4.712	4.564	4.423	4.288	4.160	4.039	3.922	3.812	3.706	3.605
8	5.146	4.968	4.799	4.639	4.487	4.344	4.207	4.078	3.954	3.837
9	5.537	5.328	5.132	4.946	4.772	4.607	4.451	4.303	4.163	4.031
10	5.889	5.650	5.426	5.216	5.019	4.833	4.659	4.494	4.339	4.192
11	6.207	5.938	5.687	5.453	5.234	5.029	4.836	4.656	4.486	4.327
12	6.492	6.194	5.918	5.660	5.421	5.197	4.988	4.793	4.611	4.439
13	6.750	6.424	6.122	5.842	5.583	5.342	5.118	4.910	4.715	4.533
14	6.982	6.628	6.302	6.002	5.724	5.468	5.229	5.008	4.802	4.611
15	7.191	6.811	6.462	6.142	5.847	5.575	5.324	5.092	4.876	4.675

s you can see the layout is the same as for the present value table. However
his time the discount factor that is shown in the **cumulative** discount factor
t that interest rate for an annuity for that time period.

Remember when we calculated the present value of £100 for each of the
next three years:

			Present value
			£
Year 1 (one year's time)	£100 x 0.9090	=	90.90
Year 2 (two years' time)	£100 x 0.8264	=	82.64
Year 3 (three years' time)	£100 x 0.7513	=	75.13
			248.67

What we could have done is simply total the three annual discount factors
and multiply this by £100.

$$£100 \times (0.9090 + 0.8264 + 0.7513) = £100 \times 2.4867 = £248.67$$

Alternatively we could have read off this cumulative discount factor from the
10% column and the time 3 row – 2.4867.

Activity 3

A business has to make a payment of £1,000 to a leasing company on 31
December from 2006 to 2010. The discount rate to use is 12%.

What is the present value of the payments if:

a)   today's date is 1 January 2006
b)   today's date is 31 December 2006?

In the exam you will be told the present value factor to apply to the given
data, correct to four places of decimal.

Perpetuity

A PERPETUITY is a cash flow of the same amount that is received every year
to infinity starting in one year's time. For example, if you were to receive
£100 every year starting in one year's time this would be a perpetuity.

You do not need any present value tables to calculate the discount factor for
this as it is so simple. The discount factor for a perpetuity is:

$$\frac{1}{r}$$

where r is the discount rate or interest rate (expressed as a decimal).

So if the interest rate is 10% and you are to receive £100 every year starting
in one year's time the present value of this is:

$$£100 \quad \times \quad \frac{1}{0.10} \quad = \quad £1,000$$

Activity 4

You are to receive £240 every year in perpetuity starting in one year's time and the interest rate is 5%. What is the present value of this income?

NET PRESENT VALUE

The computation of a present value is a **discounted cash flow (DCF technique**. We are finding the discounted (present) value of each individua cash flow or annuity.

If we are appraising a project then the technique that we can use is to find the NET PRESENT VALUE of all of the cash flows of the project. This involve calculating the present value of each individual cash flow and then totalling them all, remembering that the initial cost of the project is a cash outflow and any income or cost savings are cash inflows. The total of the present value o the inflows minus the outflows is the net present value (NPV).

Take care with the cash flows as we are dealing only with cash inflows or outflows and savings of cash outflows. Therefore any non-cash figures such as depreciation should be ignored.

If the net present value is a positive figure, a positive NPV, then the project should be accepted as this means that even after having taken account of the time value of money the cash inflows from the project exceed the cash outflows. If however the net present value is a negative figure, a negative NPV, then the project should be rejected.

HOW IT WORKS

We will return to Uckport Industrials.

Uckport Industrials is considering investment in major new plant for their factory which will cost £250,000 if purchased now, 1 January 2006. The benefit of the new plant is that it will provide major cost savings in future production. The production manager has estimated that the cost savings for each calendar year will be:

2006	£80,000
2007	£80,000
2008	£80,000
2009	£60,000
2010	£40,000

The discount rate, or COST OF CAPITAL to be used, is 10%.

We can now use discounted cash flow techniques to determine the net present value of this project. When using DCF techniques we have to be very careful about our assumptions about the timing of cash flows. As we have seen DCF techniques are used for cash flows at specific time intervals.

For this example therefore we will have to assume that the cost savings all occur on the last day of each year, but the investment occurs immediately, now, which we shall call year 0. Therefore the timings are as follows:

1 January 2006	=	Year 0
31 December 2006	=	Year 1
31 December 2007	=	Year 2

and so on.

We can now build up the net present value of these cash flows:

Year	Cash flow £	Discount factor @ 10%	Present value £
0	(250,000)	1.000	(250,000)
1	80,000	0.9090	72,720
2	80,000	0.8264	66,112
3	80,000	0.7513	60,104
4	60,000	0.6830	40,980
5	40,000	0.6209	24,836
Net present value			14,752

There are a number of points to note here:

- the initial cost occurs at year 0 or NOW, therefore the discount factor is 1.00 as £250,000 is the present value of the outflow now

- although the cost savings are not actual income they are the saving of an outflow, ie, they are reducing the cash costs of the business, and this is why they are treated as cash inflows.

- the initial cost of the machinery is a cash outflow and is therefore traditionally shown in brackets to distinguish it from the cost savings and cash inflows

The layout above shows clearly how the net present value is arrived at. An alternative layout, used by the examiner for Unit 6, is as follows:

	Year 0 £'000	Year 1 £'000	Year 2 £'000	Year 3 £'000	Year 4 £'000	Year 5 £'000
Investment	(250,000)					
Cost savings	0	80,000	80,000	80,000	60,000	40,000
PV factors	1.0000	0.9090	0.8264	0.7513	0.6830	0.6209
Discounted cash flows	(250,000)	72,720	66,112	60,104	40,980	24,836
NPV	14,752					

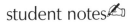

So for Uckport Industrials at their cost of capital or discount rate of 10% the project cash flows have a positive net present value and therefore the projec should be accepted.

You may have noted that the first three years of cost savings are an annuity the same amount each year. Therefore we could speed up the calculation by using the annuity tables for these cash flows.

Year	Cash flow £	Discount factor @ 10%	Present value £
0	(250,000)	1.0000	(250,000)
1 - 3	80,000	2.4867	198,936
4	60,000	0.6830	40,980
5	40,000	0.6209	24,836
Net present value			14,752

If you can spot annuities in any calculations it can make the calculations less time-consuming!

Activity 5

A business is considering investment in new machinery at a cost of £100,000 now, 1 January 2006. The machinery will be used to make a new product which will provide additional cash inflows as follows:

Year ending
31 December 2006   £30,000
31 December 2007   £40,000
31 December 2008   £40,000
31 December 2009   £20,000

The cash inflows occur the end of each year. What is the net present value at the cost of capital of 8%?

INTERNAL RATE OF RETURN

The INTERNAL RATE OF RETURN is the discount rate or interest rate that will result in a net present value of zero for a set of cash flows.

If the internal rate of return of a project is higher than the organisation's cost of capital or higher than its required return from investments the project should be accepted. If it is lower then it should be rejected.

For Unit 6 tasks will **not** be set which require the computation of a project's internal rate of return, but you should be aware of its meaning.

WRITING A REPORT

Both in practice and in assessments and exams you might be required to present information regarding payback period, net present value or internal rate of return in the form of a report. You can refer to Chapter 12 of this Course Companion for details of report writing.

The main things to remember are:

- show your calculations in an appendix to the report

- make sure that you give your conclusion, ie invest in the project or do not invest

- justify your conclusion, for example by stating that you should not invest as the project has a negative net present value

CHAPTER OVERVIEW

- long term decisions are often of the nature of large initial capital expenditure followed by benefits in terms of additional revenue or cost savings

- the payback period is a method of assessing a project based upon how quickly the inflows from the project repay the initial investment

- if the payback period for a project is shorter than the organisation's payback period limit then the project will be accepted

- the main disadvantage of the payback period is that it takes no account of the time value of money - if cash is to be received in the future it must be discounted to take account of the time value of money

- present value tables can be used so that individual discount factors do not have to be calculated

- annuity tables can be used to find the discount factor for an annuity

- one method of using discounted cash flow techniques for project appraisal is to calculate the net present value of the project cash flows - if the net present value at the organisation's cost of capital is positive then the project should be accepted but if it is negative it should be rejected

- if the internal rate of return of the project is greater than the organisation's cost of capital the project should be accepted

- you may be required to write a report incorporating your calculations and conclusions using payback or DCF techniques

KEY WORDS

Payback period the time it takes for the cash inflows from a project to repay the initial investment cost

Payback period limit the period set by an organisation within which projects must pay back their initial investment

Time value of money the fact that money received or paid in the future is worth less than money received or paid now due to risk, consumption and investment preferences

Risk preference money to be received sooner rather than later carries less risk of not materialising

Consumption preference money received sooner rather than later can be used for earlier consumption

Investment preference money received sooner rather than later can be invested to earn interest

Present value the discounted value of a future cash flow to put it on equivalent terms with cash flows now

Compound interest a system where interest is accumulated rather than being withdrawn - interest is then paid on the interest

Discount factor the factor applied to a future cash flow in order to find its present value

Discount rate the interest rate used to discount cash flows

Present value tables tables of pre-calculated discount factors for annual cash flows and annuities

Annuity equal annual cash flows in successive years starting in one year's time

Perpetuity equal annual cash flows every year to infinity starting in one year's time

Net present value the total of the individual present values of the cash flows of a project

Cost of capital the discount rate used by an organisation to appraise projects

Internal rate of return the discount rate which when applied to project cash flows gives a zero net present value

HOW MUCH HAVE YOU LEARNED?

1 A business is considering one of the following two possible investments:

	Investment A	Investment B
Cost at 1 July 2006	£120,000	£100,000
Cash inflow at 30 June 2007	£ 43,000	£21,000
Cash inflow at 30 June 2008	£ 51,000	£21,000
Cash inflow at 30 June 2009	£ 52,000	£21,000
Cash inflow at 30 June 2010	£ 38,000	£21,000
Cash inflow at 30 June 2011		£40,000
Cash inflow at 30 June 2012		£70,000

All of the cash inflows are spread evenly over the year.

The business has a policy of only investing in projects with a payback period of three years or less.

a) Which of the two investments, if either, would be accepted?

b) Using the two investments given, illustrate any problem there may be with using this method of investment appraisal.

2 Today's date is 1 January 2006. What are the present values of each of the following cash flows?

a) A receipt of £3,100 on 31 December 2008 – interest 11%

b) A payment of £15,000 on 1 January 2006 – interest 6%

c) A receipt of £1,000 on 31 December 2006 and 2007 – interest 12%

d) A payment of £4,400 on 31 December 2007 – interest 7%

3 A business is considering investment in a new production line at a cost of £500,000. This will lead to efficiencies and cost savings of £80,000 per annum for the next 8 years. The company has a cost of capital of 9%. Should the business introduce the new production line?

4 You are to receive a sum of £80 every year to infinity starting on one year's time. What is the present value of these receipts at an interest rate of 8%?

5   A business is considering investment in new machinery at a cost of £340,000 on 1 April 2006
This machinery will be used to produce a new product which will give rise to the following ne
cash inflows.

31 March 2007   £80,000
31 March 2008   £70,000
31 March 2009   £90,000
31 March 2010   £120,000
31 March 2011   £60,000

The new machinery is to be depreciated at 20% per annum on cost. The cost of capital is 7%

What is the net present value of this project?

6   A business is considering investment in new plant and machinery on 1 January 2006 at a cos
of £90,000. The cash cost savings are estimated to be:

31 December 2006   £23,000
31 December 2007   £31,000
31 December 2008   £40,000
31 December 2009   £18,000

The business has a cost of capital of 11%.

a)   What is the net present value of this project?

b)   Advise the business as to whether it should invest in the new plant and machinery anc
      justify your advice.

chapter 10:
INTERNAL INFORMATION

——— chapter coverage 📖 ———

In this opening chapter for Unit 7 we will consider in general terms the internal informational requirements of organisations. We will consider different types of information and for whom it will be provided. The chapter will also introduce the idea of separate units within an organisation for which information must be gathered and added together or consolidated.

In the following chapters the techniques and methods for providing useful information will be considered in detail – in this chapter the internal information requirements in general will be considered. The topics to be covered are:

✎ types of information requirements

✎ the time scale of information

✎ the role of management and information required by management

✎ financial and non-financial information

✎ reporting information in different organisational structures

✎ qualities of useful information

✎ divisions within organisations

✎ transfer prices

✎ groups of companies

✎ information requirements of retail and service organisations

Diploma Pathway

Students studying the Diploma Pathway do not need to study Unit 7, as the topics are covered in Unit 31, Accounting Work Skills. You do not therefore need to study the remaining chapters of this book.

Unit 7

knowledge and understanding - the organisation

16   the purpose and structure of reporting systems within the organisation

18   background understanding that recording and accounting practices may vary between organisations and different parts of organisations

Performance criteria – element 7.1

A   consolidate information derived from different units of the organisation into the appropriate form

B   reconcile information derived from different information systems within the organisation

D   account for transactions between separate units of the organisation in accordance with the organisation's procedures

TYPES OF INFORMATION

The types of information that will be required within an organisation are many and varied, and the detail will differ from organisation to organisation. However in general terms the same types of information will be required in one form or another by all organisations.

Who is it within the organisation that requires information?

The answer is that all levels of supervisor and management within an organisation will require information but their requirements will be for different levels of detail and different aspects of the information.

HOW IT WORKS

Talbot Electrical is a manufacturer of a variety of electrical goods such as washing machines, tumble dryers, microwaves etc. The goods are manufactured in a large factory and the materials are controlled by the stores department in the stores room.

Information about the cost of the materials used in the manufacture of these products will be required in different forms by a wide range of personnel in the organisation.

stores manager – the stores manager will need to have details of the quantities of materials purchased and the quantities issued to the factory in order to maintain the stores records card

purchasing manager – the purchasing manager will want details of the cost of items purchased from the suppliers that are used in order to ensure that the best suppliers offering the best price and terms are being used

accountant – the accountant will require the details of the purchase invoices in order to be able to write up the purchases day book

production manager – the production manager will be concerned about the quantity and cost of the materials used in the production runs on a daily basis

production director – the production director will be interested in any significant variances from the budgeted cost of materials each week or each month depending upon the reporting procedures

Detail of information required

As you can see, the amount of detail that is required by each level of supervisor or management is different. At the lower levels the information requirements are detailed costs and quantities of each purchase or issue. However as information is passed to higher levels of management they will not wish to be inundated with daily details, and instead they will require summaries, overviews and exceptional items such as significant variances.

Time scale of information

Information required within an organisation can be on a variety of different time scales – it can relate to performance that is past, current or future.

Past performance – this is where information is required regarding the costs and revenues for a previous period, often the previous few months or information about the same month last year

Current performance – this is where information is required regarding the costs and revenues of the current period

Future performance – this is where estimates or budgets are required for costs and revenues in future periods.

Roles of management

The three main roles of management are decision making, planning and control. In order to carry out these roles, management will require many different types of information in a variety of different forms.

Decision making – for decision making the information required is normally related to past performance and some indications of future performance

Planning – both past and current performance information will be required to plan for future developments

Control – for control purposes the current information is most vital as it is then compared to the budgeted figures for the current period in order to determine whether everything is going according to plan

Activity 1

What are the three main roles of management in an organisation?

Financial and non-financial information

Most of your studies so far have been involved with the accounting and financial aspects of a business. However the managers of an organisation will require not only financial information but also other non-financial information.

Financial information will include figures such as materials costs, labour costs, costs per unit of production, overheads etc.

or many organisations, non-financial information will be just as important, uch as the number of units of production each period, the number of mployees, the number of units produced per employee, the number of units produced per working hour etc.

REPORTING OF INFORMATION

The amount of information and the detail of information required at various levels within a business will depend upon the size and ORGANISATIONAL STRUCTURE of the business.

Organisational structure

Every business will be organised in a manner that suits its own nature and size. This will range from a small sole trader running a business on his own to a large multi- national company with business units all over the world. The organisational structure is the way in which the personnel in the business work together and how this structure is set up will affect how information is passed around the business.

HOW IT WORKS

A sole trader who runs a small retail business may have two sales assistants, a stock room assistant and an administration assistant. His organisational structure would be as follows:

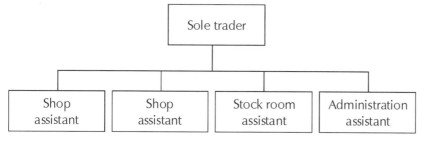

Communication of information here is quite straight forward. The owner, the sole trader, will be informed of the sales for the day by the sales assistants. He will also be informed of the stock levels by the stock assistant and the general everyday running costs of the business by the administration assistant.

A large manufacturing organisation's structure would however be much more complicated:

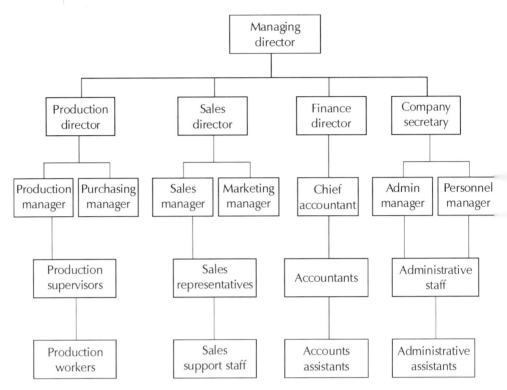

Obviously in this sort of organisational structure the requirements for information are going to be much more complex. Each level of management will require different levels of detail of information.

We will consider the production team.

The production workers will require detailed information of which shifts they are working – they will need to know when they are expected to arrive at work and how much, if any, overtime they are expected to work.

The production supervisors will require details of which production workers should be working on each shift, how much is to be produced, details of any absentees and details of materials requirements.

The production manager will require information about the total amount of materials used in each shift, the number of and cost of the production team on each shift, the amount of overtime that is being worked, any expenses incurred by the factory and the amount of production planned for future periods.

The purchasing manager will need information about stock levels, future production plans, suppliers' prices and terms.

The production director will require regular summaries of what is happening on the factory floor. These will include variances from budget for costs of materials, labour and expenses, variances from budget for the number of nits produced, variances from budget for the number of hours worked and osts per unit.

s you can see, for each individual manager to be able to carry out their uties and fulfil their responsibilities they will require a vast amount of nformation. One of the jobs of an accounting technician is to be able to rovide the correct information to the right person on time!

USEFUL INFORMATION

nformation that is required within a business must be useful to the person hat it is prepared for. In order for information to be useful it must have a umber of qualities:

Relevance – the information must be relevant to the person to whom it is sent. For example the production director of a large manufacturing firm will not need to know that Jo French worked 8 hours of overtime last week.

Reliability – the information must be reliable – when sending out information to any other person in your organisation you must be satisfied that this information is correct, therefore it should always be thoroughly checked. Remember that the information that you provide may be used as part of the decision making process. If the information is not correct then the wrong decision may be taken.

Consistency – information required by management will frequently be compared from week to week or month to month, so it is important that the information is provided in a consistent manner using the same layout or format each week or month, and using the same bases for any calculations.

Promptness – any information that is required must be provided within any deadlines that are set. If the information is late then this may totally invalidate the purpose of the request for information. If a report is requested by a particular date then it must arrive with the person by that date otherwise it may be too late to be of use.

Activity 2

What are the main requirements of information if it is to be useful?

Reliability of information

We have already seen that information that is reported must be accurate and reliable. One method of checking the accuracy of the information being provided is to ensure that it agrees in total to the same information derived from another part of the accounting system of the organisation.

Information systems within the organisation

In most organisations, other than the very small, there will be a number of different information systems within the organisation.

For example in a retail organisation the analysis of sales for the day produced by the tills should be agreed to the movements in stock during the day ie, the items that have been sold.

Similarly the labour cost charged out to each cost centre should agree in total to the amount of hours shown on the payroll system.

DIVISIONALISATION

Many organisations do not operate as a single unit. Instead they are organised into separate units which operate side by side but are dealt with in accounting terms separately. These separate units are often known as DIVISIONS. The reasons for splitting the organisation into divisions may be many and varied – they may be geographical or to do with the products that the division makes or sells.

HOW IT WORKS

Troppers Stores has three department stores in Bromley, Croydon and Sevenoaks. They each have their own accounting systems recording sales and all of the costs of those sales. Each month the senior management of Troppers Stores requires a summary of the sales and expenses of the stores in total.

For the month of May 2006 the figures for each store were as follows:

	Bromley £	Croydon £	Sevenoaks £
Sales	346,000	259,000	105,000
Cost of sales	182,000	135,000	65,000
Gross profit	164,000	124,000	40,000
Less: expenses	127,000	89,000	21,000
Net profit	37,000	35,000	19,000

The figures required for management for the month of May are the aggregated or consolidated figures showing the totals for all three stores.

	£
Sales (346,000 + 259,000 + 105,000)	710,000
Cost of sales (182,000 + 135,000 + 65,000)	382,000
Gross profit	328,000
Expenses (127,000 + 89,000 + 21,000)	237,000
Net profit	91,000

Trading between divisions

It is common practice for divisions to buy and sell products from and to each other. For example one division may make a product which is used by another division of the organisation in the manufacture of its products.

Transfer price

When goods are "sold" by one division of an organisation to another it is common practice to set a TRANSFER PRICE for these goods. This is the price agreed between the divisions that the selling division will sell at and the buying division will buy at.

The transfer price will normally be somewhere in the range of the cost of the goods through to the market price of the goods.

```
                        TRANSFER
                         PRICE

                           |
                           |
                           ↓

MANUFACTURING   ─────────────────────→    MARKET
    COST                                   PRICE
```

The transfer price will not exceed the market price as the buying division would then buy the goods from the external market. The transfer price will be above the manufacturing cost of the goods in order for the selling division to make an element of profit. The final transfer price will normally be set by negotiations between the two divisions and will eventually be arrived at as:

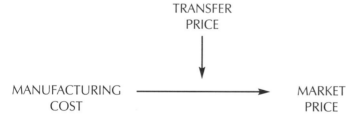

| Manufacturing cost | + | Agreed profit | = | Transfer price |

Effect of the transfer price

It is important to realise that the transfer price of the goods being transferred between divisions has no effect on the organisation's overall performance; it merely affects the performance of each division.

The selling division will be making sales not only to external customers but also to the other division at the transfer price. The buying division will be making purchases of the same amount from the selling division, as well as its external purchases.

This sale and this purchase cancel each other out in the overall organisation profit and loss account, so when reporting the overall organisational figures the value of the goods transferred between divisions must be excluded.

HOW IT WORKS

Talbot Electrical has two production divisions, A and B. The sales and manufacturing costs of each division are given below. The sales of division A and the manufacturing cost of division B include £55,400 of goods transferred between them from division A to division B.

	Division A £	Division B £
Sales	765,800	635,400
Manufacturing cost	468,900	419,200

Lets think about the performance of each individual division:

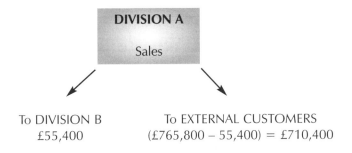

DIVISION A

Sales

To DIVISION B
£55,400

To EXTERNAL CUSTOMERS
(£765,800 – 55,400) = £710,400

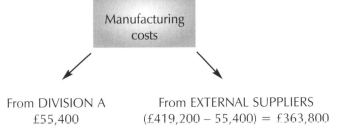

DIVISION B

Manufacturing costs

From DIVISION A
£55,400

From EXTERNAL SUPPLIERS
(£419,200 – 55,400) = £363,800

When we look at the performance of the whole organisation the sale and purchase of £55,400 cancel each other out. As far as Talbot Electrical is concerned, the sales that were made were those to the external customers of £710,400 in division A and the cost of manufacturing are the costs incurred from external suppliers of £363,800 in division B.

this is normally shown by using a consolidation adjustment column to deduct the inter-division transfer from both sales and cost of sales.

	Division A £	Division B £	Consolidation adjustment £	Total £
Sales	765,800	635,400	(55,400)	1,345,800
Manufacturing cost	468,900	419,200	(55,400)	832,700
Gross profit	296,900	216,200		513,100

Now the total figures show the true sales of the two divisions to external customers, and the manufacturing cost is the true cost of the two divisions' purchases and expenses incurred from external suppliers.

The gross profit however requires no adjustment – it is simply the total of each division's gross profit as the two adjustments made cancel each other out exactly.

GROUPS OF COMPANIES

In many large organisations, instead of the organisation being made up of one company the structure of the organisation may be that it is made up of a number of companies. There will normally be a parent company and a number of subsidiary companies which the parent company owns.

For example a group structure may be as follows:

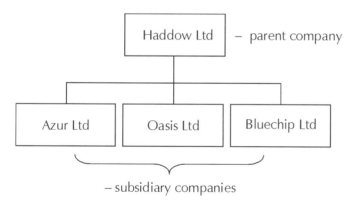

If any of the group companies transfer goods between each other and include the transfer price in their own sales or cost of sales figures, these intra-group transactions must be adjusted for in the consolidation adjustment column in exactly the same way as for transfers between divisions.

Activity 3

Daffyd Ltd owns another company, Luger Ltd. The figures for each company for the month of June 2006 are as follows:

	Daffyd Ltd £	Luger Ltd £
Sales	157,388	104,734
Cost of sales	96,365	77,446

During the month Daffyd made sales of £31,267 to Luger Ltd.

Show the consolidated sales, cost of sales and gross profit for the two companies for the month of June 2006.

MANUFACTURING, RETAIL AND SERVICE COMPANIES

So far when considering the information that may be required internally in an organisation, we have concentrated on manufacturing organisations and the type of information that might be required in this type of organisation.

However organisations that are in the retail trade or which provide a service rather than a physical manufactured product will also have detailed information requirements.

HOW IT WORKS

The management of Troppers Stores are likely to require the following type of information:

- floor space for each store
- number of employees for each store
- total employee costs per store
- number of average daily customers per store

Jenner and Partners are a small accountancy firm – typical information requirements that the partner will have may be:

- total chargeable hours in the period
- total non-chargeable hours
- administration and overhead costs
- employee costs

Activity 4

Merton Ltd is a company that runs a small group of hotels. What typical information might the management of Merton Ltd require?

CHAPTER OVERVIEW

- all levels of supervisor and management within an organisation will require information but the detail of the information requirements tends to be greatest at the lower levels of management, with overview, summaries and variances being required by more senior management

- management will require information in order to carry out their roles of decision making, planning and control – in each role they will require a mix of past information, current period information and future estimates and budgets

- the information requirements of management will not only be for financial information but also for non-financial information

- the complexity of the communication process for information will depend upon the size and organisational structure

- in order for the information reported to be useful it should be relevant, reliable, consistent and prompt

- many organisations are split into a number of separate units or divisions – when reporting the total performance of the organisation, the figures for each division must be added together or consolidated

- if divisions pass goods to each other this will normally be done at an agreed transfer price – when consolidating the divisional figures this transfer price should be deducted from both sales and purchases in order to reflect the sales and purchases to and from external customers and suppliers

- when a number of companies trade as a group, any intra-group sales and purchases must also be removed when adding the group figures together

- it is not only manufacturing organisations that have internal information requirements – the management of retail and service organisations will also require detailed information although this may be different types of information than that required by a manufacturing organisation.

HOW MUCH HAVE YOU LEARNED?

1   In a manufacturing organisation what type of information regarding the labour force for the last month is likely to be provided to:

a)   the production supervisor
b)   the managing director?

Why is there a difference between the information requirements of the two people?

2   The management of a manufacturing organisation are trying to decide whether to continue with production of one of their products, the Hedgit. What type of information do you think they would require in order to take this decision?

3   Give examples of both financial and non-financial information that might be required by the management of each of the following types of organisation:

a)   a manufacturer of double glazed window units
b)   a private nursing home
c)   a firm of solicitors
d)   a transport organisation

4   A business has three retail outlets whose performance for the month of June 2006 is given below:

	Headingly £	Leeds £	Barnsley £
Sales	163,500	104,700	126,500
Cost of sales	101,400	64,500	78,400
Other expenses	35,900	23,000	27,800

Show the sales, gross profit and net profit for the whole organisation for the month of June 2006.

5   A manufacturing organisation has two divisions and their results for the month of May 2006 are as follows:

	Division 1 £	Division 2 £
Sales	368,900	286,300
Cost of sales	236,700	183,200
Production overheads	88,500	71,500

During the month Division 2 transferred goods to Division 1 for further manufacture at a transfer price of £31,600.

Prepare the consolidated results of the two divisions for the month of May 2006.

chapter 11:
PERFORMANCE MEASURES

Unit 7

knowledge and understanding - the business environment

2   relevant performance and quality measures

knowledge and understanding - accounting techniques

8   use of standard units of inputs and outputs

11   main types of performance indicators: productivity; cost per unit; resource utilisation; profitability

12   ratios: gross profit margin; net profit margin; return on capital employed

Performance criteria – element 7.1

E   calculate ratios and performance indicators in accordance with the organisation's procedures

PERFORMANCE INDICATORS

the previous chapter we have seen how the information requirements of anagement become less detailed the higher the management level. The pres and production managers will require detailed information about stock ovements and labour hours and costs, but the production director will need verviews and summaries of the activity for the period and an indication of ny problem areas.

this chapter we will consider some of the many performance indicators at can be used in order to provide higher levels of management with the formation they require, without having to provide them with all of the etails of performance.

ERFORMANCE INDICATORS are methods of summarising the performance f all or parts of the organisation for a period using a formula.

Assessing performance

the previous chapter we saw that consistency was important when roviding information. Performance indicators are a good method of roviding consistent information, because if the same formula is used in each eriod the performance indicators can be compared over time, in order to iscover the trend of how the organisation is performing.

Areas of performance

erformance indicators can be calculated to cover many, many areas of an rganisation's activities. For Unit 7 the areas that will be covered are:

- productivity – how efficiently the product is being made or services provided from available resources

- cost per unit – how much it costs to produce a unit of product or service

- resource utilisation – how well the resources of the organisation are being used

- profitability – how profitable the business is.

Remember that we are not only dealing with manufacturing organisations but also retail and service organisations and as you will see in this chapter the performance indicators are also relevant to these types of business.

PRODUCTIVITY

PRODUCTIVITY is a measure of how hard the employees are working how productive they are being in their hours at work.

As with many performance indicators, productivity can be measured different ways but the basic calculation is to discover how many units product or service are being produced either each hour or by eac employee.

HOW IT WORKS

Division A of Talbot Electrical has produced 224,500 units of its product i the month of May 2006. In order to do this the work force of 28 productio workers have worked for a total of 4,486 hours.

The productivity of Division A could be expressed in two ways:

Method 1 – Productivity per labour hour

$$\text{Productivity per labour hour} = \frac{\text{Output in the period}}{\text{Hours worked in the period}}$$

$$= \frac{224,500 \text{ units}}{4,486 \text{ hours}}$$

$$= 50 \text{ units per labour hour}$$

This productivity level could then be compared with the previous month'. and with budgeted figures.

Suppose that the budgeted figures for the month were 230,000 units o production in 4,200 labour hours.

$$\text{Budgeted productivity} = \frac{230,000 \text{ units}}{4,200 \text{ hours}}$$

$$= 54.8 \text{ units per labour hour}$$

In this case the actual productivity during May is low compared to the standard or budgeted productivity.

Method 2 – Productivity per employee

$$\text{Productivity per employee} = \frac{\text{Output in the period}}{\text{Number of employees working on output}}$$

$$= \frac{224{,}500}{28}$$

$$= 8{,}018 \text{ units per employee}$$

Which method to use?

In a manufacturing situation the most useful method of measuring productivity is normally method 1, productivity per labour hour. This is because on the factory floor each employee is likely to be doing different tasks and it is probably not the case, in the previous example, that each of those 28 production workers produced 8,018 units.

However method 2, the productivity per employee measure, is most appropriate in a situation where each employee is doing an identical job and the job in question can take a varied amount of time.

HOW IT WORKS

Talbot Electrical has a sales department which processes all orders for goods. In May 2006 the 8 members of the telephone sales team processed 142 orders.

$$\text{Productivity per employee} = \frac{\text{Output in the period}}{\text{Number of employees}}$$

$$= \frac{142 \text{ orders}}{8 \text{ employees}}$$

$$= 17.75 \text{ orders per employee}$$

Activity 1

An advertising company has produced 123 advertisements in the quarter to June 2006 using 15 advertising executives. In the previous quarter only 88 advertisements were produced when there were 12 executives.

What is the productivity of the company for this quarter and the previous quarter?

Productivity index

The productivity measures considered looked at how hard the employee worked and how much they had produced in the time that they worked.

The PRODUCTIVITY INDEX assesses whether the employees have produced as much as was expected. It is expressed as a percentage and is calculated a

$$\text{Productivity index} = \frac{\text{Actual output in units}}{\text{Standard or expected output}} \times 100$$

HOW IT WORKS

Remember that Division A of Talbot Electrical had actual output of 224,50 units and budgeted output of 230,000.

$$\text{Productivity index} = \frac{224,500}{230,000} \times 100$$

$$= 97.6\%$$

This indicates that the output for the month is below the budgeted amoun of output.

Activity 2

A manufacturing organisation had a budgeted output planned for the month of June 2006 of 388,000 units. However 368,000 units were in fact produced.

What is the productivity index?

COST PER UNIT

COST PER UNIT is the cost of producing one unit of the organisation's product.

This product of course does not need to be a physical product: it could also be a service. Therefore in a hotel, the cost per resident could be calculated, in a restaurant the cost per diner, in an accountancy firm the cost per chargeable hour.

The calculation for cost per unit is:

$$\text{Cost per unit} = \frac{\text{Cost of production/provision of service}}{\text{Number of units produced in the period}}$$

HOW IT WORKS

In May 2006 Division A of Talbot Electrical produced 224,500 units of its product at a total manufacturing cost of £468,900. The total costs of the telephone sales department were £12,300 and the number of sales orders processed in the month were 142.

Division A   Cost per unit $= \dfrac{£468,900}{224,500}$

$= £2.09$ per unit

Sales orders   Cost per unit $= \dfrac{£12,300}{142\,\text{units}}$

$= £86.62$ per order

Activity 3

A restaurant had total costs of £66,500 for the month of June 2006 and in that month served 3,600 meals.

What is the cost per meal?

RESOURCE UTILISATION

Performance measures which indicate RESOURCE UTILISATION show how well, how productively and how efficiently an organisation is using the various resources at its disposal.

The main resources that are measured for this purpose tend to be labour, fixed assets and capital.

Labour utilisation

In a perfect world, the labour force would be working productively for every hour that they were on the premises, in which case LABOUR UTILISATION would be 100%. However in practice this is not the case. The reason for this is known as IDLE TIME.

Idle time is the time that the production workers are on the factory floor but are not actually producing the products of the organisation. Some idle time is necessary for Health and Safety reasons – workers must have time for coffee breaks, lunch breaks etc. This is known as UNAVOIDABLE IDLE TIME as it is a necessary part of working life.

Other idle time however is a consequence of the manufacturing process. There may be bottlenecks in production which mean that some production workers are not able to work when they should. There may be machine breakdowns or a lack of materials that mean that there is no production to work on. The workers may have finished the assigned tasks for the day and no other task is available. This is all known as AVOIDABLE IDLE TIME as it is not strictly necessary although it is a practical aspect of factory life.

Labour utilisation is measured as:

$$\text{Labour utilisation \%} = \frac{\text{Actual hours worked}}{\text{Hours available for work}} \times 100$$

HOW IT WORKS

The production workers of Division A in Talbot Electrical worked for 4,486 hours in May 2006. However due to unplanned overtime hours the total hours that could have been worked in the month were 4,620.

$$\text{Labour utilisation \%} = \frac{4,486 \text{ hours}}{4,620 \text{ hours}} \times 100$$

$$= 97.1\%$$

Activity 4

A manufacturing organisation had enough employees to work for 6,700 hours in the month of June 2003. In fact the employees only worked for 6,400 hours.

What is the rate of labour utilisation?

Fixed asset utilisation

Another useful indicator to management of how effectively the organisation is using its resources is a measure of how much the fixed assets, the major long term assets of the business, are earning.

FIXED ASSET UTILISATION is normally measured as an absolute figure rather than a percentage:

$$\text{Fixed asset utilisation} = \frac{\text{Sales for the period}}{\text{Net book value of fixed assets}}$$

Note that this is based upon sales for the period rather than the cost of the goods. This gives a better indication of what the fixed assets are actually earning during the period.

A further measure of the utilisation of the fixed assets can be made by comparing the sales achieved by the division to the hours that the machinery were used.

$$\text{Machinery utilisation} = \frac{\text{Sales for the period}}{\text{Machine hours for the period}}$$

This is again an absolute figure showing the sales earned for each hour that the machines are in use.

HOW IT WORKS

The sales of Division A of Talbot Electrical for May 2006 were £765,800, the net book value of the fixed assets used in Division A was £584,000 and the machines worked for 4,300 hours during the month.

$$\text{Fixed asset utilisation} = \frac{\text{Sales for the period}}{\text{Net book value of fixed assets}}$$

$$= \frac{£765,800}{£584,000}$$

$$= £1.31$$

This means that every £1 of fixed asset value is earning £1.31 of revenue. This figure is often known as fixed asset turnover.

$$\text{Machinery utilisation} = \frac{\text{Sales for the period}}{\text{Machine hours for the period}}$$

$$= \frac{£765,800}{4,300 \text{ hours}}$$

$$= £178.09$$

This means that for every hour that the machines were working they were earning £178.09 of income.

Activity 5

A manufacturing organisation produced goods which sold for £316,800 in the month of June 2006. The machinery used to make those goods had a net book value of £280,000 and was in operation for 12,200 hours during the month.

Show two measures of machine utilisation.

Capital utilisation

A further utilisation measure that can be calculated is to compare the sales for the period to the entire capital of the organisation. This is commonly known as ASSET TURNOVER and is measured as:

$$\text{Asset turnover} = \frac{\text{Sales for the period}}{\text{Total capital employed}}$$

Total capital employed is usually understood to be the assets of the organisation less the current liabilities.

HOW IT WORKS

The total sales of Talbot Electrical for May 2006 were £1,345,800 and the capital at 31 May 2006 was £845,700.

$$\text{Asset turnover} = \frac{£1,345,800}{£845,700}$$

$$= £1.59$$

This means that every £1 of capital that the business has has earned £1.59 of revenue during the month of May.

Activity 6

An accountancy firm has revenue of £420,000 in the month of June 2006 and the capital of the firm totals £350,000.

What is the asset turnover for the month?

PROFITABILITY MEASURES

he aim of most businesses is to make a profit. Therefore management will f course be interested in performance measures that indicate the level of rofitability. These tend to be known as ratios although they are in fact xpressed as a percentage figure.

Gross profit margin

The GROSS PROFIT of a business is the sales for the period less the cost of those sales. In a manufacturing business the cost of sales figure will be the manufacturing cost, and in a retail business the cost of sales will be the cost of the stocks that were actually sold during the period. You will remember from your earlier financial accounting studies that cost of sales is calculated as follows:

Cost of sales	£
Opening stock	X
Add: Purchases	X
	X
Less: closing stock	(X)
	X

For service organisations the sales for the period will be the amount of revenue that is billed to customers for the service provided. However the cost of sales figure will not be based upon physical goods because a service organisation trades in providing the service, for example an accountancy firm, rather than selling goods. The cost of sales figure in such an organisation is likely to be made up of the direct salaries of those employees providing the service together with any other direct costs of providing the service.

The GROSS PROFIT MARGIN is calculated by showing the gross profit as a percentage of the sales figure for the period:

$$\text{Gross profit margin} = \frac{\text{Gross profit}}{\text{Sales}} \times 100$$

Net profit margin

The NET PROFIT of a business is the profit shown in the profit and loss account after all of the expenses or overheads for the period have been deducted. The NET PROFIT MARGIN is again calculated by showing the net profit as a percentage of the sales figure for the period:

$$\text{Net profit margin} = \frac{\text{Net profit}}{\text{Sales}} \times 100$$

HOW IT WORKS

The summarised profit and loss account for Talbot Electrical for the month of May 2006 is shown below:

	£	£
Sales		1,345,800
Less: cost of sales		832,700
Gross profit		513,100
Less: overheads		
Selling and distribution costs	136,400	
Administration costs	154,700	
Finance charges	10,000	
		301,100
Net profit		212,000

$$\text{Gross profit margin} = \frac{\text{Gross profit}}{\text{Sales}} \times 100$$

$$= \frac{513,100}{1,345,800} \times 100$$

$$= 38.1\%$$

$$\text{Net profit margin} = \frac{\text{Net profit}}{\text{Sales}} \times 100$$

$$= \frac{212,000}{1,345,800} \times 100$$

$$= 15.8\%$$

Activity 7

A business made sales of £442,000 in the month of June 2006 and the cost of sales totalled £278,000. The business also incurred overheads totalling £104,000.

What are the gross profit margin and the net profit margin?

Return on capital employed

The RETURN ON CAPITAL EMPLOYED is sometimes known as the primary ratio as it is of great importance to the business. It is calculated as:

$$\text{Return on capital employed (ROCE)} = \frac{\text{Net profit}}{\text{Capital employed}} \times 100$$

As such it is relating the profit that has been earned for the period to the capital from the balance sheet, to determine what return has been made on the owner's investment in the business. As the capital figure is made up of the assets minus the liabilities, the ROCE can also be seen to be showing the profit that has been made by the net assets of the business.

ROCE can be calculated in different ways for different businesses. Both the return element, the net profit, and the capital employed can be calculated in different ways and it is important to ensure that the return being used matches the capital figure used.

HOW IT WORKS

Given below is the summarised profit and loss account for Talbot Electrical for the month of May 2006 together with the summarised balance sheet at the end of May.

Summarised profit and loss account

	£	£
Sales		1,345,800
Less: cost of sales		832,700
Gross profit		513,100
Less: overheads		
Selling and distribution costs	136,400	
Administration costs	154,700	
Finance charges	10,000	
		301,100
Net profit		212,000

Summarised balance sheet

	£	£
Fixed assets		919,600
Current assets	104,300	
Less: current liabilities	78,200	
Net current assets		26,100
		945,700
Less: Long-term loan		(100,000)
Total assets less liabilities		845,700
Owner's capital		845,700

ROCE is normally calculated in one of two ways.

Method 1

$$\text{ROCE} = \frac{\text{Net profit after all expenses}}{\text{Owner's capital}} \times 100$$

$$= \frac{212,000}{845,700} \times 100$$

$$= 25.1\%$$

The return figure is the profit after all expenses, including the finance charge of interest, and the capital figure is the total of all of the assets of the business minus all of the liabilities including the long-term loan.

Method 2

$$\text{ROCE} = \frac{\text{Net profit before interest}}{\text{Owner's capital plus long - term loans}} \times 100$$

$$= \frac{212,000 + 10,000}{845,700 + 100,000} \times 100$$

$$= 23.5\%$$

In this method the return used is the profit before interest has been charged – this is the profit available for all of the providers of capital including the long-term loan. The capital figure therefore must also include the long-term loan.

s there are these two methods of calculating return on capital employed two
oints here are extremely important:

- make sure that you match the correct profit and capital figures

- ensure that you write the formula that you are using out in words as
  well as just putting figures in, so that it is quite clear which formula
  is being used.

he ROCE shows the overall return that is being made by the providers of
apital – in method 1 this is the return to the owner of the business, in
method 2 this is the return to all of the providers of capital including any
ong-term loans.

Activity 8

A business has total assets less liabilities totalling £380,000. This includes
a long term loan of £80,000. The net profit of the business is £42,000 after
charging interest of £4,800.

What are the two different figures that could be calculated for return on
capital employed?

USING THE PERFORMANCE INDICATORS

The performance indicators that have been considered in this chapter are
vital tools of management, as they serve as summaries of the performance of
the business during the period. For example if the production director is
informed that productivity is 50 units per hour for the month then this has
summarised information about the number of units produced and the
number of hours worked without the need for management to have these
detailed figures.

However none of these performance indicators are of much significance on
their own. They are only useful if they are being compared to other figures.
The comparisons that are useful are:

- comparison to previous periods' performance measures
- comparison to budgeted performance measures
- comparison to industry average performance measures

HOW IT WORKS

We will now consider some of the performance measures that have been calculated for Talbot Electrical.

Productivity = 50 units per labour hour

On its own this is not particularly informative but if we know that the budgeted productivity for May was 54.8 units per labour hour then management can see at a glance that Division A has been operating below the expected productivity level.

Sales department productivity = 17.75 orders per sales representative

If the budgeted sales department productivity was 15 orders per sales representative then we can see that the productivity of the sales department is good in May.

Labour utilisation = 97.1%

On its own this indicates a degree of idle time as the hours that were worked were only 97.1% of the hours available. However what would be more useful would be to compare the measure to that of previous periods. If the labour utilisation figures were 94%, 92% and 95% in February, March and April respectively, the figure for May shows a significant improvement.

Gross profit margin = 38.1%
Net profit margin = 15.8%
ROCE = 25.1%

These are again not particularly useful on their own but they could be compared to industry average figures. Each different type of business will have a different typical gross and net profit margin. For example an antique shop would be likely to have a high gross profit margin whereas a food store would typically operate on a much lower gross profit margin.

The industry figures for makers of white goods such as Talbot Electrical are as follows:

Gross profit margin = 41%
Net profit margin = 13%
ROCE = 20%

If we compare these to the figures for Talbot Electrical, management should be pleased that both the net profit margin and ROCE are above the industry average. However the gross profit margin is below the industry average. This would indicate that either Talbot's selling price is too low or that they are paying too much to suppliers. If the gross profit margin can be improved and brought more in line with the industry average then this should improve the net profit margin and ROCE even more.

nterpreting the performance measures

s well as being able to calculate the performance measures correctly and to
understand the concepts underlying them, you may need to be able to
comment on the performance indicators and to explain what picture they
paint of the organisation.

herefore in the next example we will bring together all of the performance
indicators covered in this chapter and not only calculate them but also
comment on their significance.

HOW IT WORKS

Grant Productions Ltd is a manufacturing company with three separate
factory units in Tamworth, Solihull and Barnsley each producing the same
range of products. A summary of the performance of the three divisions for
the most recent three month period is given below.

	Tamworth £'000	Solihull £'000	Barnsley £'000	Total £'000
Profit and loss details				
Sales	800	750	600	2,150
Cost of sales	520	525	380	1,425
Gross profit	280	225	220	725
Overheads	180	165	150	495
Net profit	100	60	70	230
Balance sheet details				
Capital	1,250	1,200	900	3,350
Production details				
Units produced	120,000	115,000	90,000	325,000
Budgeted production in units	120,000	125,000	85,000	330,000
Hours worked	32,400	37,100	23,000	92,500
Available hours	33,500	40,000	23,500	97,000
Budgeted hours	33,333	34,722	23,611	91,666

student notes✐

Procedure

- Draw up a table showing the performance indicators that you ca
  calculate from the figures – use the following headings to help t
  guide you:

    - productivity
    - cost per unit
    - resource utilisation
    - profitability

- Calculate any budgeted figures that you can to compare to th
  actual figures

- Comment on the position shown by the performance indicators fo
  each of the three divisions and for the company as a whole.

Performance indicator

PRODUCTIVITY	Tamworth	Solihull	Barnsley	Total
Labour productivity Units produced/hours worked	3.7	3.1	3.9	3.5
Productivity index Units produced/budgeted units	100%	92%	105.9%	98.5%
COST PER UNIT				
Cost of sales/units produced	£4.33	£4.57	£4.22	£4.38
RESOURCE UTILISATION				
Labour utilisation Hours worked/hours available	96.7%	92.8%	97.9%	95.4%
Asset turnover Sales/capital employed	0.64	0.63	0.67	0.64
PROFITABILITY				
Gross profit margin Gross profit/sales	35%	30%	36.7%	33.7%
Net profit margin Net profit/sales	12.5%	8%	11.7%	10.7%
Return on capital employed Net profit/capital employed	8%	5%	7.8%	6.9%

BUDGETED FIGURES

Budgeted productivity = Budgeted production/Budgeted hours

= 330,000/91,666

= 3.6 units per labour hour

omments

PRODUCTIVITY

Labour productivity is above the budgeted figure of 3.6 units per hour in both Tamworth and Barnsley but is significantly below target in Solihull.

Similarly both Tamworth and Barnsley have met or exceeded their budgeted production but Solihull's productivity index is only 92%, meaning that production is well below the target figure.

However overall the productivity index for the total company shows a fairly healthy 98.5%.

In conclusion the productivity at Solihull should be investigated.

COST PER UNIT

The cost per unit overall is £4.38 with both Tamworth and Barnsley products costing less than this figure.

Again there seems to be some problem at Solihull with the cost per unit being significantly higher than in the other two divisions.

RESOURCE UTILISATION

The labour utilisation indicates a significant amount of idle time in Solihull which will have an effect on the productivity of this branch.

The asset turnover figures are all very similar with all three divisions earning between 63 pence and 67 pence for every £1 of capital employed.

Although there appears to be a problem with the production at Solihull the problem would appear to be isolated to the production as the asset turnover shows that the sales level of the division is reasonable.

PROFITABILITY

The gross profit margins of Tamworth and Barnsley seem reasonable but the overall gross profit margin is pulled down by the performance of Solihull probably due to the productivity and cost per unit problems there.

The net profit margin indicates a problem at Barnsley. Although Barnsley has a higher gross profit margin than Tamworth the net profit margin is lower. This might indicate that overheads at Barnsley should be investigated to find out why they are comparatively high.

The ROCE is reasonable for Tamworth and Barnsley but the poor performance of Solihull reduces the overall ROCE.

CONCLUSION

All of the divisions are profitable and they are all achieving reasonable leve of productivity and resource utilisation. However the production problems Solihull indicated by the low productivity and high cost per unit should k investigated. The other problem is the net profit percentage of Barnsle which could perhaps be improved with more control over its overheads.

AAT simulation guidance

The guidance notes to Unit 7 make it clear that open-ended tasks in this are will be avoided. Instead, when performance measures are to be calculate you will be directed along reasonably restricted lines. For example you ma be told that certain specific ratios are to be included in the report, or tha comment is required on specific ratios or trends.

HAPTER OVERVIEW

performance indicators are used to summarise the performance of the organisation using formulae to provide management with information

productivity can be measured by the number of units produced per labour hour, or per employee, or by a productivity index comparing the actual output to the budgeted output

cost per unit is calculated by taking the total production cost for the period and dividing by the number of units produced in the period

the main resources of a manufacturing business will be its labour force, its fixed assets and its capital – performance indicators can be calculated to show how well these resources have been used in the period – the utilisation indicator for capital is generally known as asset turnover

there are three profitability measures that are required – gross profit margin, net profit margin and return on capital employed

when calculating the return on capital employed, you should be aware that both return and capital employed can be defined differently – if profit after interest is used as the return then the capital is simply the owner's capital – if profit before interest is used as the return then this is the return for all providers of capital, and therefore the long term loans must be included as capital employed

performance indicators in isolation are of little use – they must be compared to either previous periods' figures, budgeted figures or industry average figures in order to provide information about how the organisation is performing

---

KEY WORDS

Performance indicators methods of summarising information about the performance of the organisation using formulae

Productivity a measure of how hard the employees have worked

Productivity index a comparison of the actual output for the period to budgeted output expressed as a percentage

Cost per unit the cost of producing one unit of the organisation's product or providing one unit of its service

Resource utilisation a measure of how well, productively and efficiently an organisation has used its resources

Labour utilisation the hours of work performed in relation to the available hours

Idle time time that the work force is being paid for but is not producing products or services

Unavoidable idle time necessary down time for employees such as coffee breaks etc.

Avoidable idle time time when employees are not working due to manufacturing problems when they should be working

Fixed asset utilisation the amount of sales income per £ of investment in fixed assets

Asset turnover the amount of revenue earned by the business per £ of capital employed

Gross profit sales revenue less the cost of those sales

Gross profit margin gross profit as a percentage of sales

Net profit gross profit minus all expenses of the business

Net profit margin net profit as a percentage of sales

Return on capital employed the net profit expressed as a percentage of the capital employed

---

HOW MUCH HAVE YOU LEARNED?

1   Given below are the production figures for a factory for four months.

	February	March	April	May
Output in units	136,700	154,200	144,600	139,800
Budgeted output	140,000	145,000	142,000	144,000
Hours worked	13,200	14,600	13,600	13,700

Calculate the productivity per labour hour each month and the productivity index each month

2   Given below are the production figures for a factory for three months.

	April	May	June
Production costs	£416,400	£452,300	£425,500
Output in units	120,500	137,000	121,500
Hours worked	11,200	13,400	11,500
Budgeted output	120,000	140,000	140,000
Hours available	12,000	13,900	12,600
Sales revenue	£765,000	£790,000	£725,000
Machine hours	10,200	12,000	10,800

Calculate the following performance indicators for each of the three months and for the three months in total:

a)   productivity per labour hour
b)   productivity index
c)   labour utilisation
d)   cost per unit
e)   machine utilisation (revenue per machine hour)

3   A travel firm employs 7 sales representatives. Sales of holidays are seasonal and you are provided with the following figures for the last year:

	July – Sept	Oct – Dec	Jan – March	April – June
Holidays sold	8,300	6,200	9,800	7,200
Budgeted holidays	7,500	7,000	11,000	8,000
Total costs	£104,500	£110,200	£116,500	£109,000

For each quarter of the year and for the year in total you are to calculate:

a)   the productivity per sales representative
b)   the productivity index
c)   the cost per holiday sold

Why do you think that the cost per holiday sold fluctuates so much?

4 A small firm of solicitors employs a number of qualified and part qualified solicitors who work a standard 40 hour week, although overtime is often worked. Given below is a summary of the business for the last four quarters.

	July – Sept	Oct – Dec	Jan – March	April – June
Chargeable hours	350	380	420	410
Completed cases	84	90	115	120
Revenue	£226,300	£240,600	£263,200	£270,400
Capital	£100,000	£100,000	£130,000	£130,000

For the first six months of the year there were 8 qualified and part-qualified employees working on cases. In January the partners paid £30,000 additional capital into the business and employed two more qualified solicitors, in order to ease the current workload and to bring in new business.

a) Calculate the following performance indicators for each quarter of the year:

   i)   productivity index (chargeable hours compared to standard weekly hours)
   ii) productivity per employee (completed cases per employee)
   iii) productivity per chargeable hour (completed cases per chargeable hour)
   iv) asset turnover

b) Comment upon the effect of the introduction of the additional capital and the new employees.

5 Given below is a summary of a business's performance for six months:

	Jan £000	Feb £000	Mar £000	April £000	May £000	June £000
Sales	250	300	280	320	350	340
Cost of sales	130	170	160	200	210	210
Overheads	85	90	88	85	98	95
Capital	150	150	170	190	200	200

For each month you are to calculate the following performance indicators:

a) gross profit margin
b) net profit margin
c) return on capital employed
d) asset turnover

Comment on what your performance measures indicate about the business activities for the six month period.

6   Given below is a summary of the performance of a business for four quarters:

	July Sept £000	Oct – Dec £000	Jan March £000	April June £000
Sales	620	650	660	700
Cost of sales	340	345	340	350
Overheads	190	205	205	220
Capital	300	300	360	360

For each of the quarters you are to calculate the following performance measures and t comment on what the measures indicate about the performance of the business over the year

a)   gross profit margin
b)   net profit margin
c)   return on capital employed
d)   asset turnover

chapter coverage 📖

In the previous chapter we looked at the calculation of various performance indicators that might be required to be reported to management. In this chapter we will consider the form that such a report will take. The topics to be covered are:

✍ different types of reporting systems

✍ the importance of accuracy and promptness

✍ the format for a report

✍ how to write a successful report

KNOWLEDGE AND UNDERSTANDING AND PERFORMANCE CRITERIA COVERAGE

Unit 7

knowledge and understanding - accounting techniques

14 methods of presenting information: written reports

knowledge and understanding - the organisation

16 the purpose and structure of reporting systems within the organisation

Performance criteria - element 7.1

F prepare reports in the appropriate form and present them to management within the required timescales

REPORTING SYSTEMS

As we have seen in an earlier chapter the detail of information regarding an organisation's day to day operations is dealt with at the lower management levels. This detail will then be assessed, summarised and reported in the appropriate form, usually to the next level of management upwards.

The precise reporting structure or system will depend upon the organisation structure. As we saw in an earlier chapter, a simple organisational structure such as that of a small sole trader will have a very straightforward reporting system, whereas in a larger organisation with directors, senior management line management and supervisors the reporting system will be more complex.

Importance of accuracy and promptness

Before looking at the layout of a report it is important to stress two factors to bear in mind when providing a report to someone else in the organisation:

- the information that you provide must be accurate
- the report must be presented on time

Accuracy

We have already seen that for information to be useful it must be reliable Only accurate information is reliable.

You should always ensure that the information that is required for the report has been taken from the correct source and that you have copied that information down correctly.

Any calculations that you make, such as calculating performance measures, should be thoroughly checked and re-checked.

The worst scenario is that you provide inaccurate information to management and this may then result in a wrong decision being made – this could be as major as shutting down an element of the organisation. Beware!

Timing

For information to be useful it must be provided promptly. If a manager has asked for a report for Thursday 22 June then he will expect that report on his desk on Thursday at the very latest.

If a manager requests a report for a certain date this will mean that he does need it on that date. This may be due to the fact that he has a meeting scheduled for Friday for which he requires the information, or that he himself has a reporting deadline to a senior level of management and he needs your report to meet that deadline.

u must be able to schedule your work in such a way that you find the time complete the report at the latest by Wednesday evening.

ways be honest about any problems that you have with completing a report thin the required timescale. If there is some problem that means that the port is unlikely to be completed by the due date, inform the manager as on as possible. It is an element of human nature that most of us will put this f hoping that we do in fact finish it on time. However from the point of view the manager, if he expects the report to arrive on his desk on Thursday and does not he is likely to be very unhappy. However if you went to see the anager on Monday and explained the reasons why the report may not be ady for Thursday then he has four days to alter his schedules to :commodate this.

ORM OF A REPORT

eports can range in size from a short, one or two page internal report, to a uge Government report on a matter of public concern.

or the purposes of Unit 7 you will be required to prepare the short version f these reports. However a formal report of whatever size will have the same najor elements and overall form.

ear in mind that different organisations may have detailed formats for eports – the type of report considered in this chapter is the general type of eport that most organisations will use with some additional details to suit heir own requirements.

ach of the major elements of a report will now be considered and then ummarised in a typical report format on the following page.

Overall structure

When writing a report it is important to plan it carefully and to consider its overall structure. In simple terms the report must have a beginning, a middle and an end.

The beginning sets the scene for the reader of the report as to what the report is about, where the information has come from and what the overall purpose of the report is.

The middle contains the main body of the information and the analysis and arguments.

The end provides the conclusions or recommendations that were requested.

student notes✍

Title and details

A report must always have a title so that the reader immediately knows wh area of the organisation or operations the report is dealing with.

The report is a formal document and therefore must show the name and jc title of the person that it is addressed to and your name and job title as th writer of the report.

As with all correspondence the report must also bear the date on which it w prepared.

If the report is to be sent to a number of people within the organisation the it is common practice to provide a list of the people that it has been sent tc

Terms of reference

The TERMS OF REFERENCE or introductory section of the report set th background for the report. They will explain the reasons for the report bein written and its scope. The important details that should be included here are

- the person who requested the report

- the date by which it must be presented

- the areas that it must cover

- the purpose – whether it is to provide information, draw conclusion or make recommendations

When preparing a report you must be quite clear about its purpose. In some cases you will simply be requested to provide information. In most case: however you will be required to analyse that information, to draw conclusions from it and possibly to make recommendations about future actions to be taken.

If it is to be a long report this section may also include a table of the contents of the report by major headings.

Summary of the report

It is common practice to provide a summary of the report and its conclusions and recommendations, if any, here at the start of the report.

It may seem strange to present the summary and conclusion of the report at the beginning, but this will help the reader of the report to decide whether he needs to read the whole report and also to focus the reader on the main issues in the report.

In practice you will probably not be able to write this section of the report until the entire report is completed, as you will not necessarily know your conclusions or recommendations.

Main body of the report

This is the "middle" of the report. This is where the main FINDINGS of the information that has been requested from you are set out. This section of the report is normally headed up as findings.

This section, again rather confusingly, does not include any detailed information or calculations that you have made, since these will appear in the appendix at the end of the report (see later in the chapter) .

What you must focus on in this section of the report are:

- the main points of the information that you have found
- significant figures or events
- any trends that the information has highlighted
- comments on any performance measures that have been calculated

This section of the report may cover a number of different areas and it is often useful to the reader of the report to include sub-headings here to highlight these different areas.

Conclusion

Here we are at the end of the report. This is where we have to produce a CONCLUSION section.

In this section the key points of the body of the report are summarised, evaluated and a logical conclusion must be made as to the what the report shows.

The conclusion must be based totally upon the information provided in the body of the report – there should be no new information introduced at this point.

Recommendations

RECOMMENDATIONS are not always required in a report. Often the purpose of a report is simply to provide information and conclusions. However if you are required to make a recommendation as to a course of action then this should be considered extremely carefully.

If a recommendation is required you should consider the information and conclusions in your report in the context of the purpose of report and then make the recommendations that you consider are the most appropriate. These recommendations may not be followed but they must be made if they are required.

Appendix

The APPENDIX to a report was mentioned earlier in the chapter. As you w
have realised from the previous chapter, the purpose of a report is to provic
the vital information in the clearest possible way. This can normally only k
done by excluding from the main body of the report the details of th
information and calculations that have been made.

Therefore here in the appendix tables of calculations of performanc
measures and any other diagrams or graphs that you have used (see ne
chapter) will be included. They are therefore available for the manager 1
refer to if necessary, but it means that the main body of the report contair
only references to the significant areas of these calculations.

If the calculations and diagrams cover different areas that are bein
investigated in the main body of the report, it is common practice to have
number of appendices, for example Appendix A, Appendix B etc. The mai
body of the report can then refer to each of these appendices when requirec

TYPICAL REPORT LAYOUT

REPORT TITLE

Report to: Name and job title

Report from: Name and job title

Report date:

Terms of reference

The reasons for the report, who requested it, the areas that it will cover,
why it is being written and where the information in the report has been
taken from.

Summary

The main conclusions and/or recommendations – written when the
report is completed.

Findings

The main points of the information, significant figures and trends and
comments on any performance measures – these key features will be
referenced through to the detailed figures in the appendices.

Conclusion

Summary and evaluation and the findings and conclusions drawn.

Recommendations

Any recommendations required based upon the conclusions drawn.

Appendices

The detailed calculations, diagrams, graphs etc on which the main body
of the report is based.

Activity 1

What are the main elements of a formal report?

HOW IT WORKS

You work in the accounts department of Julian Products Ltd and you have received the following memo from the production manager.

MEMO

To: Jane Thomas – Accounts assistant

From: Pet Lincoln – Production manager

Date: 13 July 2006

I am a little concerned about the performance of our Teddington division. Please send me a report outlining the production and sales performance of the division for the first six months of this year. I need this information by 20 July at the latest.

You now go to the relevant files and find the following information:

	Jan	Feb	Mar	Apr	May	June
Sales £'000	320	300	340	300	270	250
Cost of sales £'000	200	180	210	190	170	160
Overheads £'000	70	80	80	70	70	60
Capital £'000	600	600	600	600	600	600
Actual output units in thousands	480	480	520	470	420	400
Budgeted output units in thousands	500	500	500	500	500	500
Labour hours in thousands	20.0	21.0	22.1	20.4	18.2	18.2

Now you must prepare the report. Start with the appendices showing the calculations of the performance measures. The performance measures that you will calculate fall neatly into profitability measures and production measures so we will use two appendices, A and B, for this.

student notes ✎

Appendix A – Profitability Performance Indicators

	Month					
	Jan	**Feb**	**Mar**	**Apr**	**May**	**June**
Gross profit margin	37.5%	40.0%	38.2%	36.7%	37.0%	36.0%
Net profit margin	15.6%	13.3%	14.7%	13.3%	11.1%	12.0%
Return on capital employed	8.3%	6.7%	8.3%	6.7%	5.0%	5.0%
Asset turnover – in pence for every £ of capital employed	53.3	50.0	56.7	50.0	45.0	41.7

Appendix B – Production Performance Indicators

	Jan	**Feb**	**Mar**	**Apr**	**May**	**June**
Output per labour hour – units	24.0	22.9	23.5	23.0	23.1	22.0
Productivity index	96%	96%	104%	94%	84%	80%
Cost per unit – in pence	41.7	37.5	40.4	40.4	40.5	40.0

These appendices will appear at the end of the report. Now for the report itself.

REPORT

TEDDINGTON DIVISION PERFORMANCE JANUARY TO JUNE 2006

Report to: Pet Lincoln – Production manager

Report from: Jane Thomas – Accounts assistant

Report date: 14 July 2006

Terms of reference

This report has been prepared on the request of Pet Lincoln, Production manager, in order to highlight the production and sales performance of the Teddington Division of Julian Products Ltd for the months of January to June 2006.

Summary

The Teddington division has problems with sales, profitability and production. Sales have fallen with significant decreases in gross profit margin and net profit margin. Production levels have also decreased with production well below budget and a decrease in productivity as well.

Findings

The sales, expenses and production figures have been summarised and analysed in Appendices A and B of this report. The main findings are now summarised.

Sales performance and profitability

Sales of the division reached a peak of £340,000 in March but by June had slumped to £250,000. This is accompanied by a decline in the gross profit margin from a peak of 40% in February to 36% in June. This would indicate either a fall in selling price or an increase in cost of sales. It is possible that as production levels have fallen over the 6 month period bulk purchasing discounts have been lost, which may account for the falling gross profit margin.

The net profit percentage has also suffered, falling from 15.6% in January to 12% in June. This will partly be accounted for by the fall in gross profit margin but whereas the gross profit margin has fallen by 10% from the highest point the net profit margin has decreased at more than twice that rate. Therefore there would appear that there is some problem with the control of overheads. This may be due to the fact that many of the overheads are fixed in nature and therefore are not decreasing as sales and production decrease.

The fall in profit is reflected by a severe reduction in return on capital employed from 8.3% to just 5%. As well as the fall in profitability the return on capital employed will also be affected by the fall in sales reflected in the reduction of asset turnover from a high of 56.7 pence to 41.7 pence for every £1 of capital.

cont.

Production performance

The production levels have decreased in line with the decrease in demand for the product as illustrated by the reduced sales, with production levels falling by over 20%. With the exception of March production has been below the budgeted level in each month with the productivity index falling as low as 80% in June. Productivity has also decreased with the number of units produced per labour hour falling from 24 to 22.

One positive factor in the production figures is that the cost per unit has remained largely constant for the last four months.

Conclusion

The sales and profitability of the division are in serious decline. The gross profit percentage is decreasing and the net profit percentage is falling even faster. This in turn has caused a significant decrease in the return on capital employed.

Production levels have fallen by nearly 17% over the six month period and are largely significantly below the budgeted levels of output. To further add to the production problems, productivity has decreased over the period although cost per unit appears to be fairly stable.

Recommendations

The significant decreases in both gross profit margin and net profit margin should be investigated. The productivity decline should also be looked into further.

WRITING A SUCCESSFUL REPORT

Knowing how to prepare a report is only part of the process. The report must be written well too. A report is a form of communication and therefore as with any form of communication you should aim to get your message across clearly and accurately.

Language and style

The type of language that you use in a report and style of your writing will be of almost as much importance as the actual content of the report. Given below are some pointers on how to communicate in writing in a clear and effective manner.

Length of the report

A report should be as brief as possible without losing any information. This can be achieved by using short words rather than longer ones and short, succinct sentences.

"The sales and profitability of the division are in serious decline"

is preferable to:

"The sales of the division have decreased in value by large amounts and the levels of profitability have also been on the decline."

Clear wording

Try to avoid using complex words or phrases – they are much harder to read and understand than simple words and statements.

"Sales have fallen with significant decreases in gross and net profit margins"

is preferable to:

"With regard to sales the level of turnover recorded in the division has shown a sharp reduction. In connection with this the gross profit margin has declined and there is evidence of a diminishing net profit margin."

Jargon and slang

Wherever possible avoid using jargon which may not be readily understood by the person using the report. In general, simple accounting terms such as gross and net profit margins can be assumed to be understood by management . For example the phrase *"the impairment test indicated that the intangible asset's carrying value was below the economic value as measured by the discounted cash flows of the asset"* may be understood by a qualified accountant but not necessarily by the average non-accountant.

Slang words and "in-phrases" should be avoided.

"Cost per unit is stable"

is preferable to:

"Cost per unit is cool"

Objectivity

Try to avoid writing in the first person – avoid using "I" or "you"

"The productivity decline should be looked into further"

is preferable to:

"In my view I think that you should investigate the productivity decline"

Presentation of your report

First impressions are important – make sure that the report that you submit not crumpled or dirty or covered in yesterday's lunch.

Use the spell check facility of your computer or word processor to ensure tha there are no spelling mistakes. But remember that it will only detect mi. spelled words; not incorrect words.

Break up any longer sections of the report by using headings. Make sure an heading is informative and tells the reader what the next section of the repo is about.

Accuracy

A final word on accuracy – remember to check and double check all figure and calculations. An error in the calculation of a performance indicator coul alter your conclusions completely.

Activity 2

Given below are the performance indicators calculated for the three factories of Grant Productions Ltd for the most recent three month period from Chapter 11. You are to use these as the appendix to a report that you are to write to the production director Philip Martin concerning the performance of the three factories. You are the accounts assistant Fred Harvey and today's date is 22 June 2006.

PERFORMANCE INDICATORS

	Tamworth	Solihull	Barnsley	Total
PRODUCTIVITY				
Labour productivity				
Units produced/hours worked	3.7	3.1	3.9	3.5
Productivity index				
Units produced/budgeted units	100%	92%	106%	98%
COST PER UNIT				
Cost of sales/units produced	£4.33	£4.57	£4.22	£4.38
RESOURCE UTILISATION				
Labour utilisation				
Hours worked/hours available	97%	93%	98%	95%
Asset turnover				
Sales/capital employed	0.64	0.63	0.67	0.64
PROFITABILITY				
Gross profit margin				
Gross profit/sales	35%	30%	37%	34%
Net profit margin				
Net profit/sales	12.5%	8%	11.7%	10.7%
Return on capital employed				
Net profit/capital employed	8%	5%	7.8%	6.9%

BUDGETED FIGURES

Budgeted productivity = Budgeted production/Budgeted hours

$$= \frac{330,000}{91,666}$$

$$= 3.6 \text{ units per labour hour}$$

CHAPTER OVERVIEW

- reporting structure is the way in which information is passed up the organisation from the detailed information required by line managers to the summaries and highlights required by more senior management – the complexity of the reporting structure will depend upon the size of the organisation and THE complexity of the organisational structure

- when providing a report to a manager it must be accurate and provided within the time scale set by the manager

- a report should have a beginning, a middle and an end

- the report should start with its title, the names and job titles of the person to whom the report is to be sent and who it is from

- the terms of reference section sets out the purpose of the report, who requested it and the areas and information that it covers

- there should then be a brief summary of the findings and conclusions

- the main body of the report should not be full of detailed figures – these are shown in appendices at the end of the report. Instead the findings section of the report should highlight significant figures and trends and comment on the performance measures calculated

- the conclusion section should summarise and evaluate the key points of the findings and a logical conclusion should be drawn based upon those findings

- the recommendation section should set out any recommendations that are required of you based upon the contents of the report and your conclusions

- writing a report is a form of communication, so care should be taken with language and style – use short words and sentences, avoid complex words or phrases, avoid jargon and slang, be objective

- ensure that your report looks professional, check all spellings and check and re-check any calculations

HOW MUCH HAVE YOU LEARNED?

1   A retail business has three small department stores in Worksop, Mansfield and Newark. The figures for the first six months of 2006 are given below:

	Worksop £	Mansfield £	Newark £
Financial details			
Sales	450,000	330,000	510,000
Cost of sales	180,000	165,000	230,000
Overheads	210,000	125,000	215,000
Capital	550,000	410,000	650,000
Non-financial details			
Floor area	2,000sq m	1,400sq m	2,500sq m
Employees	24	15	24
Hours worked	20,800	14,000	20,000

You are required to write a report to the sales director, John Hartman, comparing the performance of the three stores over the six month period. He has asked you to make recommendations about any further investigations that should be made. You are the accounts assistant and your name is Philip Oliver. Today's date is 15 July 2006.

2   The details of the results of a business for the six months ending 31 March 2006 are given below:

	Oct £000	Nov £000	Dec £000	Jan £000	Feb £000	Mar £000
Sales	300	360	340	380	420	400
Cost of sales	150	200	190	240	250	250
Overheads	100	110	105	100	120	115
Capital	180	180	200	230	240	240

You are the accounts assistant in the business and your name is Kevin Burne. You have been requested by the sales director, Janis Robbins, to write a report commenting on these results (no recommendations are required). Today's date is 22 April 2006.

chapter 13:
TABLES AND DIAGRAMS

chapter coverage 📖

In the last two chapters you have learnt how to write a report and how to calculate performance indicators to use in the reporting process. When providing information in a report or in the appendix to a report, you may wish to show the information in the form of a table or indeed to present it in the form of a diagram. In this chapter we will consider setting up tables and also the various types of diagram that you might be required to prepare. The topics to be covered are:

✎   tabular information

✎   using spreadsheets

✎   simple bar charts

✎   compound bar charts

✎   component bar charts

✎   pie charts

✎   pictograms

✎   graphs

✎   uses of the various presentation tools

KNOWLEDGE AND UNDERSTANDING AND PERFORMANCE CRITERIA COVERAGE

Unit 7

knowledge and understanding - accounting techniques

13   tabulation of accounting and other quantitative information using spreadsheets
14   methods of presenting information: written reports; diagrammatic; tabular

Performance criteria – element 7.1

F   prepare reports in the appropriate form and present them to management within the required timescales

TABULATION OF DATA

When preparing the performance indicators in the previous chapters, w
used a simple form of tabulation. The time periods or divisions were listed a
columns across the top of the page and the performance indicators were the
listed in rows.

HOW IT WORKS

An example of a TABLE is given below:

TALBOT ELECTRICAL – PROFIT AND LOSS ACCOUNT SUMMARY

	APRIL 2006 £'000	MAY 2006 £'000	JUNE 2006 £'000
Sales	1,289	1,346	1,463
Cost of sales	801	833	906
Gross profit	488	513	557
Overheads	289	301	322
Net profit	199	212	235

You should note the following points:

- the table has been given a title which clearly describes the
  information in the table

- each column represents a time period which is clearly stated – this
  case it is months but the time period could be a year or a week

- in other types of table the column headings may relate to each
  division in the organisation if the table is to show a comparison
  between divisions in a period

- the units that each column is showing are clearly shown – in this
  case thousands of pounds (£'000) so that the table is not confused
  with lots of zeros

PREPARING TABLES USING SPREADSHEETS

SPREADSHEETS are computer packages that can be used to help in the tabulation of data and calculation of figures to appear in the table.

What is a spreadsheet?

You will have come across computer spreadsheet packages either at work or on your own PC. In essence a spreadsheet is a number of columns and rows and might typically look like this:

	A	B	C	D	E
1					
2					
3					
4					

Each column and each row will represent different factors, so the columns may be the months of the year and the rows may represent sales, cost of sales, gross profit etc.

	A	B	C	D
1	2006	May	June	July
2	Sales	100,000	93,000	95,000
3	C of S	65,000	33,480	35,150
4	Gross profit	35,000	59,520	59,850
5	Expenses	25,000	49,755	49,400
6	Net profit	10,000	9,765	10,450

The columns can be continued as each month's profit figures become known.

However this is simply a tabulation of profit and loss account information as we have seen earlier. The point of a computer spreadsheet is that it can be used to make large numbers of calculations very rapidly providing that the package is programmed by the use of formulae to make the correct calculations.

HOW IT WORKS

Ken Bowman, the owner of Bowman Enterprises, wishes to use a computer spreadsheet package to calculate the gross profit margin and net profit margin for each month of trading.

The initial input to the spreadsheet will be the basic profit and loss account for each month.

		A	B	C	D
1			June	July	August
2		Sales	64,300	71,200	62,700
3		Cost of sales	45,010	49,130	42,640
4		Gross profit	19,290	22,070	20,060
5		Expenses	12,860	14,600	13,160
6		Net profit	6,430	7,470	6,900
7		Gross profit margin			
8		Net profit margin			

The next step is to input the formulae required to calculate gross profit margin and net profit margin, based upon the figures in each column and row.

First consider the gross profit margin for June:

$$\text{Gross profit margin} = \frac{\text{Gross profit}}{\text{Sales}} \times 100$$

For June the figure for sales is in column B row 2. Therefore June sales are recognised by the computer as B2.

The June figure for gross profit is in column B row 4 so June's gross profit is recognised by the computer as B4.

To get the gross profit margin gross profit must be divided by sales and multiplied by 100. This gives us the spreadsheet formula for the gross profit margin of:

Gross profit margin = (B4/B2) *100

Take some care with this formulation:

■ for the computer spreadsheet the multiplication sign (x) is replaced by *

■ the B4/B2 element must be in brackets as this must be done first by the computer as a separate calculation otherwise the computer would divide B4 by 100 times B2.

This formula for calculating the gross profit margin for June can now be entered onto the spreadsheet in column A row 7 where the gross profit

...argin will be shown by the computer when it has processed the ...readsheet.

	A	B	C	D
1		June	July	August
2	Sales	64,300	71,200	62,700
3	Cost of sales	45,010	49,130	42,640
4	Gross profit	19,290	22,070	20,060
5	Expenses	12,860	14,600	13,160
6	Net profit	6,430	7,470	6,900
7	Gross profit margin =(B4/B2)*100			
8	Net profit margin			

Now we will do the same exercise for the net profit margin.

$$\text{Net profit margin} = \frac{\text{Net profit}}{\text{Sales}} \times 100$$

...ales for June are B2.
Net profit for June is B6.

The formula for the spreadsheet for net profit margin is therefore:

= (B6/B2)*100

Again this is input into the spreadsheet in the net profit margin row for June.

	A	B	C	D
1		June	July	August
2	Sales	64,300	71,200	62,700
3	Cost of sales	45,010	49,130	42,640
4	Gross profit	19,290	22,070	20,060
5	Expenses	12,860	14,600	13,160
6	Net profit	6,430	7,470	6,900
7	Gross profit margin =(B4/B2)*100			
8	Net profit margin =(B6/B2)*100			

The formulae are then determined for July and August:

July

Gross profit margin	=	(C4/C2)*100
Net profit margin	=	(C6/C2)*100

August

Gross profit margin	=	(D4/D2)*100
Net profit margin	=	(D6/D2)*100

253

student notes✎

These will then also be input to the spreadsheet:

	A	B	C	D
1		June	July	August
2	Sales	64,300	71,200	62,700
3	Cost of sales	45,010	49,130	42,640
4	Gross profit	19,290	22,070	20,060
5	Expenses	12,860	14,600	13,160
6	Net profit	6,430	7,470	6,900
7	Gross profit margin = (B4/B2)*100	= (C4/C2)*100	= (D4/D2)*100
8	Net profit margin = (B6/B2)*100	= (C6/C2)*100	= (D6/D2)*100

(In fact in most spreadsheet packages you can copy the formulae for June into July and August - the computer will automatically change 'B4' to 'C4' etc.)

Once this has been done the computer spreadsheet package can be run and the result will be the gross profit margins and net profit margins for each month.

	A	B	C	D
1		June	July	August
2	Sales	64,300	71,200	62,700
3	Cost of sales	45,010	49,130	42,640
4	Gross profit	19,290	22,070	20,060
5	Expenses	12,860	14,600	13,160
6	Net profit	6,430	7,470	6,900
7	Gross profit margin	30.0%	31.0%	32.0%
8	Net profit margin	10.0%	10.5%	11.0%

This technique can be extended to draw up tables of information regarding all areas of the business. It can be used for other performance measures and also in areas such as time series analysis and indices (see the next chapter).

Activity 1

For the last three months the actual and budgeted units of production for a manufacturing company have been as follows:

	Actual Units	Budgeted Units
September	102,000	105,000
October	108,000	104,000
November	110,000	106,000

i) Produce a spreadsheet showing the actual and budgeted figures for the three months and the formulae necessary to calculate the productivity index for each month.

ii) Show the spreadsheet once the computer has processed the information thereby calculating the productivity index.

ADDITIONAL FEATURES OF SPREADSHEETS

You may have met in practice some of the features of spreadsheets that can make life easier for the user. We shall consider here:

- conditional statements
- sort facilities
- spreadsheets to graph
- rounding buttons

Conditional statements

In some situations, companies may make (or receive) payments dependent on conditional factors, which at the time of setting up the spreadsheet are as yet uncertain. For example:

- a company may award a bonus to those of its staff who exceed a sales target by more than a certain sum

- a company may offer a discount to customers who order goods in excess of a certain value

The spreadsheet can be made to reflect the fact that some payments are triggered only if a specific condition is met.

HOW IT WORKS

Discounts

A company offers a discount of 5% to customers who order more than £1,000 worth of goods. A spreadsheet showing what customers will pay might look like this.

	A	B	C	D
1	**Marvellous Motorspares**			
2	*Sales analysis - April 2006*			
3	Customer	Sales	5% discount	Sales (net)
4		£	£	£
5	Adam	956.00	0.00	956.00
6	David	1423.00	71.15	1351.85
7	Fred	2894.00	144.70	2749.30

The formula in cell C5 is: =IF(B5>1,000,(0.05*B5),0). This means, if the value in B5 is greater than £1,000 multiply it by 0.05, otherwise the discount will be zero. Cell D5 will calculate the amount net of discount, using the formula: =B5–C5. The same conditional formula with the cell references changed will be found in cells C6, C7 and C8.

Strictly, the variables £1,000 and 5% should be entered in separate cells in different part of the spreadsheet so that the trigger level for the discount, and the discount rate can be changed easily. The formula in cell C5 would now refer to the cells containing the values 1,000 and 0.05 rather than the absolute values. Then, if the company decides that a discount can now b given for sales over £500, only the cell with the trigger level stored in it need be changed for all the formula to reflect this.

Delivery charges

A company charges £10 for delivery on all orders of less than £200. The following spreadsheet shows the amounts payable by three customers.

	A	B	C	D
1	**Books Ltd**			
2	*Delivery charges - week ended 23 June 2006*			
3				
4	Customer	Sales	Delivery charge	Invoice amount
5		£	£	£
6	Geoff	156	10	166
7	Henry	247	0	247
8	Cyril	201	0	201

Cell C6 will contain a formula: =IF(B6<200,10,0). Cell D6 will add together the contents of cells B6 and C6. Again, strictly the variables (£200, £10) should be entered in a separate part of the spreadsheet.

Note that in this spreadsheet we have reduced the font size in the column headings to improve presentation. The alternatives would have been to have even wider columns or to have tables almost running into one another. Spreadsheets should be presented with care to try to maintain an easily understandable layout.

Sort facilities

Spreadsheets often have databases - like facilities for manipulating tables of data (although they should not be regarded as true databases). Sort facilities within a spreadsheet provide a good example.

In the following illustration, data has been sorted by highlighting columns A to C and then clicking on Data and then Sort. It has been sorted into **ascending** product name order and **descending** order of number of parts used in that product. Then the data has been copied into columns E to G where it can be re-sorted according to part number and product name.

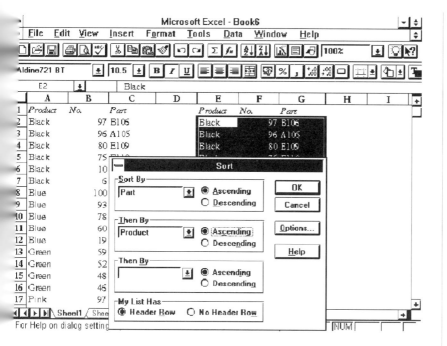

Spreadsheet to graph facilities

It is usually possible to convert tabulated data in a spreadsheet into a variety of bar chart or graphical formats. We will look again at the Marvellous Motorspares Ltd example, reproduced below.

	A	B	C	D
1	**Marvellous Motorspares**			
2	*Sales analysis - April 2006*			
3	Customer	Sales	5% discount	Sales (net)
4		£	£	£
5	Adam	956.00	0.00	956.00
6	David	1423.00	71.15	1351.85
7	Fred	2894.00	144.70	2749.30
8	Peter	842.00	0.00	842.00

This could be used to generate any of the charts shown over the page.

student notes✐

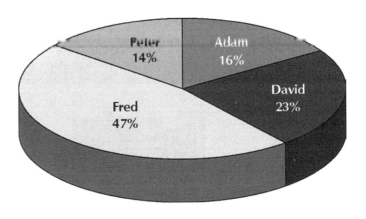

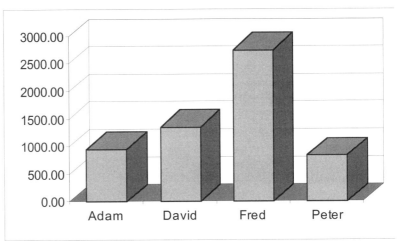

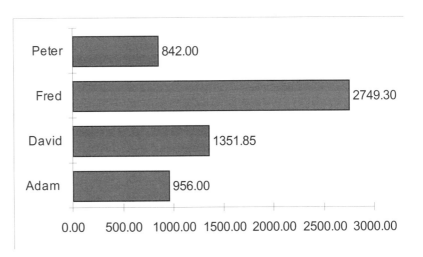

Very impressive graphics can be generated simply by selecting the range of figures to turn into a chart and then clicking on a chart icon and following the step-by-step instructions on screen.

![ounding]

he variety of formats available means that the number displayed may be
fferent from the one actually in the cell. This can cause apparent errors. If
ou check the arithmetic in a spreadsheet by hand or with a calculator, you
ay not obtain exactly the same numbers as appear in the spreadsheet.

HOW IT WORKS

he following spreadsheet shows how apparent rounding errors can arise.

	A	B	C	D
1	Petty cash			
2	Week ended 16 August 2006			
3		£		
4	Opening balance	231		
5	Receipts	33		
6	Payments	-105		
7	Closing balance	160		
8				

Cell B7 contains the formula =SUM(B4:B6). It appears that 231 + 33 − 105
s equal to 160, which is not true (check it). The reason for the discrepancy
s that the cells actually contain the following values.

	A	B	C	D
1	Petty cash			
2	Week ended 16 August 2006			
3		£		
4	Opening balance	231.34		
5	Receipts	32.99		
6	Payments	(-104.67)		
7	Closing balance	159.66		
8				

The spreadsheet has been formatted as fixed with no decimal places. Thus
the numbers would be rounded up or down to the nearest whole number.

A report produced by a spreadsheet should be no more prone to such
discrepancies than a report produced by hand or using a calculator. It would
of course be possible to go through the spreadsheet manually correcting such
errors, but this would defeat the object of using a spreadsheet, which is to
save time.

One possible solution to this difficulty is to use the ROUND function. The
ROUND function has the following structure: ROUND (value, places)

'Value' is the value to be rounded. 'Places' is the number of places to whic the value is to be rounded. In the above example, to round 231.34 to zer decimal places the formula would be =ROUND(231.34,0).

The difference between using the ROUND function and formatting a valu to some number of decimal places is that using the ROUND function actual changes the value itself, while formatting the value only changes th appearance of the value. Thus, in our example, the values to be added wou actually become 231, etc, and the total would therefore be 159.

If the ROUND function is selected to eliminate decimal places fc presentation purposes, the result of the calculation will be inaccurate due t the rounding. A possible strategy for dealing with this would be to calculate on a separate spreadsheet or part of the spreadsheet, the 'real' result. Yo would then find the difference between this and the rounded result an present it separately as 'Rounding ' difference.

Which way to round?

A value of 1.5 would be rounded up to 2 using the ROUND function Suppose you wanted it rounded down?

Excel also has functions called ROUNDUP and ROUNDDOWN. Thu =ROUNDUP(1.4, 0) would return the value 2, and =ROUNDDOWN(1.6 0) would give you 1.

DIAGRAMS

Although figures shown in a table are informative they do not give an immediate impression of what is happening – with a table a certain amount of time is needed in order to study it in order to discover the details of the information.

A more immediate way of showing the impact of information is to show it in the form of a diagram. The three main diagrams that you are likely to use are:

- bar charts
- pie charts
- pictograms

Each type will be considered in turn.

BAR CHARTS

A BAR CHART is a chart which sets out a series of bars with the height of each bar representing the size of the variable being illustrated.

There are three types of bar chart each of which will be considered in turn:

- simple bar charts
- compound bar charts
- component bar charts

Simple bar charts

A SIMPLE BAR CHART is a series of normally vertical bars of different heights.

HOW IT WORKS

Given below is a summary of the sales for Jesmond Trading for the last three years:

	Year 1 £'000	Year 2 £'000	Year 3 £'000
Product A	120	150	200
Product B	200	220	240
Product C	60	120	180
Total sales	380	490	620

This information for the total sales will now be shown in the form of a simple bar chart.

student notes

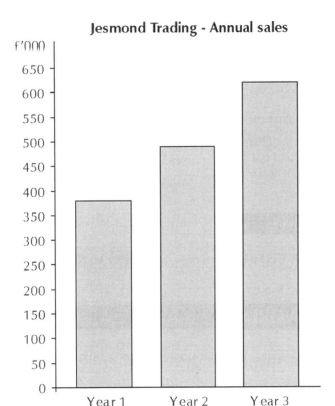

Note the following points about the bar chart:

- it has a title showing clearly what the bar chart illustrates

- the values on the vertical axis are clearly labelled as £'000

- the values on the vertical axis start from zero

- there are gaps between the bars although it is also possible to draw a bar chart with the sides touching.

The bar chart clearly and immediately shows the trend of how the sales have increased over the three years, although it is harder to read off the precise sales figure each year.

Activity 2

Johnston & Co has the following trading results for the last three years:

	Year 1	Year 2	Year 3
	£'000	£'000	£'000
Sales	300	380	450
Cost of sales	120	150	180
Gross profit	180	230	270
Overheads	100	130	150
Net profit	80	100	120

Prepare a simple bar chart showing the sales over the three years.

Compound bar chart

If more than one figure is to be illustrated for each year in a bar chart then this can be done by preparing a COMPOUND BAR CHART with a bar for each element of the total.

HOW IT WORKS

Returning to Jesmond Trading's sales, using a simple bar chart we were only able to show the sales in total for each year. If we wished to show the sales of each of the three products then we would need a compound bar chart showing a bar for each product for each year.

student notes ✍

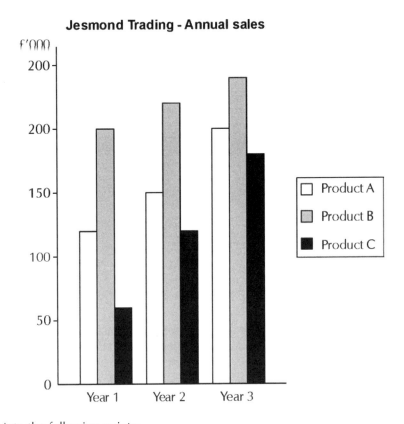

Jesmond Trading - Annual sales

Note the following points:

- each product's bar is shaded differently

- there is a key showing which shading relates to which product

From this compound bar chart it is possible to clearly see the trend of increases in sales of each product but again it is difficult to read off the precise total of each product's sales each year.

Activity 3

Johnston & Co has the following trading results for the last three years:

	Year 1 £'000	Year 2 £'000	Year 3 £'000
Sales	300	380	450
Cost of sales	120	150	180
Gross profit	180	230	270
Overheads	100	130	150
Net profit	80	100	120

Prepare a compound bar chart to show sales, gross profit and net profit for the three years.

omponent bar chart

COMPONENT BAR CHART can be used when the requirement is to show e proportion of a total that relates to each individual element of that total.

HOW IT WORKS

e will now show the sales of Jesmond Trading in a component bar chart. mply show product A's total then add Product B's to find the top of B's aded bar and then add product C's to find the top of C's shaded bar.

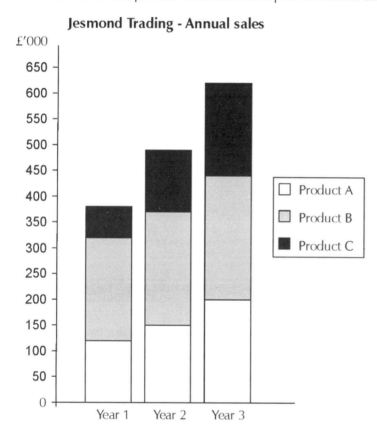

Jesmond Trading - Annual sales

Note again that the part of the bar representing each different product is shaded differently and there is a key to show which product relates to which shading.

The component bar chart does not show as clearly as the compound bar chart the trend of increases in each product's sales, but it does clearly show the trend of the proportion of total sales for each product.

Activity 4

Given below are the sales for a business for the last three years.

	Year 1 £'000	Year 2 £'000	Year 3 £'000
Division A	210	280	320
Division B	140	240	340
Division C	180	230	300
Total	530	750	960

Prepare a component bar chart to show sales in each division for each of the three years.

PIE CHARTS

A PIE CHART is another method of showing the proportions of a total made up by each individual element.

A pie chart is a circle which is split up into slices or segments representing each portion of the total.

Computer packages will prepare pie charts but if they are to be prepared by hand you will need a protractor and a pair of compasses.

HOW IT WORKS

We will continue with the sales for Jesmond Trading for the three years.

Starting with the Year 1 sales we will construct a pie chart.

The circle represents the total sales for the year of £380,000. This will then be split into three slices or segments representing the proportion of sales for each of the three products.

A circle has 360° therefore it is necessary to work out how many degrees relate to each of the three products using the following formula:

$$\text{Angle of segment for each product} = \frac{\text{Product sales}}{\text{Total sales}} \times 360$$

For Year 1 the calculations are:

Product A $\dfrac{120}{380} \times 360 = \quad 114$

Product B $\dfrac{200}{380} \times 360 = \quad 189$

Product C $\dfrac{60}{380} \times 360 = \quad \dfrac{57}{360}$

Note that the total of the three degrees must be 360.

The pie chart for Year 1 sales can now be drawn.

Jesmond trading – Year 1 sales

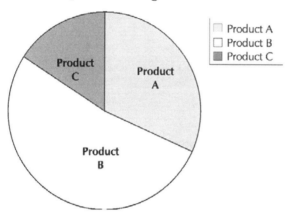

☐ Product A
☐ Product B
■ Product C

Note that the shading is different for each product and again there is a key to show which shading relates to which product.

The pie charts for Years 2 and 3 sales can also be drawn.

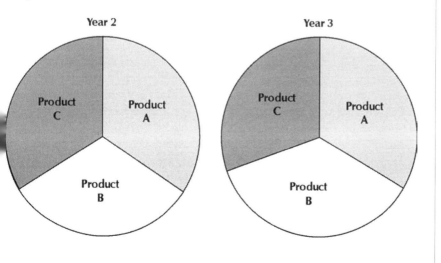

267

student notes✎

Comparison of the three pie charts shows clearly the changes in t
proportions of sales of each product, but gives no indication of the actu
amount of the sales for each product.

On some pie charts the actual proportion is shown for each slice as
percentage. If we redraw the Year 3 pie chart we can show it with t
proportions as well.

Product A $\dfrac{200}{620} \times 100 =$ 32.3%

Product B $\dfrac{240}{620} \times 100 =$ 38.7%

Product C $\dfrac{180}{620} \times 100 =$ 29.0%

100.0%

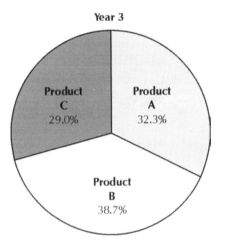

Year 3

Product C 29.0%

Product A 32.3%

Product B 38.7%

Activity 5

Given below are the sales for a business for the last three years:

	Year 1 £'000	Year 2 £'000	Year 3 £'000
Division A	210	280	320
Division B	140	240	340
Division C	180	230	300
Total	530	750	960

Draw a pie chart to represent the sales of each division for each of the
three years.

ICTOGRAMS

PICTOGRAM is the simplest form of diagram for information. A picture is
ed to represent a certain number of sales, services provided etc and the
tal for the period is then presented as the correct number of these pictures
us a proportion of the picture to make up the actual amount.

HOW IT WORKS

gymnasium currently has 530 male members and 480 female members.

his could be represented in a pictogram.

ymnasium – current membership

Note the following points:

- there is a title indicating clearly what the diagram is showing
- there is key showing what each picture means

pictogram has an immediate visual impact but can only be used for very
imple information, and it is never possible to determine the exact number
hat a part of one of the pictures represents.

Activity 6

A car dealer illustrates the number of car sales each month in its quarterly
sales report using a picture of a car for every 100 cars sold.

The sales for the last quarter were:

	Number of cars
April	320
May	390
June	270

Show these sales figures in a pictogram where one car equals 100 cars
sold.

GRAPHS

One of the most commonly used methods of presenting financial informati[on] is in the form of a graph. A GRAPH is a method of showing the relationsh[ip] between two variables. Graphs are simple and have immediate visual impa[ct] but there are some rules regarding the drawing of a graph.

Rules for graph drawing:

- there are two axes on a graph – the vertical axis and the horizon[tal] axis
- the vertical axis is the y axis
- the horizontal axis is the x axis
- there are two variables when drawing a graph – the x variable an[d] the y variable
- the x variable is always the INDEPENDENT VARIABLE – this is th[e] one that is not affected by the other variable
- the y variable is always the DEPENDENT VARIABLE – this is th[e] variable whose value depends upon the independent variable
- each axis should start at zero (there are exceptions to this – see late[r]

Typical graph

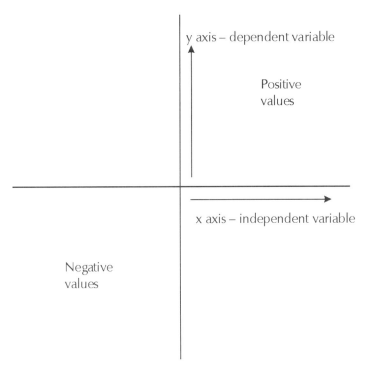

y axis – dependent variable

Positive
values

x axis – independent variable

Negative
values

- graphs can show negative figures, but normally the area to be used is the top right hand quarter

xamples of independent and dependent variables

dependent variable	Dependent variable
me (months/years)	Sales/costs/profits
nits produced	Time taken
nits produced	Costs of production

HOW IT WORKS

iven below is a summary of the sales for Jesmond Trading for the last three ears:

	Year 1 £'000	Year 2 £'000	Year 3 £'000
Product A	120	150	200
Product B	200	220	240
Product C	60	120	180
Total sales	380	490	620

he total sales will now be plotted on a graph.

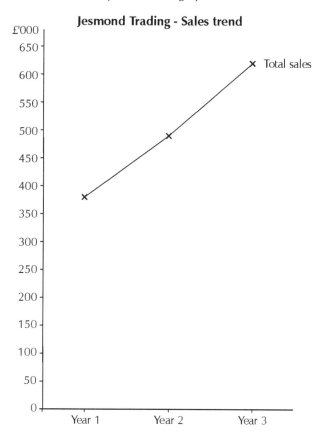

Jesmond Trading - Sales trend

271

Note the following points about the graph:

■ it is given a title which explains what the graph shows

■ both axes are labelled

– the y axis is the dependent variable – the sales figure
– the x axis is the independent variable – the year

■ both axes start from zero – take care with the scale – you need to ensure that you can fit all of your figures onto the graph and also that it is not so small that the trend of the graph line cannot be seen

It is quite possible to have more than one line on a graph. We will now add in the graph lines for the sales of each of the individual products as well as the total sales.

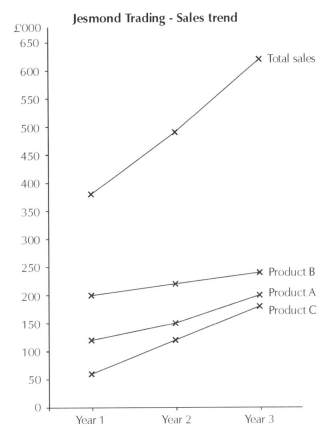

Jesmond Trading - Sales trend

■ as you now have more than one line, each line must be labelled and you may show them in different colours or in different styles (dotted, dashed or solid)

■ note how useful the graph is in showing the comparative trends of sales in total and for each of the products

scales of axes

a business was plotting its sales for a six month period and these sales were between £10,000 and £13,000 it would not be practical to start the y axis zero. In this case the axes of the graph would look like this – the break on the y axis indicates that it does not start at zero.

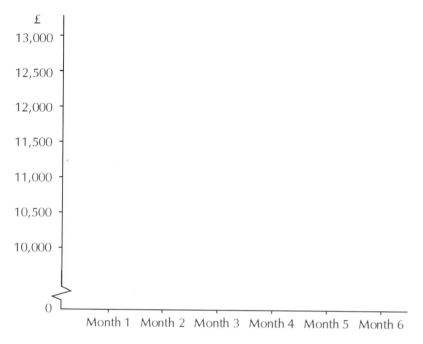

Activity 7

A business has the following trading results for the last three years:

	Year 1 £'000	Year 2 £'000	Year 3 £'000
Sales	300	380	450
Cost of sales	120	150	180
Gross profit	180	230	270
Overheads	100	130	150
Net profit	80	100	120

You are to plot a graph showing lines for sales, gross profit and net profit.

USES OF THE VARIOUS PRESENTATION TOOLS

In this chapter we have looked at a number of different ways of illustratir data. To conclude the chapter we will consider the usefulness of each these methods:

Tables – tables show the precise detail of the information but they normal require fairly detailed study in order to be able to determine trends

Spreadsheets – spreadsheets are capable of calculating the same figure fc many periods very rapidly

Bar charts – bar charts have immediate visual impact and the use compound and component bar charts can show trends in individu; elements as well as the totals. However it is difficult to read off any exac figures from a bar chart.

Pie chart – this is a good method of presentation for showing the proportio that each element is of the total. However although trends in proportions ca be illustrated no exact figures can be read off a pie chart.

Pictogram – this gives an immediate impression of the information provide that it is fairly simple information but no exact figures can be determined.

Graphs – graphs give an immediate visual feel for the trend of the data an also the approximate figures can be read from the graph.

CHAPTER OVERVIEW

- a table of data should have a clear heading, the columns should be clearly headed and the units should be shown

- a simple bar chart shows a number of normally vertical bars indicating the amount of a variable – the bars can be compared over time to indicate any trend

- a compound bar chart shows the same information but more than one element can be shown

- a component bar chart is useful for illustrating the proportion of the total that each element makes up – the total is shown in the bar chart but the bar is split into the elements that make up that total

- a pie chart is another diagram that indicates the proportion of a total that is made up by each element – it is a circle that is split into segments to represent the amount of each of the elements of the total

- a pictogram is the simplest form of showing information, by representing the amount that is to be portrayed by a number of complete and partially complete pictures

- graphs are an excellent way of illustrating data – an independent variable is plotted on the x axis against a dependent variable on the y axis

HOW MUCH HAVE YOU LEARNED?

1   Given below are the production figures for a factory for the last four months.

	February	March	April	May
Output in units	136,700	154,200	144,600	139,800
Budgeted output	140,000	145,000	142,000	144,000
Hours worked	13,200	14,600	13,600	13,700

i)   Produce a spreadsheet schedule (given below) which will calculate the productivity p␣
labour hour each month and the productivity index each month by inserting th␣
appropriate formulae.

	A	B	C	D	E
1					
2					
3					
4					
5					
6					
7					

ii) Show the information that would be produced by the spreadsheet regarding productivit␣
per labour hour and the productivity index each month.

	A	B	C	D	E
1					
2					
3					
4					
5					
6					
7					

2   Given below are the production figures for a factory for the last three months.

	April	May	June
Production costs	£416,400	£452,300	£425,500
Output in units	120,500	137,000	121,500
Hours worked	11,200	13,400	11,500
Budgeted output	120,000	140,000	140,000
Hours available	12,000	13,900	12,600
Sales revenue	£765,000	£790,000	£725,000
Machine hours	10,200	12,000	10,800

a)   Produce a computer spreadsheet that will calculate each of the following performance indicators for each of the last three months and for the three months in total by inserting the appropriate formulae:

i)   productivity per labour hour

ii)   productivity index

iii)   labour utilisation

iv)   cost per unit

v)   machine utilisation (revenue per machine hour)

	A	B	C	D	E	F
1						
2						
3						
4						
5						
6						
7						
8						
9						
10						
11						
12						
13						

b)   Show the results of the spreadsheet package.

	A	B	C	D	E	F
1						
2						
3						
4						
5						
6						
7						
8						
9						
10						
11						
12						
13						

3   Given below is a summary of a business's performance for the last three months:

	Jan	Feb	Mar
	£000	£000	£000
Sales	250	300	280
Cost of sales	130	170	160
Overheads	85	90	88
Capital	150	150	170

a)   Prepare a computer spreadsheet that will calculate for each month the following performance indicators by inserting the appropriate formulae:

i)   gross profit margin

ii)   net profit margin

iii)   return on capital employed

iv)   asset turnover

	A	B	C	D	E	F
1						
2						
3						
4						
5						
6						
7						
8						
9						
10						
11						

b)   Show the completed spreadsheet with the results after the computer program has been run.

	A	B	C	D	E	F
1						
2						
3						
4						
5						
6						
7						
8						
9						
10						
11						

4   Given below are the divisional production cost figures for Latham Products for the last four months.

	March £'000	April £'000	May £'000	June £'000
Division I	180	200	170	220
Division II	240	290	260	300
Division III	100	130	110	120
	520	620	540	640

Prepare a simple bar chart showing the total production costs for the last four months.

5 Given below are the divisional production cost figures for Latham Products for the last four months.

	March £'000	April £'000	May £'000	June £'000
Division I	180	200	170	220
Division II	240	290	260	300
Division III	100	130	110	120
	520	620	540	640

Prepare a compound bar chart showing the production costs for each division for the last four months.

6 Given below are the divisional production cost figures for Latham Products for the last four months.

	March £'000	April £'000	May £'000	June £'000
Division I	180	200	170	220
Division II	240	290	260	300
Division III	100	130	110	120
	520	620	540	640

Prepare a component bar chart showing the production costs of each division for the last four months.

7 Latham Products' sales figures for its three main product types are given below for the last four months.

	March £'000	April £'000	May £'000	June £'000
Product A	230	270	300	250
Product B	350	350	360	340
Product C	100	150	180	220
Total sales	680	770	840	810

Prepare a pie chart for each of the four months showing the breakdown of sales in each month.

8 Latham Products' sales figures for its three main product types are given below for the last four months.

	March £'000	April £'000	May £'000	June £'000
Product A	230	270	300	250
Product B	350	350	360	340
Product C	100	150	180	220
Total sales	680	770	840	810

Prepare a graph showing the sales in total for the four months and for each of the product types.

Chapter 14:
REPORTING FIGURES OVER TIME

chapter coverage 📖

In the last few chapters we have been considering the methods of reporting sales, costs and other figures. In this chapter we will be looking at the problems of reporting and comparing figures over a number of years and methods of making these figures more meaningful. The topics to be covered are:

✍ time series analysis

✍ averages and moving averages

✍ calculating a trend

✍ extrapolation

✍ time series analysis and spreadsheets

✍ index numbers

✍ the retail price index

✍ index numbers and spreadsheets

KNOWLEDGE AND UNDERSTANDING AND PERFORMANCE CRITERIA COVERAGE

Unit 7

knowledge and understanding - accounting techniques

9   time series analysis
10   use of index numbers
13   tabulation of accounting and other quantitative information using spreadsheets

Performance criteria – element 7.1

C   compare results over time using an appropriate method that allows for changing price levels

TIME SERIES ANALYSIS

When reporting information about costs or revenues, it is common practic
to look at the figures for a number of years in order to get a feel for how th
figures are changing over time.

The same figure reported for a number of years, such as sales, is known as
TIME SERIES. One of the key elements of information that managemer
might require from a time series is an indication of the TREND. The trend
a feel for how the figure in question is changing over time – is it increasin
rapidly, is it decreasing slightly?

The technique for determining the trend of a series of figures is known a
TIME SERIES ANALYSIS. Time series analysis can become quite complicate
but for Unit 7 only an outline understanding of determining the trend i
required. This is done by calculating a number of AVERAGES to summaris
the figures that have been given.

Averages

An average is simply the total of a number of figures divided by the number
of figures used.

Suppose that we are told the production costs for the months of January,
February, March and April are £13,000, £17,000, £15,000 and £12,000
respectively. The average production cost for the four month period is:

$$\frac{£13,000 + £17,000 + £15,000 + £12,000}{4} = £14,250$$

The average effectively summarises the four months of costs – sometimes
they were above this figure and sometimes below it.

Activity 1

The number of employees employed by a factory over the past three years
is as follows:

2003	2,340
2004	2,860
2005	2,280

What is the average number of employees for the three years?

Moving averages

The technique of calculating a MOVING AVERAGE is a key tool in time series analysis and is a method of finding averages for a number of consecutive periods.

HOW IT WORKS

Suppose that the sales figures for a business for the first six months of the year are as follows:

	£
January	26,000
February	30,000
March	28,000
April	34,000
May	22,000
June	38,000

What is required is a three month moving average. This is done by firstly totalling the figures for January, February and March and then finding the average:

$$\frac{26,000+30,000+28,000}{3} = £28,000$$

Then the average for February, March and April sales are calculated:

$$\frac{30,000+28,000+34,000}{3} = £30,667$$

Then the average for March, April and May:

$$\frac{28,000+34,000+22,000}{3} = £28,000$$

Then finally the average for April, May and June:

$$\frac{34,000+22,000+38,000}{3} = £31,333$$

Now we can show these moving averages together with the original figures – the convention is to show the moving average next to the middle month of those used in the average.

	Sales	Moving average
	£	£
January	26,000	–
February	30,000	28,000
March	28,000	30,667
April	34,000	28,000
May	22,000	31,333
June	38,000	–

Activity 2

Given below are the production costs for a factory for a six month period:

	£
March	125,600
April	135,800
May	129,200
June	133,600
July	138,900
August	142,600

Show the three month moving averages for these figures.

Calculating a trend

The trend for a time series is essentially the moving average for the time series. However if the number of periods used for the moving average is an even number, such as the four quarters of the year, then there is a further calculation to make – the CENTRED MOVING AVERAGE. The reason for this is that if the moving average is based upon an even number of periods then there is no central period to place the moving average against – a further average, the centred average, is required in order to find the trend.

HOW IT WORKS

The quarterly sales figures for D Martin Trading for the last three years are given below:

			£
2003	Quarter 1		46,800
	Quarter 2		52,800
	Quarter 3		33,600
	Quarter 4		39,600
2004	Quarter 1		48,200
	Quarter 2		54,600
	Quarter 3		34,800
	Quarter 4		40,200
2005	Quarter 1		50,200
	Quarter 2		55,800
	Quarter 3		36,200
	Quarter 4		40,600

In order to find the trend of the time series a four quarterly centred moving average must first be calculated. Start with the four quarterly moving average:

First average: $\dfrac{46,800+52,800+33,600+39,600}{4} = 43,200$

Second average: $\dfrac{52,800+33,600+39,600+48,200}{4} = 43,550$

and so on.

student notes✎

			£	Moving average £
2003	Quarter 1		46,800	
	Quarter 2		52,800	
				43,200
	Quarter 3		33,600	
				43,550
	Quarter 4		39,600	
				44,000
2004	Quarter 1		48,200	
				44,300
	Quarter 2		54,600	
				44,450
	Quarter 3		34,800	
				44,950
	Quarter 4		40,200	
				45,250
2005	Quarter 1		50,200	
				45,600
	Quarter 2		55,800	
				45,700
	Quarter 3		36,200	
	Quarter 4		40,600	

As the average being calculated is an even number, a 'four quarter moving average', then it is shown in between the second quarter and the third quarter each time – the middle of the four quarters used.

Now in order to find the trend line the centred moving average must be calculated. This entails taking each consecutive pair of moving average figures and in turn averaging them and showing them against quarter 3, quarter 4 etc.

First average: $\dfrac{43,200 + 43,550}{2} = 43,375$

Second average: $\dfrac{43,550 + 44,000}{2} = 43,775$

and so on.

		£	Moving average £	Trend £
2003	Quarter 1	46,800		
	Quarter 2	52,800		
			43,200	
	Quarter 3	33,600		43,375
			43,550	
	Quarter 4	39,600		43,775
			44,000	
2004	Quarter 1	48,200		44,150
			44,300	
	Quarter 2	54,600		44,375
			44,450	
	Quarter 3	34,800		44,700
			44,950	
	Quarter 4	40,200		45,100
			45,250	
2005	Quarter 1	50,200		45,425
			45,600	
	Quarter 2	55,800		45,650
			45,700	
	Quarter 3	36,200		
	Quarter 4	40,600		

We can now plot the quarterly sales and the trend line on a graph:

D Martin Trading – quarterly sales and trend

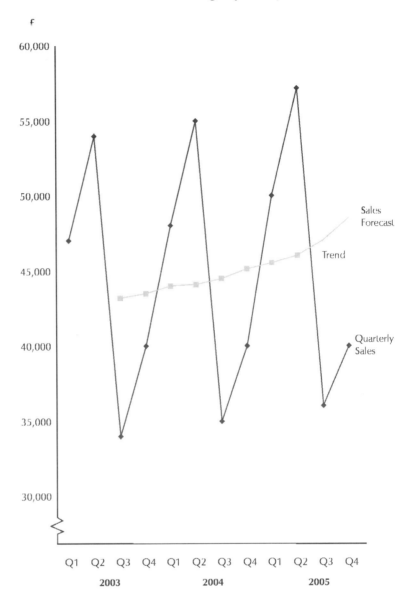

Using the trend

As you can see in the graph the sales of D Martin Trading are irregular – quite high in quarters one and two, low in quarter three and higher again in quarter 4. This is known as a seasonal business.

The trend line however smooths out the seasonal elements and shows how the sales are generally increasing over the three years.

ıe trend line can then be extended, as the dotted line shows, to indicate
e likely sales in future years. This process of estimating a future figure from
line on a graph is known as EXTRAPOLATION.

Activity 3

Given below are the annual sales figures for a business for the last eight
years:

	£
1998	226,700
1999	236,500
2000	240,300
2001	242,500
2002	240,100
2003	245,600
2004	247,600
2005	248,200

You are to calculate a four year moving average and a then a trend line
using the centred average.

TIME SERIES ANALYSIS AND SPREADSHEETS

As you have seen there are a lot of calculations involved in time series
analysis and therefore this is another area in which a computer spreadsheet
package could be used. Once the initial time series is input onto the spread
sheet formulae can be entered for calculation of the moving averages and any
centred moving average.

HOW IT WORKS

Dunn Enterprises has the following quarterly sales figures for the last two
years.

		£
2004	Quarter 1	84,500
	Quarter 2	89,600
	Quarter 3	61,400
	Quarter 4	72,100
2005	Quarter 1	85,700
	Quarter 2	90,300
	Quarter 3	63,100
	Quarter 4	74,500

student notes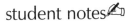

We will set up a spreadsheet to calculate the trend.

The first step is to enter the time series on the spreadsheet. As we will k calculating four period moving averages we must leave a line in betwee each entry in order for the initial moving average to be entered between th second and third quarters used in the calculation.

	A	B	C	D
1		2004	Quarter 1	84,500
2				
3			Quarter 2	89,600
4				
5			Quarter 3	61,400
6				
7			Quarter 4	72,100
8				
9		2005	Quarter 1	85,700
10				
11			Quarter 2	90,300
12				
13			Quarter 3	63,100
14				
15			Quarter 4	74,500
16				

Now the calculations for the moving average must be entered in the rov between the second and third quarters used each time.

$$\text{1st moving average} = \frac{\text{Quarters } 1 + 2 + 3 + 4}{4}$$

$$\text{Formula} = (D1 + D3 + D5 + D7)/4$$

$$\text{2nd moving average} = \frac{\text{Quarters } 2 + 3 + 4 + 5}{4}$$

$$\text{Formula} = (D3 + D5 + D7 + D9)/4$$

and so on.

	A	B	C	D	E
1		2004	Quarter 1	84,500	
2					
3			Quarter 2	89,600	
4					=(D1+D3+D5+D7)/4
5			Quarter 3	61,400	
6					=(D3+D5+D7+D9)/4
7			Quarter 4	72,100	
8					=(D5+D7+D9+D11)/4
9		2005	Quarter 1	85,700	
10					=(D7+D9+D11+D13)/4
11			Quarter 2	90,300	
12					=(D9+D11+D13+D15)/4
13			Quarter 3	63,100	
14					
15			Quarter 4	74,500	
16					

inally the centred moving average must be calculated in order to find the
end.

Quarter 3 centred moving average = (E4 + E6)/2
Quarter 4 centred moving average = (E6 + E8)/2

nd so on.

	A	B	C	D	E	F
1		2004	Quarter 1	84,500		
2						
3			Quarter 2	89,600		
4					=(D1+D3+D5+D7)/4	
5			Quarter 3	61,400		=(E4+E6)/2
6					=(D3+D5+D7+D9)/4	
7			Quarter 4	72,100		=(E6+E8)/2
8					=(D5+D7+D9+D11)/4	
9		2005	Quarter 1	85,700		=(E8+E10)/2
10					=(D7+D9+D11+D13)/4	
11			Quarter 2	90,300		=(E10+E12)/2
12					=(D9+D11+D13+D15)/4	
13			Quarter 3	63,100		

student notes✍

The final result after the computer programme has been run will be follows:

	A	B	C	D	E	F
1		2004	Quarter 1	84,500		
2						
3			Quarter 2	89,600		
4					76,900	
5			Quarter 3	61,400		77,050
6					77,200	
7			Quarter 4	72,100		77,288
8					77,375	
9		2005	Quarter 1	85,700		77,588
10					77,800	
11			Quarter 2	90,300		78,100
12					78,400	
13			Quarter 3	63,100		
14						
15			Quarter 4	74,500		
16						

We can now see that the trend is a gradual increase in sales revenue.

Activity 4

Given below are the monthly sales figures for a business for 2006:

	£
January	47,600
February	48,100
March	50,200
April	45,300
May	44,900
June	42,700
July	41,100
August	42,700
September	45,900
October	48,600
November	49,900
December	51,500

Enter the monthly sales figures on the computer spreadsheet given below and enter formulae that will calculate the trend in sales using a three month moving average.

	A	B	C
1			
2			
3			
4			
5			
6			
7			
8			
9			
10			
11			
12			

student notes✍

INDEX NUMBERS

Given a time series, a number of equivalent figures for a number of periods, as we have seen the need will often be to get a feel for how the figures are changing over time. One simple and convenient method of doing this is to convert the actual figures to a series of INDEX NUMBERS.

This is done by determining firstly a BASE YEAR which is the year for which the actual figure is equated to an index of 100. Each subsequent year's figure is converted to the equivalent index using the following formula:

$$\text{Index} = \frac{\text{Current year figure}}{\text{Base year figure}} \times 100$$

HOW IT WORKS

The sales figures for a business for the first six months of the year are as follows:

	£
January	26,000
February	30,000
March	28,000
April	34,000
May	22,000
June	38,000

We will set the January figure as the base year with an index of 100.

This means that the index for February is calculated as:

$$\frac{\text{Current year figure}}{\text{Base year figure}} \times 100 = \frac{30,000}{26,000} \times 100 = 115$$

The index for March is: $\dfrac{28,000}{26,000} \times 100 = 108$

The index for April is: $\dfrac{34,000}{26,000} \times 100 = 131$

The index for May is: $\dfrac{22,000}{26,000} \times 100 = 85$

The index for June is: $\dfrac{38,000}{26,000} \times 100 = 146$

Activity 5

The profit of a business for the last eight quarters is given below:

		£
2005	Quarter 1	35,600
	Quarter 2	32,100
	Quarter 3	38,700
	Quarter 4	33,400
2006	Quarter 1	36,500
	Quarter 2	31,400
	Quarter 3	40,200
	Quarter 4	36,800

Using quarter 1 2005 as the base year, you are to produce an index showing how the profit figures have changed over the two years.

RETAIL PRICE INDEX

One index that is regularly used and is a published statistic is the RETAIL PRICE INDEX published by the Office for National Statistics. This is an index that is published monthly based upon the price of a particular "shopping basket" of products compared to the price in the base month.

sing the Retail Price Index

₁e Retail Price Index gives an indication of the general level of prices in the
< economy. This can then be used in businesses to determine whether their
vn sales, costs and profits have moved in line with any general price
creases or have over or under performed.

HOW IT WORKS

business has had the following sales for an eight-year period:

	£
1999	368,900
2000	370,200
2001	372,300
2002	375,900
2003	384,600
2004	390,200
2005	392,500
2006	393,500

we use 1999 as the base year and then index these sales figures on that
asis the index will be as follows:

		Index
1999		100.0
2000	370,200/368,900 x 100	100.4
2001	372,300/368,900 x 100	100.9
2002	375,900/368,900 x 100	101.9
2003	384,600/368,900 x 100	104.3
2004	390,200/368,900 x 100	105.8
2005	392,500/368,900 x 100	106.4
2006	393,500/368,900 x 100	106.7

⁀his index shows a small but steady increase in sales over the years.

However we will now consider the general increases in prices over these
₁ears by looking at the average retail price index (RPI) for each of the years:

	RPI
1999	140.7
2000	144.1
2001	149.1
2002	152.7
2003	157.5
2004	162.9
2005	165.4
2006	170.2

We will now apply the RPI to the annual sales figures in order to show t.
RPI adjusted figures. This is done by using the following formula:

$$\text{Sales for current year} \times \frac{\text{RPI for year 1}}{\text{RPI for current year}}$$

1999   Adjusted sales figure   = 368,900 x 140.7/140.7   =   368,900

2000   Adjusted sales figure   = 370,200 x 140.7/144.1   =   £361,46!

2001   Adjusted sales figure   = 372,300 x 140.7/149.1   =   £351,325

and so on:

	Sales £	Adjusted sales £
1999	368,900	368,900
2000	370,200	361,465
2001	372,300	351,325
2002	375,900	346,360
2003	384,600	343,576
2004	390,200	337,024
2005	392,500	333,886
2006	393,500	325,296

If we now calculate an index based upon these adjusted sales figure a ver
different picture is shown:

	Sales £	Adjusted sales £	Index
1999	368,900	368,900	100.0
2000	370,200	361,465	98.0
2001	372,300	351,325	95.2
2002	375,900	346,360	93.9
2003	384,600	343,576	93.1
2004	390,200	337,024	91.4
2005	392,500	333,886	90.5
2006	393,500	325,296	88.2

This shows that the sales for the last eight years have in fact dramatically failec
to keep up with the general rise in prices as shown by the retail price inde>
adjusted sales index.

Activity 6

Given below are the monthly sales for a business for the last year together with the retail price index for each month:

		Sales £	RPI
2005	June	33,100	171.1
	July	33,800	170.5
	Aug	33,600	170.8
	Sept	34,600	171.7
	Oct	35,800	171.6
	Nov	35,100	172.1
	Dec	35,600	172.1
2006	Jan	34,700	171.1
	Feb	35,900	172.0
	Mar	36,200	172.2
	Apr	36,500	173.1
	May	36,700	174.2

You are to show the adjusted sales figures for the year based upon the retail price index.

Index numbers and spreadsheets

As with time series analysis as there are a lot of calculations to be made when calculating index numbers a computer spreadsheet can be used to tabulate the data and perform the calculations.

HOW IT WORKS

Give below are the monthly sales figures for Mindstation, a computer software company for the first six months of 2006.

	£
January	120,450
February	122,580
March	123,640
April	119,220
May	118,640
June	120,520

We will prepare a computer spreadsheet that will calculate the index with January as the base month.

First enter the monthly sales figures on the spreadsheet.

student notes✍

	A	B	C
1	January	120,450	
2	February	122,580	
3	March	123,640	
4	April	119,220	
5	May	118,640	
6	June	120,520	

Then we must determine the formulae to use to calculate the index:

$$\text{Index} = \frac{\text{Current year figure}}{\text{Base year figure}} \times 100$$

For January	=	B1/B1*100
For February	=	B2/B1*100
For March	=	B3/B1*100

and so on ......

	A	B	C
1	January	120,450	=B1/B1*100
2	February	122,580	=B2/B1*100
3	March	123,640	=B3/B1*100
4	April	119,220	=B4/B1*100
5	May	118,640	=B5/B1*100
6	June	120,520	=B6/B1*100

Finally we can show how the index would appear once the computer programme has been run.

	A	B	C
1	January	120,450	100.0
2	February	122,580	101.8
3	March	123,640	102.6
4	April	119,220	99.0
5	May	118,640	98.5
6	June	120,520	100.1

Retail Price Index

We will now add in the complication of adjusting figures for changes in the Retail Price Index before determining the index. Again the calculations can be simplified by using a computer spreadsheet package.

OW IT WORKS

well as knowing the monthly sales for Mindstation we are now also given
e RPI for each month.

	£	RPI
January	120,450	171.1
February	122,580	172.0
March	123,640	172.2
April	119,220	173.1
May	118,640	174.2
June	120,520	175.0

rst enter the sales figures and the RPI figures onto the spreadsheet.

	A	B	C
1	January	120,450	171.1
2	February	122,580	172.0
3	March	123,640	172.2
4	April	119,220	173.1
5	May	118,640	174.2
6	June	120,520	175.0

n column D we will enter formulae to calculate the RPI adjusted sales
gures:

$$\text{Sales for current month} \quad \times \quad \frac{\text{January RPI}}{\text{Current month RPI}}$$

January	=	B1*(C1/C1)
February	=	B2*(C1/C2)
March	=	B3*(C1/C3)

	A	B	C	D
1	January	120,450	171.1	=B1*(C1/C1)
2	February	122,580	172.0	=B2*(C1/C2)
3	March	123,640	172.2	=B3*(C1/C3)
4	April	119,220	173.1	=B4*(C1/C4)
5	May	118,640	174.2	=B5*(C1/C5)
6	June	120,520	175.0	=B6*(C1/C6)

Finally the index can be calculated using the column D figures in column E.

$$\text{Index} \quad = \quad \frac{\text{Current month adjusted sales}}{\text{January adjusted sales}} \times 100$$

January	=	(D1/D1)*100
February	=	(D2/D1)*100
March	=	(D3/D1)*100

student notes✎

Note that you need the brackets around D3/D1, using the March examp
in order for the calculations to be carried out in the correct order. This p
of the calculation must be done first and then multiplied by 100.

	A	B	C	D	E
1	January	120,450	171.1	=B1*(C1/C1)	(D1/D1)*10
2	February	122,580	172.0	=B2*(C1/C2)	(D2/D1)*10
3	March	123,640	172.2	=B3*(C1/C3)	(D3/D1)*10
4	April	119,220	173.1	=B4*(C1/C4)	(D4/D1)*10
5	May	118,640	174.2	=B5*(C1/C5)	(D5/D1)*10
6	June	120,520	175.0	=B6*(C1/C6)	(D6/D1)*10

Finally the figures can be shown after the computer program has been run

	A	B	C	D	E
1	January	120,450	171.1	120,450	100.0
2	February	122,580	172.0	121,939	101.2
3	March	123,640	172.2	122,850	102.0
4	April	119,220	173.1	117,843	97.8
5	May	118,640	174.2	116,529	96.7
6	June	120,520	175.0	117,834	97.8

CHAPTER OVERVIEW

a time series is information about a variable such as sales or costs over a period of time, and time series analysis is concerned with determining the trend of that figure over time

the trend of a time series is determined by calculating a series of moving averages which summarise the overall movement of the figures

if the number of periods that the moving average is being calculated for is an odd number, such as a three year moving average, then this is the trend figure – however if the number of periods is an even number then a further stage is required, calculation of the centred moving average

the periodic figures can be plotted on the same graph as the trend figures – the trend line gives an indication of future figures – if such figures are estimated from the trend line this is known as extrapolation

a computer spreadsheet can also be used to calculate the trend figures

a further method of analysing a time series is to show it in the form of an index which clearly and simply shows any increases or decreases in the figures over the period

an index shows a figure that compares the current year to a base year which has been given an index of 100

the Retail Price Index is a nationally published index indicating in general terms how prices are changing in the UK economy – this can be used by businesses to determine whether their own sales, costs or profits are keeping up with the general levels of inflation

a business's periodic figures can be converted into RPI adjusted figures by dividing by the RPI for the current period and multiplying by the RPI for the base period - again a computer spreadsheet can be used for the calculations

---

KEY WORDS

Time series the same figures – sales, costs, profits – that are reported over a number of time periods

Trend how the time series figure is changing over time

Time series analysis the technique for determining the trend of a time series

Average the total of a number of figures divided by the number of figures used

Moving average a method of finding averages for a number of consecutive periods

Centred moving average used when a moving average is based upon an even number of periods in order to determine the trend figure

Extrapolation a method of estimating a future figure from a trend line on a graph

Index numbers a method of comparing time series numbers by converting the actual figures to an index based upon an initial base year with an index of 100

Base year the year or period that is designated to have the index of 100 and to which all subsequent years are compared with their index

Retail Price Index a published statistic showing the index of the price of a particular "shopping basket" of products each month

HOW MUCH HAVE YOU LEARNED?

1   Given below are the production cost figures for a business for the last year.

	£
July	305,800
August	310,600
September	307,600
October	311,800
November	312,400
December	314,200
January	313,800
February	315,700
March	320,000
April	317,800
May	321,500
June	324,500

You are to calculate a three month moving average for these figures.

2   Given below are the quarterly sales figures for a business for three years:

		£
2004	Quarter 1	479,600
	Quarter 2	484,600
	Quarter 3	452,200
	Quarter 4	410,800
2005	Quarter 1	482,400
	Quarter 2	490,500
	Quarter 3	440,600
	Quarter 4	423,600
2006	Quarter 1	490,600
	Quarter 2	501,600
	Quarter 3	461,200
	Quarter 4	430,500

You are to calculate a four quarter moving average and then the trend using a centred movin average.

3   Plot the quarterly sales from the previous question, together with the trend line, on a graph.

4   Using the figures in question 2 set up a computer spreadsheet to calculate the trend by inserting appropriate formulae.

	A	B	C	D	E
1					
2					
3					
4					
5					
6					
7					
8					
9					
10					
11					
12					
13					
14					
15					
16					
17					
18					
19					
20					
21					
22					
23					

5   Given below are the profits of a business for the last six months:

	£
January	59,700
February	62,300
March	56,900
April	60,400
May	62,400
June	66,700

Using January as the base month calculate an index for each month's profits.

6   Given below are the sales of a business for the last six months together with the retail price index for those months:

	Sales £	RPI
January	127,600	171.1
February	129,700	172.0
March	130,400	172.2
April	131,600	173.0
May	130,500	172.1
June	131,600	171.3

Calculate the RPI adjusted sales figures for each of the six months.

7   Using the RPI adjusted sales figures from the previous question calculate an index for the sales for each month with January as the base period.

8   Using the figures from question 6 set up a computer spreadsheet to calculate the RPI adjusted sales index by inserting appropriate formulae.

	A	B	C	D	E
1					
2					
3					
4					
5					
6					

chapter 15:
EXTERNAL REPORTING

chapter coverage 📖

This chapter largely covers the types of reports that may be required to be prepared not for internal use but for various types of external use. However we start the chapter with a consideration of the main source of external statistics from government departments, namely National Statistics. The topics to be covered are:

✎ National Statistics

✎ types of report to external agencies

✎ applications for a grant or award

✎ information collection

✎ trade associations

✎ authorisation

Unit 7

knowledge and understanding - the business environment

1   main sources of relevant government statistics

3   main types of outside organisations requiring reports and returns: regulatory; grant awarding; information collecting; trade associations

knowledge and understanding - the organisation

17   background understanding that a variety of outside agencies may require reports and returns from organisations and that these requirements must be built into administrative and accounting systems and procedures

Performance criteria – element 7.2

A   identify, collate and present relevant information in accordance with the conventions and definitions used by outside agencies

B   ensure calculations of ratios and performance indicators are accurate

C   obtain authorisation for the despatch of completed reports and returns from the appropriate person

D   present reports and returns in accordance with outside agencies' requirements and deadlines

NATIONAL STATISTICS

We have already seen in the previous chapter how a business might wish to use one particular statistic published by a government department, the Retail Price Index. There are also a number of other statistics and information published by the government that may be of use to the management of a business and which you may be required to research and provide.

When the management of a business are taking long term strategic decisions about the future of the business, and indeed shorter term operational decisions, they will often require information about the economy and the social trends of the UK in order to make informed decisions.

Background

The government appreciate the importance of statistics regarding the state of the nation both for their own purposes and for those of businesses and the public, and as such launched the new NATIONAL STATISTICS in June 2000. A Statistics Commission was established together with the appointment of a National Statistician who has overall responsibility for all National Statistics output. The website address is www.statistics.gov.uk.

Themes

The statistics available are divided into 13 separate THEMES covering distinct areas of national life. The themes are:

- agriculture, fishing and forestry
- commerce, energy and industry
- compendia and reference
- crime and justice
- economy
- education and training
- health and care
- labour market
- natural and built environment
- population and migration
- social and welfare
- transport, travel and tourism
- other

Each of these themes can be accessed via the website or by registering with the National Statistics office.

Importance of the National Statistics

No business can operate in a vacuum and on many occasions it is likely the information about the economy, the population, social trends etc will be required. All of this information can now easily be accessed from the National Statistics.

Activity 1

If you were interested in finding out if the population of the UK has changed its main areas of residence over the past 20 years, which theme of the National Statistics might be most useful?

REPORTS TO EXTERNAL AGENCIES

The main element of this chapter concerns a variety of possible reports that you may be involved in preparing for external agencies. As an accounting technician, probably the most common report that you will be involved in preparing will be the quarterly VAT return and this will be dealt with in detail in the following chapter.

The VAT return must be completed on a regular basis and sent to HM Revenue & Customs (HMRC) and this is therefore an example of a regulatory return.

In the remainder of this chapter we will consider other reports that might be sent to external agencies under the headings of:

- grant awarding applications
- information collecting returns
- trade association information

Most returns or reports that are required by external agencies will require information about the business to be entered onto pre-printed standard forms or PRO-FORMA FORMS. Therefore you will need to be able to understand the forms and to find the correct information that is required on the form. Each report or return will be different but below are some examples of the typical information that you may need to extract from the accounting and other records of the organisation in order to be able to prepare the report or return.

Grant awarding

Many government and private agencies offer grants to businesses in order to help them to achieve their full potential. When applying for a grant it is likely that a large amount of financial and other operating information about your business will be required in order for the grant awarding agency to be able to judge the merits of your business.

HOW IT WORKS

Fielden Potteries is a small pottery set up by Jamie Marchant in 1999. It is situated in Fielden House, Priory Road, Westchester, WC4 3NB. The business telephone number is 0135 2645 and the fax number is 0135 2646. Jamie's email address is jamie@fieldenpotteries.co.uk.

Since 2000 it has become increasingly successful with 10 potters and decorators now employed and significant increases in both UK sales and exports. Jamie now wishes to expand into the tourist industry by providing demonstrations and tours of the pottery and as such is applying to the Local Tourist Board for a grant of £24,000 in order to help with the provision of the equipment and staff necessary for this new venture. A grant application form is shown below and you have been provided with the task of finding the information required.

WESTCHESTER TOURIST BOARD

GRANT APPLICATION

PART 1   **BUSINESS DETAILS**

Business name

Business address

Business telephone
Business fax
Email

Chief executive/managing director

Type of business

PART 2   **FINANCIAL DETAILS**

2A   **TURNOVER AND PROFIT**

Figures are to be provided for annual turnover and reported net profit for the last three complete financial years

Financial year ended: Month	Year	UK turnover £	Export turnover £	Net profit £

2B   **WORKING CAPITAL**

Figures are to be provided for working capital at the end of the most recent financial year.

Year ending:

£

Current assets
Minus: current liabilities
Working capital

FIXED ASSETS

gures are to be provided for fixed asset totals at the
d of the most recent financial year.

ar ending:

£

nd and buildings
ant and machinery
her
tal fixed assets

ART 3   **NON FINANCIAL DETAILS**

A   **EMPLOYMENT DETAILS**

igures are to be provided for the number of employees
or the last three financial years.

inancial year ended:	Number of full time employees	Number of part time employees
onth Year		

B   **BUSINESS DETAILS**

ate business started:

usiness type –   Sole trader
                     Partnership
                     Company

PART 4   **GRANT APPLICATION**

Indicate in the space provided the reasons for the grant
application. If the grant application is processed
further more detail will be requested at a later date.

311

You are now required to find the information required for completion of the grant application.

The profit and loss account summaries for the last three years and summarised balance sheet for the year ended 31 March 2006 have been extracted from the filing system and are given below.

Profit and loss account summaries:

	Year ending:		
	31 March 2004	31 March 2005	31 March 2006
	£	£	£
Turnover – UK	332,820	364,905	439,356
Export	36,980	64,395	96,444
Costs	314,330	356,320	428,640
Net profit	55,470	72,980	107,160

Balance sheet summary as at 31 March 2006:

Fixed assets:

	£
Buildings	120,000
Machinery	64,000
Shop fittings	31,000
Motor vehicle	12,000
	227,000
Current assets	35,400
Current liabilities	(27,600)
Total net assets	234,800

In the year ending 31 March 2004 Jamie employed 6 potters and decorators, four of whom were full time and two part time, as well as a full time shop assistant. In the year ending 31 March 2005 a further 2 full time potters were employed and in the most recent year one more full time and one more part time potter were taken on.

e complete form is shown below.

WESTCHESTER TOURIST BOARD

GRANT APPLICATION

PART 1   BUSINESS DETAILS

Business name   *Fielden Potteries*

Business address   *Fielden House*
                         Priory Road
                         Westchester
                         WC4 3NB

Business telephone   *0135 2645*
Business fax   *0135 2646*
Email   *jamie@fieldenpotteries.co.uk*

Chief executive/managing director   *Jamie Marchant*

Type of business   *Pottery*

PART 2   FINANCIAL DETAILS

2A   TURNOVER AND PROFIT

Figures are to be provided for annual turnover and reported net profit for the last three complete financial years

Financial year ended:		UK turnover	Export turnover	Net profit
Month	Year	£	£	£
March	2004	332,820	36,980	55,470
March	2005	364,905	64,395	72,980
March	2006	439,356	96,444	107,160

2B   WORKING CAPITAL

Figures are to be provided for working capital at the end of the most recent financial year.

Year ending: *31 March 2006*

	£
Current assets	35,400
Minus: current liabilities	27,600
Working capital	7,800

2C   FIXED ASSETS

Figures are to be provided for fixed asset totals at the end of the most recent financial year.

Year ending: *31 March 2006*

	£
Land and buildings	*120,000*
Plant and machinery	*64,000*
Other	*43,000*
Total fixed assets	*227,000*

PART 3   NON FINANCIAL DETAILS

3A   EMPLOYMENT DETAILS

Figures are to be provided for the number of employee for the last three financial years.

Financial year ended:		Number of full time employees	Number of part time employees
Month	Year		
March	*2004*	*5*	*2*
March	*2005*	*7*	*2*
March	*2006*	*8*	*3*

3B   BUSINESS DETAILS

Date business started: *1999*

Business type –   Sole trader   ✔
                     Partnership
                     Company

PART 4   GRANT APPLICATION

Indicate in the space provided the reasons for the grant application. If the grant application is processed further more detail will be requested at a later date.

Grant applied for to aid in expansion of business to provide demonstrations and tours of the pottery for tourists.

formation collecting

saw earlier in this chapter that the government publishes National tistics in order to help itself as well as businesses and the public. In order gather these statistics information may be required of businesses. Again :h information will normally be required on a pro-forma form as this will sure that the same information is provided by each business questioned.

OW IT WORKS

nie Marchant has recently received a form from the local Chamber of ommerce requesting information about his business for the purposes of eir annual economic review.

CHAMBER OF COMMERCE

ANNUAL ECONOMIC REVIEW

Please tick the appropriate box in answer to each question – all answers v
be treated in the strictest confidence. All answers should be based upon t
business performance for the last full financial year.

1   BUSINESS DETAILS

End of last full financial year:

Turnover range:

Up to £50,000	
£50,000 – £100,000	
£100,000 – £250,000	
£250,000 – £500,000	
£500,000 – £1,000,000	
Over £1,000,000	

Main business activity:

Engineering	
Construction	
Agriculture	
Energy	
Retail	
Education	
Health	
Art and design	
Transport	
Tourism	
Other (please state)	

Turnover

rcentage of total turnover accounted for by export sales:

0%	
upto 10%	
11% to 20%	
21% to 30%	
31% to 50%	
51% to 75%	
76% to 100%	

ercentage increase/decrease in turnover compared to previous financial ear:

Decrease up to 20%	
Decrease of 21% to 50%	
Decrease of more than 50%	
Increase up to 20%	
Increase of 21% to 50%	
Increase of more than 50%	

BUSINESS CONFIDENCE

Do you consider that over the following 12 months:

urnover	will increase	
	remain the same	
	decrease	
Profitability	will increase	
	remain the same	
	decrease	

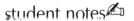

Jamie has told you that he is confident that both turnover and profitability increase in the following year. You have now completed the Chamber Commerce form on Jamie's behalf and it is shown below.

CHAMBER OF COMMERCE

ANNUAL ECONOMIC REVIEW

Please tick the appropriate box in answer to each question – all answers be treated in the strictest confidence. All answers should be based upon business performance for the last full financial year.

1   BUSINESS DETAILS

End of last full financial year: 31 March 2006

Turnover range:

Up to £50,000	
£50,000 – £100,000	
£100,000 – £250,000	
£250,000 – £500,000	
£500,000 – £1,000,000	✓
Over £1,000,000	

Main business activity:

Engineering	
Construction	
Agriculture	
Energy	
Retail	
Education	
Health	
Art and design	✓
Transport	
Tourism	
Other (please state)	

Turnover

Percentage of total turnover accounted for by export sales:

0%	
up to 10%	
11% to 20%	✓
21% to 30%	
31% to 50%	
51% to 75%	
76% to 100%	

Percentage increase/decrease in turnover compared to previous financial year:

Decrease up to 20%	
Decrease of 21% to 50%	
Decrease of more than 50%	
Increase up to 20%	
Increase of 21% to 50%	✓
Increase of more than 50%	

3   BUSINESS CONFIDENCE

Do you consider that over the following 12 months:

Turnover	will increase	✓
	remain the same	
	decrease	
Profitability	will increase	✓
	remain the same	
	decrease	

319

Trade association information

TRADE ASSOCIATIONS are groups that protect the interests and work fo the benefit of a particular type of business. For example the Association c British Travel Agents, ABTA, is the trade association to which all reputabl travel agents belong and the Association of Professional Rugby Union Player is the trade association that protects the interests of professional rugby unior players. As well as serving the interests of their members, trade association will often require information from their members, in order to fully appreciate the businesses of their members and their problems and successes.

Activity 2

Jamie Marchant has received a short form from The Master Craftsman's Guild, of which Fielden Potteries is a member, requesting information about the debtor levels for members.

MASTER CRAFTSMAN'S GUILD
AGED DEBTOR QUESTIONNAIRE

Business name and address:

Total debtors at 30 April 2006   £.............................

Ageing of debtors:

Current   £.............................

30 to 60 days   £.............................

60 to 90 days   £.............................

More than 90 days   £.............................

Do you offer a settlement discount for early payment?   Yes/No

Please note that all information provided will be treated in the strictest confidence. Thank you for your cooperation.

You have found the aged debtor listing as at 30 April 2006 and this is given below. Jamie does not offer credit customers any settlement discount for early payment.

Aged debtor listing – April 2006

	90 days £	60–90 days £	30–60 days £	<30 days £	Total £
TOTALS	537	3,669	15,490	17,668	37,364

You are to complete the trade association return on Jamie's behalf.

AUTHORISATION OF REPORTS AND RETURNS

When a report or a return for an external agency has been completed three factors are of great importance:

- accuracy
- authorisation
- deadline

Accuracy

Just as it is important to ensure that any performance indicators or calculations made for an internal report are accurate, it could be argued that this is even more important when a report or return is being sent out to an external agency. The external agency will be using the figures given in the return to generate statistics and therefore in order not to distort these statistics the information that you provide must be accurate. In some cases, such as the VAT return, the business can indeed be fined for any errors that are made, however accidental.

Authorisation

Before any information is sent out to an external agency it is vital that the information should be authorised by a senior member of the management of the business. Often the information being reported can be highly sensitive and it is therefore extremely important that all internal procedures are followed before a report or return is sent to the external agency, and that appropriate authorisation of the content of the report or return is sought.

Deadlines

The information required by external agencies will normally be required to be received by a particular date in order that all the information received can be collated. It is therefore important that any deadlines set by the agency are strictly adhered to. With some regulatory returns there are even fines for the late arrival of the information required.

AAT simulation guidance

The guidance notes to Unit 7 indicate that when simulations require you to complete a form for an external agency, the form will relate to consolidated figures. Therefore you may have to add together the relevant figures for a number of divisions (see Chapter 10).

Take care when completing external agency forms as the guidance notes indicate that the form will invariably contain definitions of the ratios and statistics required. These definitions may be different from those used when preparing performance indicators.

CHAPTER OVERVIEW

- June 2000 saw the launch of a government initiative, National Statistics, which are available under 13 separate themes covering different areas of national life in order to provide reliable statistics for use by government, businesses and the public

- on occasions a business may be required or requested to provide information about its activities to external agencies – usually this information will be provided on a standard form or pro-forma although sometimes a written report may be required

- typical of such reports or returns to external agencies might be an application for a grant or award from a government department or other grant awarding agency, provision of information for collation to provide National Statistics or provision of information to a trade association

- whenever information about the business is sent out to an external agency the data and any calculations must be thoroughly checked, the report or return must be authorised by the correct level of management and the information must be sent out on time to meet any deadline set by the external agency

KEY WORDS

National Statistics statistics published by the government covering all areas of national life

Themes the thirteen separate categories of the National Statistics

Pro-forma form a standard pre-printed form that must be completed

Trade associations groups of businesses in the same line of work or profession formed in order to promote and protect the interests of their members

HOW MUCH HAVE YOU LEARNED?

1   The business that you work for has a loan from a bank of £60,000. When the loan was granted detailed monthly budgets showing budgeted sales and budgeted costs were submitted to the bank and it was agreed that each month the actual sales and costs and any variances from budget would be reported to the bank.

For the month of June 2006 the actual sales and costs were £135,700 and £108,400. The budgeted figures for the same period were £140,000 and £110,000 respectively.

You are to complete the bank's form given below showing the required figures for June 2006.

NORTHERN BANK

LOAN MONITORING

Month:

	Budget £	Actual £	Variance £
Sales			
Costs			

2   You have received the following form from the trade association to which your firm belor requesting certain information

WINE MERCHANTS ASSOCIATION

QUARTERLY PROFIT SURVEY

Please provide the following information for the quarter ended 3 June 2006 – all information provided will be treated with th strictest confidentiality.

Gross profit percentage

Net profit percentage

Return on capital employed

A summary of the profit and loss figures for April to June 2006 are provided below:

Summarised profit and loss accounts

	April 2006 £	May 2006 £	June 2006 £
Sales	268,366	251,378	270,892
Cost of sales	177,122	160,882	184,207
	91,244	90,496	86,685
Expenses	59,040	62,845	54,178
Profit	32,204	27,651	32,507

The capital of the business is £750,000.

You are required to complete the trade association return.

hapter 16:
ALUE ADDED TAX

chapter coverage 📖

Although you will have come across Value Added Tax (VAT) in your earlier studies, we will begin this chapter with a reminder of how the VAT system works. We will then consider some of the more detailed areas of dealing with and accounting for VAT. In chapter 17 we will then go on to consider the VAT records that must be kept and in particular the completion of the VAT return. The topics to be covered are:

- ✍ the value added tax system

- ✍ rates of VAT

- ✍ registration for VAT

- ✍ non-reclaimable VAT

- ✍ VAT invoices

- ✍ calculation of VAT

- ✍ less detailed VAT invoices and modified invoices

- ✍ credit notes and debit notes

- ✍ VAT and bad debts

- ✍ errors on VAT invoices

- ✍ imports and exports

- ✍ the VAT Guide

Unit 7

knowledge and understanding - the business environment

4   basic law and practice relating to all issues covered in the range statement and referred to in the performance criteria. Specific issues include: the classification of types of supply; registration requirements; the form of VAT invoices; tax points

5   sources of information on VAT: HMRC Guide

6   administration of VAT: enforcement

7   special schemes: annual accounting; cash accounting; bad debt relief

knowledge and understanding - the organisation

19   the basis of the relationship between the organisation and the VAT Office

Performance criteria – element 7.3

B   correctly identify and calculate relevant inputs and outputs
D   ensure guidance is sought from the VAT Office when required, in a professional manner

VALUE ADDED TAX – THE SYSTEM

What is VAT?

Value Added Tax (VAT) is essentially a sales tax – it is a tax on spending and an important source of revenue for the government. Similar forms of sales tax are also charged in many other countries, although you only need to be aware of the system in the UK.

VAT regulation

The VAT system in the UK is administered by HM Revenue & Customs (HMRC), which is the combined body that used to be both the Inland Revenue and HM Customs and Excise (the body responsible for VAT). HMRC issues VAT 700 "The VAT Guide", which provides a business with all the information it needs about accounting for, recording and paying over VAT. The VAT Guide will be referred to throughout this chapter and the next, and if you are involved with VAT in the workplace it is important that you read it. The VAT Guide can be sent to you free of charge by simply contacting your local HMRC office, although it is likely that your business will already have a copy. Alternatively, you can access it at www.hmrc.gov.uk. You are not expected to know all of the details of the VAT Guide but the main elements will be covered in this chapter and the following chapter.

Before we begin to look at the details of how a business must record and account for VAT we will start with a brief reminder of the VAT system works.

VAT registration

If the sales of a business exceed a certain amount for a year then a business must register for VAT. This means that they have a VAT registration number which must be included on invoices and other business documents. From April 2006 the registration threshold is £61,000. The detailed rules regarding registration will be considered later in the chapter.

What this also means is that the business must charge VAT on all of its taxable supplies or sales normally at the standard rate of 17.5%. This is known as OUTPUT VAT.

There is however a benefit in that the VAT that the business pays when buying from suppliers or paying expenses can be recovered back from HMRC and is known as INPUT VAT.

Every three months (usually) the business must complete a VAT return (see next chapter) showing the output and input VAT. The excess of output VAT over input VAT must be paid with the VAT return. However if the input VAT exceeds the output VAT then a refund is due from HMRC (this will be dealt with in detail in the next chapter).

HOW IT WORKS

Let's follow a simple manufacturing process through the VAT payment process.

Business	Transaction		HMRC VAT due
Supplier of wood	Sells wood to table manufacturer for £160 + VAT of £28		
	Sale value	£160	
	Output VAT	£28	£28
Table manufacturer	Purchases wood from supplier for £160 + VAT of £28 Sells table to retailer for £280 + VAT of £49		
	Sale value	£280	
	Purchases value	£160	
	Output VAT – Input VAT (49 – 28)	£21	£21
Retailer	Purchases table from manufacturer for £280 + VAT of £49		
	Sells table to customer for £360 + VAT of £63		
	Sale value	£360	
	Purchases value	£280	
	Output VAT – Input VAT (63 – 49)	£14	£14
Customer	Purchases table for £360 + VAT of £63		
	Pays retailer (360 + 63)	£423	£0
Total VAT paid to HMRC			£63

Note that it is the final consumer who bears the cost of the VAT. The table cost him £423 not £360, but the consumer does not have to pay this to HMRC as this has already been done throughout the chain of manufacture and sale.

Activity 1

Business A sells goods to Business B for £1,000 plus £175 of VAT. Which business treats the VAT as Input tax and which treats it as output tax?

ATES OF VAT

ere are three rates of VAT in the UK:

- standard rate of 17.5%
- reduced rate on domestic fuel and power of 5%
- zero rate 0%

ere are also exempt supplies which, like zero-rated supplies, do not have
AT charged on them. However there is a difference between zero-rated
pplies and exempt supplies.

ero-rated supplies

ERO-RATED SUPPLIES are supplies of goods and services which are
chnically taxable but the law states that the rate of VAT on these goods is
%. The main reason for this is that these zero-rated supplies are normally
sential items which if they were taxed would be an additional burden to
e less well-off.

he details of supplies that are zero-rated are set out in Appendix A of the
AT Guide.

xamples of zero-rated supplies are:

- young children's clothes and shoes
- food purchased in shops (although not in restaurants)
- bus and train fares
- books
- newspapers and magazines

he effect on a business which sells zero-rated supplies is that although they
o not charge any output VAT on their sales they are allowed to reclaim any
nput VAT on their purchases. Therefore a bus company charges no VAT on
ts fares but it is able to reclaim from HMRC any VAT on its purchases and
xpenses such as fuel and service costs.

Exempt supplies

EXEMPT SUPPLIES are supplies on which no VAT is charged at all, at any rate.
As with zero-rated supplies details of exempt supplies are found in Appendix
A of the VAT Guide. Examples of exempt supplies are:

- Post Office postal services
- education
- healthcare
- insurance
- betting and gambling

The difference between exempt supplies and zero-rated supplies is that supplier sells exempt supplies then he cannot reclaim the input VAT on a of his purchases and expenses. Therefore an insurance company can reclaim the VAT on its expenses as its supplies are exempt.

REGISTRATION FOR VAT

It has already been mentioned that a business must register for VAT if turnover exceeds the registration limit, which from April 2006 is £61,0C However the situation is slightly more complicated than that. There are tv situations in which a business must register for VAT:

- when the TAXABLE TURNOVER for a twelve month period, t value of a business's taxable supplies, has exceeded the registratic limit, £61,000, then the business must apply within 30 days of t end of that twelve month period to register

- when the taxable turnover (before any VAT is added) is expected exceed the annual registration limit within the next 30 days the again the business must register for VAT

Therefore a business must be extremely careful to ensure that if either i current turnover for the last twelve months or its expected turnover with the next 30 days for the last twelve months will exceed the registration lir then it must apply to register for VAT. If a business does not apply to registe in these circumstances within the 30 day limit then it is liable to a fine Additionally if discovered at a future date by HMRC the business may hav to repay all output VAT that should have been charged if it had registere without reclaiming any input VAT.

These rules apply to suppliers of both standard rated and zero-rated gooc and services.

In order to register for VAT the business must apply to the local HMRC offic and complete a form VAT 1.

Once registered for VAT you are known as a REGISTERED PERSON.

Voluntary registration

If a business's taxable turnover is below the annual registration limit it is stil possible for the business to register for VAT on a voluntary basis. Why migh a business do this?

If a business supplies zero-rated goods and services then it may be advantageous to register for VAT – no output VAT has to be charged on its sales but if registered for VAT it can reclaim the input VAT on its purchases and expenses.

registration

AT registered business may find that its taxable turnover either falls or is
ected to fall. If this fall or expected fall is beneath the deregistration limit,
ch from April 2006 is £59,000 for taxable suppliers and £60,000 for
uisitions from other EU member states, then the business can apply to
IRC to deregister.

e de-registration, VAT is due on all stock and capital assets on which input
T was claimed, unless this is less than £1,000. VAT is not due if the
iness is sold as a going concern to another taxable person.

ON-RECLAIMABLE VAT

hough we have said that businesses can reclaim VAT on purchases and
penses there are some items of expenditure on which VAT cannot be
claimed from HMRC. The main examples of this are:

- business entertainment expenses

- cars purchased for use within the business (company cars for
  salespeople etc.), including fitted accessories and delivery charges.

AT INVOICES

a business is registered for VAT if it sends out an invoice to another VAT
gistered business then it must supply a VAT invoice within 30 days of the
pply as shown below:

student notes

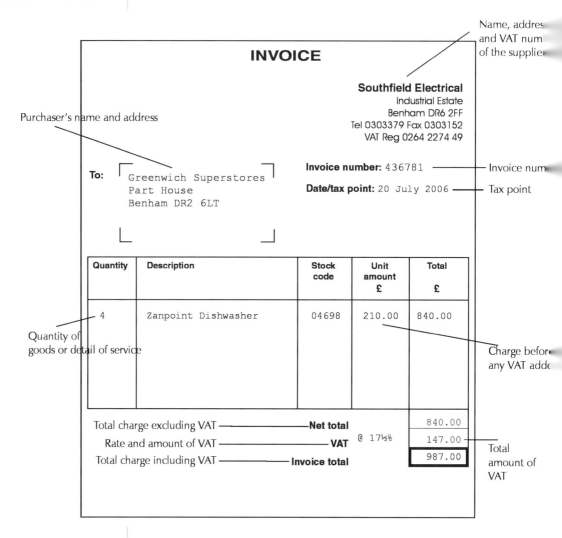

Name, address and VAT number of the supplier

INVOICE

Southfield Electrical
Industrial Estate
Benham DR6 2FF
Tel 0303379 Fax 0303152
VAT Reg 0264 2274 49

Purchaser's name and address

To: Greenwich Superstores
Part House
Benham DR2 6LT

Invoice number: 436781 — Invoice number

Date/tax point: 20 July 2006 — Tax point

Quantity	Description	Stock code	Unit amount £	Total £
4	Zanpoint Dishwasher	04698	210.00	840.00

Quantity of goods or detail of service

Charge before any VAT added

Total charge excluding VAT —— **Net total**		840.00
Rate and amount of VAT —— **VAT** @ 17½%		147.00
Total charge including VAT —— **Invoice total**		987.00

Total amount of VAT

We will now consider some of the details of this VAT invoice in more detail.

Tax point

You will note the date/TAX POINT on the invoice. This is an important date as it is the date on which the taxable supply will be taken as having occurred for the purposes of the VAT return. Therefore the output tax must be paid over to HMRC at the end of the period which covers this tax point.

When goods are supplied the BASIC TAX POINT is normally the date on which the goods are either taken away by the customer or sent to the customer. When services are provided the basic tax point is normally the date on which the service was provided.

in there are some rules here. The basic tax point is over-ridden if there is ACTUAL TAX POINT.

actual tax point is created if:

- the invoice is issued or payment is received before the goods or services are delivered then the date of invoice or the payment is the actual tax point depending upon which happens first

- if the issue of the VAT invoice is up to 14 days after the date of supply of the goods or services the date of the issue of the invoice is the tax point

s 14 day rule may be varied provided that you write to the VAT Business vice Centre for your area. For example you may require an extension of : 14 day rule if you normally issue invoices monthly.

ou issue a VAT invoice more than 14 days after the basic tax point without proval to extend the 14 day rule, the tax will be due at the basic tax point, the date on which the goods or services were supplied.

nportance of the tax point

e importance of the tax point, be it the basic tax point or the actual tax int, is that you must account for the VAT in your VAT return for the period vering the tax point.

Activity 2

A business sends goods out to a customer on 15 May 2006. The VAT nvoice is then sent later and is dated 20 May 2006. What is the tax point or these goods?

ype of supply

he following types of supply must be identified separately on a VAT invoice:

- sale
- hire purchase or conditional sale
- loan
- exchange
- hire, lease or rental
- process (making goods from someone else's materials)
- sale on commission, for example by an auctioneer
- sale or return

Zero-rated and exempt supplies

If a VAT invoice is issued which includes zero-rated or exempt supplies, th
items must show clearly that there is no VAT payable and their values n
be totalled separately.

Calculation of VAT

The VAT is calculated based upon the cost of the goods or services after
trade discount has been deducted.

When VAT is calculated for individual lines on an invoice, the calculation
be rounded in either of two ways.

- round down to the nearest 0.1p (so 86.76p would be 86.7p), or
- round to the nearest 0.5p, so 86.7p would be 87p.

The total VAT on an invoice should be rounded to the nearest 1p.

Cash or settlement discounts

If a cash or settlement discount is offered to a customer, the VAT is calcula
on the basis that the customer will take advantage of the discount. If
customer does not in fact take the settlement discount but pays the invo
in full there is no requirement to charge any additional VAT. The VAT tha
charged and is shown on the invoice is the amount that should be account
for on the VAT return.

HOW IT WORKS

Goods are supplied to a customer with a total VAT exclusive list price
£865.80. The customer is allowed a 10% trade discount and is also offered
3% settlement discount.

The VAT would be calculated as follows:

	£
List price	800.00
Less: trade discount	80.00
Net price	720.00
Less: settlement discount	21.60
	698.40
VAT £698.40 x 17.5%	122.22

On the invoice you would see:

	£
VAT@17.5%	122.22
Invoice total	842.22

e customer could pay £842.22, or (£842.22 – £21.60) = £820.62 if the ms for receiving cash discount are complied with. In either case, no justment is made to the amount of output tax.

Activity 3

A business sells goods to a customer for £1,000. The customer is allowed 20% trade discount and is offered a 2% settlement discount for payment within 14 days. If the goods are standard-rated how much VAT would be charged on them?

Foreign currency invoices

a VAT invoice is issued in a foreign currency then the VAT must be calculated on the amounts expressed in sterling. The foreign currency amounts should be converted using the UK market selling rate as published national newspapers or a period rate of exchange published by HMRC.

Less detailed VAT invoice

your business is in the retail trade then you should always give your customer a VAT invoice if this is requested by the customer.

However if the charge for the goods is less than £250, including VAT, then you can issue a LESS DETAILED VAT INVOICE showing:

- your name, address and VAT registration number
- the time of supply
- a description of the goods or services supplied
- for each VAT rate applicable, the total amount payable including the VAT and the VAT rate charged.

herefore on such an invoice the actual amount of VAT charged is not shown separately. In order to calculate the amount of VAT included in this invoice he VAT fraction of 17.5/117.5 or 7/47 must be used.

HOW IT WORKS

An invoice shows a total VAT inclusive amount of £47.00. The amount of VAT included in this amount can be calculated in one of two ways:

£47.00 x 17.5/117.5 = £7.00

or

£47.00 x 7/47 = £7.00

Activity 4

Goods are sold for £51.11 including VAT. How much VAT is included i▬ this figure?

Modified invoice

If the amount charged for the goods or services exceeds £250, if asked fo▬ VAT invoice you must supply a full VAT invoice or, if the customer agrees, MODIFIED INVOICE.

The amounts that must be shown on a modified invoice are the VAT inclusi▬ amount of each standard rated or reduced rate supply rather than the net VAT amount

At the bottom of the modified invoice the following must be shov▬ separately:

- total VAT inclusive amount of the standard rated or reduced ra▬ supplies

- total VAT payable on those supplies

- total value, net of VAT, of the supplies

- total value of any zero rated supplies included on the invoice

- total value of any exempt supplies included on the invoice

The modified invoice must also show all of the other factors included on full VAT invoice such as the tax point and VAT registration number.

Pro-forma invoice

A PRO-FORMA INVOICE is often used in order to offer goods to a potenti▬ customer at a certain price and to invite the customer to send a payment i return for which the goods will be dispatched. This is often the case when business does not wish to sell on credit but instead needs payment up from before the goods are dispatched.

When the pro-forma invoice is received by the potential customer it canno▬ be used by the customer as evidence to reclaim the VAT element. Therefor▬ any pro-forma invoice should be clearly marked "THIS IS NOT A VA INVOICE".

If the customer does decide to buy the goods or sends payment then a prope▬ VAT invoice must be issued.

REDIT NOTES AND DEBIT NOTES

customer returns goods then it is customary to issue a CREDIT NOTE to lect the value of these goods, including the VAT element. Alternatively the stomer may, if both parties agree, issue a DEBIT NOTE which reflects the ue of the goods returned and the VAT element. Credit notes and debit tes can also be issued to correct errors that have been made on the original oice.

be a valid credit or debit note for VAT purposes the following must occur:

- the credit/debit note must reflect a genuine mistake or change in value of the goods supplied and must be issued within one month of the mistake or alteration being discovered or agreed;

- it must be headed clearly as a credit note or debit note;

- it must include all of the following details:

  - identifying number and date of issue

  - name, address and registration number of the supplier

  - name and address of the customer

  - the reason for the issue

  - a description of the goods or services to which the credit relates

  - the quantity and amount for each description

  - the total amount of the credit excluding VAT

  - the rate and amount of VAT

  - the number and date of the original VAT invoice

- any zero-rated or exempt supplies can be included on the credit/debit note but must be totalled separately and it must show clearly that there is no VAT on these items.

Replacement of returned goods

f a customer returns goods and these are replaced with similar goods there are two options:

- allow the original VAT invoice to stand – therefore there is no need to account for VAT on the replacement goods; or

- cancel the original VAT invoice by issuing a credit note – then charge VAT on the replacement goods with a new invoice.

If the replacement goods are supplied at a different price to the original goods, there are again two options:

- if the replacement goods are at a lower price than the originals then the VAT charge can be reduced by issuing a credit note;

- if the replacement goods are issued at a higher price than the original goods then the additional VAT must be accounted for issuing a further invoice for the additional amount.

VAT AND BAD DEBTS

If goods or services are supplied on credit the VAT will have been accounted for when the original VAT invoice was issued. If the debt is never paid by the customer and is written off as bad in the accounting records, it is possible to reclaim the VAT that will have been paid to HMRC on that supply provided that certain conditions are met, most importantly that:

- the debt must be more than 6 months overdue
- the VAT must have been paid to HMRC
- the debt must be written off in the business's accounts.

ERRORS ON VAT INVOICES

Whether invoices are generated by computer or by hand it is entirely possible that errors can be made such as using the wrong rate of VAT or simply calculating the amount incorrectly.

If the VAT on the invoice should have been higher than the amount shown the correct amount of VAT must be accounted for to HMRC, even if this is not corrected with the customer by, for example, issuing an additional invoice.

If the VAT on the invoice should have been lower than the amount shown you must account to HMRC for the higher amount unless you correct the error with the customer by issuing a credit note.

IMPORTS AND EXPORTS

The treatment of VAT on imports from other countries and exports to other countries is fairly complicated and depends upon whether the import or export is from or to another country within the European Union (EU) or outside it. The treatment also differs depending upon whether the import/export is of goods or of services.

We will look at each situation in turn.

Goods purchased from outside the EU

If goods are imported into the United Kingdom from a country that is not part of the EU the following treatment is required for VAT:

- the VAT is normally deemed to be at the same rate as on a supply of the same goods in the UK

- VAT on these goods must be paid when you import the goods – the VAT is treated as input tax.

Goods acquired from inside the EU

Goods that are purchased from another country within the EU are known as ACQUISITIONS rather than imports. If goods are purchased by a UK buyer from a VAT registered business in another EU country, and the goods are sent to the UK, the VAT can be treated as input tax as well as being an amount of output tax due to HMRC

Services received from outside the UK

If your business receives certain services from outside the UK then for VAT purposes the services are treated as though your business has supplied them and the VAT on them is treated as output tax. Their value counts towards your taxable turnover.

The services for which this is the appropriate treatment are listed in Appendix D of the VAT Guide and include the following:

- advertising services
- transfer of copyright, patents, licenses, trademarks etc
- services of consultants, engineers, lawyers, accountants etc
- banking, financial and insurance services.

Goods exported

Goods exported to any country whether within or outside the EU are normally treated as zero-rated supplies provided that there is documentary evidence of the export and that this is obtained by the supplier within three months of the supply.

Services exported

Some supplies of services to customers overseas are zero-rated whilst others are standard-rated. Details of the VAT rate on services can be found in Appendix A of the VAT Guide.

Supplies of goods within the EU

Since 1 January 1993 any UK VAT registered business which makes suppl[ies] of goods to traders registered for VAT in another EU country must comple[te] a sales list showing the value of these supplies of goods. This is done on fo[rm] VAT 101 normally on a quarterly basis and sent to HMRC.

EU statistics

The value of the supply or acquisition of goods from other EU countries mu[st] be shown on the VAT return (see next chapter). However if the value of yo[ur] business's EU trade in goods (not services) exceeds a certain limit then yo[ur] business must also submit more detailed figures. These are known [as] INTRASTAT SUPPLEMENTARY DECLARATIONS. These INTRAST[AT] supplementary declarations are designed to provide statistics on movemer[t] of taxable goods within the EU.

THE VAT GUIDE

In this chapter we have covered many of the detailed rules for VAT whic[h] may seem excessively complex. Remember however that these rules do n[ot] necessarily have to be memorized as they are all contained in the VAT Guid[e.] If you are dealing with VAT at work then it is important that you are famili[ar] with the VAT Guide and that you are able to use it for reference to find ou[t] a particular treatment.

CHAPTER OVERVIEW

VAT is a sales tax administered by HMRC – VAT registered businesses must account for output tax on their sales and input tax on purchases and expenses – the difference between the output tax and input tax for a period is paid over to or reclaimed from HMRC

in the UK there are three rates of VAT – the standard rate of 17.5%, a reduced rate of 5% for domestic fuel and power and the zero rate – other goods are services are entirely exempt from VAT

there is no VAT charged on either zero-rated supplies or exempt supplies – however if a business makes exempt supplies it cannot reclaim the input tax on its purchases and expenses – however if the supplies made by the business are zero-rated then input VAT can be reclaimed

when a business's taxable turnover reaches the registration limit then the business must register for VAT within 30 days otherwise the business is liable to be fined

some businesses may find it advantageous to register for VAT although the registration limit has not been met – this is known as voluntary registration

if a business's taxable turnover falls below the deregistration limit then the business can apply to HMRC to deregister

the VAT on business entertainment expenses and the purchase of cars for use within a business is non-reclaimable

if supplies are made by a VAT registered business to another VAT registered business then a valid VAT invoice must be supplied within 30 days

the basic tax point is the date on which goods are sent to a customer or services are provided

KEY WORDS

Output VAT VAT on the sale of goods and the provision of services

Input VAT VAT on the purchases of goods and payment of expenses

Zero-rated supplies goods and services which are taxable but the rate of tax on them is 0%

Exempt supplies supplies on which no VAT is charged

Taxable turnover the value of a business's taxable supplies

Registered person a business that is registered for VAT

VAT invoice an invoice that allows input VAT to be claimed

Tax point the date which determines when the VAT must be accounted for to HMRC

Basic tax point the date on which goods are delivered or services provided

Actual tax point a further date that can override the basic tax point if certain conditions are met

Less detailed VAT invoice an invoice for goods supplied costing £100 or less, including VAT, showing only the VAT inclusive amount and the rate of VAT

Modified invoice an invoice for goods supplied costing more than £100 which shows the totals only for the net amount, VAT and gross amount

for a customer. This basic tax point can be over ridden by the actual tax point – the actual tax point can be created if an invoice is issued or a payment received before the goods or services are sent out or by sending out an invoice after the supply of the goods providing that this is within 14 days of the supply

CHAPTER OVERVIEW cont.

- VAT is calculated on the cost of the goods or services after deduction of any trade discount – if a settlement discount is offered the VAT is calculated on the invoice amount less the discount – VAT is always rounded down to the nearest penny

- if goods are supplied for less than £100, including VAT, a less detailed VAT invoice can be issued which shows only the VAT inclusive amount and the rate of VAT – however if the customer asks for a full VAT invoice then this must be supplied

- if the amount charged for the goods exceeds £100 and the customer agrees, a modified VAT invoice can be issued – this shows the net, VAT and gross amounts of the supplies in total

- if a pro-forma invoice is sent out to a potential customer this must be clearly marked "This is not a VAT invoice" as the customer cannot use it to reclaim any input VAT

KEY WORDS

Pro-forma invoice a document sent to a potential customer to offer goods to that customer

Credit note a document sent from a supplier to a customer in order to alter an original invoice

Debit note a document sent from a customer to a supplier in order to alter an original invoice

Acquisitions goods purchased from another European Union country

INTRASTAT Supplementary declarations statistics that must be provided by some businesses regarding their trade in goods in the EU

- in order to correct errors or to deal with returns of goods a business may issue a credit note to their customer or receive a debit note from the customer – in order to be able to reclaim any VAT difference shown on the credit/debit note then the credit/debit note must be issued in a manner similar to a VAT invoice although clearly stating that it is a credit note or debit note

- if a business writes off a bad debt that is more than six months old and the output VAT on the supply has already been paid to HMRC, this VAT can be reclaimed from HMRC

- goods imported from outside the EU are normally deemed to be at the same rate as goods in the UK

- services received from outside the EU are treated as if your business has supplied them and the output tax must be included on the VAT return

- the VAT on acquisitions of goods from other EU countries is treated as output tax

- exports of goods to another country are normally treated as zero-rated supplies – services supplied to a customer in another country may be either zero-rated or standard-rated

- if a business makes sales of goods within the EU a sales list, form VAT 101, must be completed quarterly and sent to HMRC

- some businesses will also have to provide further details of their trade in goods (not services) on INTRASTAT Supplementary Declarations

- although the rules regarding VAT appear complex the VAT Guide is an invaluable source of explanation and guidance

HOW MUCH HAVE YOU LEARNED?

1   Which organisation administers VAT in the UK?

2   Explain the difference between output VAT and input VAT.

3   Explain how it is that the final consumer pays the full amount of VAT to the seller but never pays any money to HMRC.

4   Business C sells goods to Business D for £384.00 plus VAT. Both businesses are VAT registered. How much is the VAT and which business will treat it as output tax and which will treat it as input tax?

5   What are the three rates of VAT in the UK?

6   Give four examples of zero-rated supplies.

7   Give four examples of exempt supplies.

8   If you needed to check whether a supply was zero-rated or exempt how would you do this?

9   What is the effect on a business of supplying exempt services rather than zero-rated goods?

10 Explain when a business must register for VAT.

11 State two items for which the VAT cannot be recovered from HMRC.

12 In each of the following situations state the tax point and whether this is a basic tax point or an actual tax point:

   i)   an invoice is sent out to a customer for goods on 22 June 2006 and the goods are dispatched on 29 June 2006;

   ii) goods are sent out to a customer on 18 June 2006 and this is followed by an invoice on 23 June 2006;

   iii) a customer pays in full for goods on 27 June 2006 and they are then delivered to the customer on 2 July 2006.

13 In each of the following situations calculate the amount of VAT that would appear on the invoice:

   i)   goods with a list price of £356.79 plus VAT

   ii) goods with a list price of £269.00 plus VAT and a trade discount is given of 15%

   iii) goods with a list price of £250.00 plus VAT and a settlement discount of 2.5% is offered

   iv) goods with a list price of £300.00 plus VAT, a trade discount of 10% is given and a settlement discount of 3% is offered.

14 You have received four invoices from suppliers which show only the total VAT inclusive pric and the fact that all of the goods are standard rated. For each invoice total determine th amount of VAT that is included:

    i)   £42.88
    ii)   £96.35
    iii) £28.20
    iv) £81.07

15 What is a pro-forma invoice and what wording should always appear on one?

16 When can the VAT on a bad debt be reclaimed from HMRC?

17 A UK VAT registered business is exporting goods which are standard -rated in the UK to a Frenc business. How will these goods be treated for VAT purposes in the UK?

chapter 17:
VAT RECORDS

Unit 7

knowledge and understanding - the business environment

6   administration of VAT: enforcement

7   special schemes: annual accounting; cash accounting; bad debt relief

knowledge and understanding - the organisation

19   the basis of the relationship between the organisation and the VAT Office

Performance criteria – element 7.3

A   complete and submit VAT returns correctly, using data from the appropriate recording systems, within the statutory time limits

B   correctly identify and calculate relevant inputs and outputs

C   ensure submissions are made in accordance with current legislation

D   ensure guidance is sought from the VAT Office when required, in a professional manner

VAT AND ACCOUNTING RECORDS

VAT affects most of the everyday transactions of a business. A VAT registered business will charge VAT on its sales and will pay VAT on its purchases and expense payments. These sales, purchases and expenses may be on credit or they may be for cash.

The VAT Guide sets out in detail the records that must be kept by a VAT registered business. Each individual business accounting system will be different but in general terms you must keep records of all taxable goods and services which you receive or supply. You must also be able to distinguish between standard-rated, reduced rate, zero-rated and exempt supplies.

The records must be kept up to date in order that each quarter the correct amount of VAT due to or from HMRC can be calculated and entered onto the VAT return. Whatever method of keeping these records that the business uses, they must be kept in such a way that HMRC officers can easily check that the figures on the VAT returns are correct.

Information that must be recorded

The information that must be kept by all businesses in order to be able to correctly calculate the VAT due includes the following:

- details of all goods or services the business received on which VAT has been charged

- any services that are received from abroad

- details of all trade within the European Union

- details of all supplies made by the business including zero-rated and exempt supplies

- details of any goods exported

HMRC require that these records should normally be kept for six years although if a business has storage problems then a request can be made to HMRC to keep the records for a shorter period.

Sales records

In order to be able to determine the correct total for the output tax of a business then detailed records of all sales made must be kept. If you send VAT invoices out to customers then copies of these should be kept and the details required can be summarised from them on a quarterly basis. Remember that you not only need the invoice totals but also the amounts of the supplies made including zero-rated and exempt supplies. If any credit notes are sent out to customers or debit notes received from customers which alter VAT invoices, copies of these should also be kept.

The accounting records that most businesses will keep in order to record the sales are the following:

Sales day book – this is a record of all of the invoices sent out to credit customers showing the net amount of the sale, the VAT and the invoice total.

Sales returns day book – this is a record of all of the credit notes sent out to credit customers or debit notes received from credit customers for returns and alterations to invoice amounts – again this will show the net amount of the credit/debit note, the VAT and the full value of the credit/debit note. Some businesses do not keep a separate sales returns day book; instead the details are recorded in the sales day book with brackets around each of the figures to indicate that they should be deducted.

Cash receipts book – this will record receipts from credit customers as well as other receipts for cash sales. You will remember from your accounting studies that the amount to be recorded for the receipts from credit customers is the full invoice total – the VAT does not need to be analysed here as this has already been done in the sales day book. However where cash sales are made and VAT has been charged on the sale then the cash receipts book should show the net amount of the sale, the VAT and the final total.

Purchases and expenses records

When a business receives invoices for purchases or expenses then these must all be kept. The business must keep invoices for goods and services received that are not only standard rated but also zero-rated and reduced rate supplies. They must be kept and filed in such a way that they can be easily produced for HMRC if necessary. Remember that you can only claim input VAT if you have a valid VAT invoice. Therefore any pro-forma invoices that the business receives cannot be used for this purpose – a proper VAT invoice must be sought from the supplier.

There is an exception for the requirement for a valid VAT invoice in order to reclaim input tax. For the following types of expenditure, if the total is £25 or less including VAT then no invoice is required:

- telephone calls from public or private telephones

- purchases through coin operated machines

- car park charges (although on-street parking meters are not subject to VAT)

As well as keeping the VAT invoices the business must also keep detailed records of all taxable supplies including any zero-rated supplies. This will normally be done in the following accounting records.

Purchases day book – this is a record of all of the invoices received from credit suppliers showing the net amount of the supply, the VAT and the invoice total.

Purchases returns day book – this is a record of all of the credit notes received by your business and any debit notes that you have issued. Again these will be analysed to show the net amount of the credit, any VAT and the total of the credit/debit note. Some businesses will not keep a separate purchases returns day book. Instead the details of any credit/debit notes will be shown in the purchases day book with each figure in brackets to indicate that it should be deducted from the invoice totals.

Cash payments book – this is a record of all of the payments made by the business. The payments to credit suppliers will be recorded as the total payment with no analysis of the VAT element as this has already been analysed out in the purchases day book. However all other payments for goods or expenses that have attracted VAT should be recorded as the net amount, the VAT and the full amount of the payment.

It is important to note that not only must all sales, purchases and expenses be recorded in the accounting records, but copies of all documentation, sales invoices and purchases/expenses invoices, credit notes and debit notes must also all be kept.

Activity 1

On what type of expenditure can input tax be reclaimed without a valid invoice?

THE VAT ACCOUNT

The central record that is used to record the overall VAT position and will be used to complete the VAT return is the VAT account, or as it is often called in a business's ledger the VAT CONTROL ACCOUNT. Here all of the entries from the accounting records such as the sales and purchases day books are entered and the amount of tax due for the quarter to HMRC or due to be reclaimed back from them is calculated.

HOW IT WORKS

Given below is a typical VAT account set out in the manner suggested in th
VAT Guide.

VAT ACCOUNT

VAT deductible – input tax	£	VAT payable – output tax	£
VAT on purchases – from the purchases day book	3,578.90	VAT on sales – from the sales day book	5,368.70
VAT on purchases – from the cash payments book	586.73	VAT on sales – from the cash receipts book	884.56
	4,165.63		6,253.26
VAT allowable on EU acquisitions	211.78	VAT due on EU acquisitions	211.78
Net overclaim of input tax from previous returns	–104.56	Net understatement of output tax on previous returns	315.67
Bad debt relief	33.60		
Sub-total	4,306.45	**Sub-total**	6,780.71
Less:		Less:	
VAT on credit notes from suppliers – purchases returns day book	–49.70	VAT on credit notes to customers – sales returns day book	–69.80
Total tax deductible	4,256.75	**Total tax payable**	6,710.91
		Less: total tax deductible	4,256.75
		Payable to HMRC	2,454.16

These entries will now be explained:

VAT deductible

- the VAT on credit purchases is taken from the VAT column of the purchases day book and the VAT on cash purchases is taken from the VAT column of the cash payments book – these totals should be posted regularly from the day books to the VAT control account, usually on a weekly or a monthly basis

- the VAT on acquisitions from other European Union countries is shown as both input tax and output tax as the VAT must be paid on the import but can also be deducted as an allowable input tax

- any errors from previous VAT returns (provided that they are from accounting periods ending in the previous three years) can be adjusted for in the VAT account provided that the net value of the error is £2,000 or less

- the bad debt relief is a claim for repayment of VAT already paid on a sale to a customer who has never paid, the debt is over 6 months old and the bad debt has been written off in the accounting records

- the deduction for VAT on credit notes and debit notes is taken from the VAT column total of the purchases returns day book. If credit notes are recorded in the purchases day book then the VAT on them must be totalled and not included in the earlier total for the purchases day book.

VAT payable

- the VAT on credit sales is taken from the VAT column of the sales day book and the VAT on cash sales is taken from the VAT column of the cash receipts book – these totals should be posted regularly from the day books to the VAT control account usually on a weekly or monthly basis

- the VAT due to be paid on acquisitions from other EU countries is shown as both input tax and output tax

- the net understatement of output tax from previous periods is an error in a previous period which can be adjusted for in the VAT account provided that it is from within the last three years and is for £2,000 or less

- the deduction for VAT on credit notes to customers is taken from the VAT column of the sales returns day book. If credit notes are alternatively recorded in the sales day book then the total of VAT on these credit notes will have to be calculated and not included when posting the total of the sales day book VAT earlier in the VAT control account.

Tax payable

- the total of the tax payable then has the total of the tax deductible subtracted from it to find the amount that is due to HMRC for the period

- if the amount of tax payable is less than the amount of tax deductible the difference is the amount that can be reclaimed from HMRC for the period.

Clearing the VAT account

- when the amount of tax due to HMRC is paid then the double entry will be to credit the bank account and debit the VAT account, thereby clearing the account of any balance before the postings for the next period take place – this is illustrated below:

VAT ACCOUNT

VAT deductible – input tax	£	VAT payable – output tax	£
VAT on purchases – from the purchases day book	3,578.90	VAT on sales – from the sales day book	5,368.7
VAT on purchases – from the cash payments book	586.73	VAT on sales – from the cash receipts book	884.56
	4,165.63		6,253.26
VAT allowable on EU acquisitions	211.78	VAT due on EU acquisitions	211.78
Net overclaim of input tax from previous returns	–104.56	Net understatement of output tax on previous returns	315.67
Bad debt relief	33.60		
Sub-total	4,306.45	**Sub-total**	6,780.71
Less:		Less:	
VAT on credit notes from suppliers – purchases returns day book	–49.70	VAT on credit notes to customers – sales returns day book	–69.80
Total tax deductible	4,256.75	**Total tax payable**	6,710.91
		Less: total tax deductible	4,256.75
Cash paid	2,454.16	**Payable to HMRC**	2,454.16

PARTIAL EXEPTION

A taxable person may only recover the VAT paid on supplies to that person so far as it is attributable to taxable supplies made by that person. Where a trader makes a mixture of taxable and exempt supplies, there may be **partial exemption**. Where a trader is partially exempt, not all input VAT is recoverable because some of it is attributable to exempt supplies made by that person.

A partially exempt business has the problem of trying to analyse the input tax suffered into two categories.

- **Attributable to making taxable supplies** (fully recoverable)

- **Attributable to making exempt supplies** (not recoverable unless very small)

HMRC may agree various methods with a trader to allow this apportionment to be calculated. The most popular method used is called the **standard method**, which involves the following steps.

> Step 1   Calculate the amount of input VAT suffered on supplies made to the taxable person in the period.

Step 2 Calculate how much of the input VAT suffered relates to supplies which are wholly used or to be used by him in making taxable supplies. This input VAT is deductible in full.

Step 3 Calculate how much of the input VAT suffered relates to supplies which are wholly used or to be used by him in making exempt supplies. This input VAT is not deductible.

Step 4 Calculate how much of any remaining input VAT is deductible. This is calculated using a percentage. The percentage is (taxable turnover excluding VAT/total turnover excluding VAT) × 100%, rounded to the nearest whole percentage above.

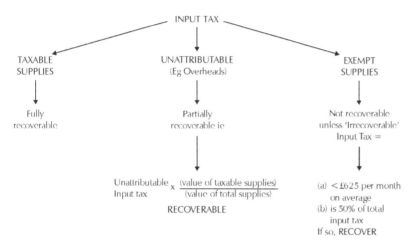

If the exempt input tax is small it can be recovered. To be 'small' two conditions must be met.

- the input VAT wholly attributable to exempt supplies plus the VAT apportioned to exempt supplies is no more than £625 a month on average

- the exempt input tax is also no more than 50% of all input VAT

This limit is known as the **de minimis limit**.

THE VAT RETURN

A VAT RETURN, Form VAT 100, will normally need to be completed for each three month accounting period, known as the tax period. When a business registers for VAT it will be allocated to one of three groups of tax periods.

Group 1 – tax periods ending on the last day of March, June, September and December

Group 2 – tax periods ending on the last day of April, July, October and January

Group 3 – tax periods ending on the last day of May, August, November and February

A business can apply to have a tax period that fits in with its financial year.

Completing the VAT return

Towards the end of each tax period a business will receive a VAT return, Form VAT 100 from the Customs & Excise VAT CENTRAL UNIT. The return must be completed and then returned to the VAT Central Unit together with any payment due, arriving no later than one month after the end of the tax period.

A VAT Notice 700/12 Filling in your VAT return is available from your local VAT Business Advice Centre and can help in completing the return.

The VAT return should be completed in ink and all boxes should be completed, writing "none" if necessary.

OW IT WORKS

e will now use the VAT control account from earlier in the chapter to ıstrate how to complete the VAT return for the period.

VAT ACCOUNT

ıT deductible – input tax	£	VAT payable – output tax	£
ıT on purchases – from the purchases day book	3,578.90	VAT on sales – from the sales day book	5,368.70
ıT on purchases – from the cash payments book	586.73	VAT on sales – from the cash receipts book	884.56
	4,165.63		6,253.26
ıT allowable on EU acquisitions	211.78	VAT due on EU acquisitions	211.78
ıet overclaim of input tax from previous returns	–104.56	Net understatement of output tax on previous returns	315.67
ad debt relief	33.60		
ub-total	4,306.45	**Sub-total**	6,780.71
ess:		Less:	
ʾAT on credit notes from suppliers – purchases returns day book	–49.70	VAT on credit notes to customers – sales returns day book	–69.80
ʾotal tax deductible	4,256.75	**Total tax payable**	6,710.91
		Less: total tax deductible	4,256.75
		Payable to HMRC	2,454.16

ʾot all of the information for the VAT return is found in the VAT control ıccount so the various day books will need to be consulted as well. These are ʒiven below:

Sales day book summary

	Zero-rated sales	Standard rated sales	VAT	Total
	£	£	£	£
Total	3,581.67	30,678.28	5,368.70	39,628.65

Purchases day book summary

	Zero-rated purchases	Standard rated purchases	VAT	Total
	£	£	£	£
Total	2,669.80	20,450.85	3,578.90	26,699.55

Sales returns day book summary

	Zero-rated sales £	Standard rated sales £	VAT £	Total £
Total	25.59	398.86	69.80	494.25

Purchases returns day book summary

	Zero-rated purchases £	Standard rated purchases £	VAT £	Total £
Total	15.89	284.00	49.70	349.59

Cash receipts book summary

	Net £	VAT £	Total £
Cash sales	5,054.63	884.56	5,939.19

Cash payments book summary

	Net £	VAT £	Total £
Cash purchases	3,352.75	586.73	3,939.48

There were no sales to other countries but the value of the acquisitions from EU countries was £1,210.18 plus VAT.

The business's name and address is Far Flung Creations, Zebra House, Horniman Street, Belsing, BE4 6TP. The VAT return is for the tax period ending 30 June 2006 and the business's VAT registration number is 382 6109 14.

How to complete the VAT return

First complete the administrative details at the top of the form – name, address, VAT registration number. The return is for the second period in 2006 and as this is to 30 June 2006 then the due date is 31 July 2006.

Now move on to completing the boxes.

		£
x 1	VAT on sales from the sales day book	5,368.70
	VAT on sales from the cash receipts book	884.56
	Net understatement of output tax from previous return	315.67
	Less: VAT on credit notes	(69.80)
		6,499.13
x 2	EU acquisitions	211.78
x 3	Total of box 1 and box 2 £6,499.13 + £211.78	6,710.91
x 4	VAT on purchases from purchases day book	3,578.90
	VAT on purchases from cash payments book	586.73
	VAT on EU purchases	211.78
	Net overclaim of input tax from previous returns	(104.56)
	Bad debt relief	33.60
	Less: VAT on credit notes from suppliers	(49.70)
		4,256.75
ox 5	Net VAT due Box 3 minus box 4 £6,710.91 – £4,256.75	2,454.16

Boxes 6 to 9 deal with sales and purchases before any VAT is added. Note that for these boxes no pence are needed.

ox 6	Zero-rated credit sales	3,581.67
	Standard rated credit sales	30,678.28
	Cash sales	5,054.63
	Less: zero-rated credit notes	(25.59)
	standard rated credit notes	(398.86)
		38,890.13
ox 7	Zero-rated credit purchases	2,669.80
	Standard rated credit purchases	20,450.85
	Cash purchases	3,352.75
	EU acquisitions	1,210.18
	Less: zero-rated credit notes	(15.89)
	standard rated credit notes	(284.00)
		27,383.69
Box 8		"none"
Box 9		1,210.17

student notes

Finally the payment box should be ticked as a payment for the amount VAT due must be sent with the VAT return. Then the VAT return must checked thoroughly including all calculations and then passed to a con member of management for the declaration to be signed.

Value Added Tax Return

For the period
01 03 06 to 30 06 06

For Official Use

Registration number	Period
382 6109 14	0606

You could be liable to a financial penalty if your completed return and all the VAT payable are not received by the due date.

Due date: 31 July 2006

FAR FLUNG CREATIONS
ZEBRA HOUSE
HORNIMAN STREET
BELSING
BE4 6TP

For
Official
Use

If you have a general enquiry or need advice please call our National Advice Service on 0845 010 9000.

Before you fill in this form please read the notes on the back and the VAT Leaflet "*Filling in your VAT return*" and "*Flat rate schemes for small businesses*", if you use the scheme. Fill in all boxes clearly in ink, and write 'none' where necessary. Don't put a dash or leave any box blank. If there are no pence write "00" in the pence column. Do not enter more than one amount in any box.

For official use			£	p
	VAT due in this period on sales and other outputs	1	6,499	13
	VAT due in this period on acquisitions from other EC Member States	2	211	78
	Total VAT due (the sum of boxes 1 and 2)	3	6,710	91
	VAT reclaimed in this period on purchases and other inputs (including acquisitions from the EC)	4	4,256	75
	Net VAT to be paid to Customs or reclaimed by you (Difference between boxes 3 and 4)	5	2,454	16
	Total value of sales and all other outputs excluding any VAT. Include your box 8 figure	6	38,890	00
	Total value of purchases and all other inputs excluding any VAT. Include your box 9 figure	7	27,384	00
	Total value of all supplies of goods and related services, excluding any VAT, to other EC Member States	8	NONE	00
	Total value of all acquisitions of goods and related services, excluding any VAT, from other EC Member States	9	1,210	00

If you are enclosing a payment please tick this box.

✓

DECLARATION: You, or someone on your behalf, must sign below.

I, _____ declare that the
(Full name of signatory in BLOCK LETTERS)
information given above is true and complete.

Signature_____ Date .... 20 ....

A false declaration can result in prosecution.

---

e will now summarise the necessary steps for completing the VAT return:

Step 1 Fill in the business details and VAT registration number at the top of the form and the VAT period and due date of the form

Step 2 Fill in box 1 with the details of the VAT on sales, less the VAT on any credit notes issued together with any adjustments for earlier period errors of £2,000 or less

Step 3 Fill in box 2 with the VAT due on any acquisitions from other European Union countries

Step 4 Fill in box 3 with the total of boxes 1 and 2

Step 5 Fill in box 4 with the total of the VAT on purchases and expenses being reclaimed less the VAT on any credit notes received. This total also includes the VAT on any acquisitions from other EU countries and any adjustments for errors on previous VAT returns of £2,000 or less

Step 6 Deduct the figure in box 4 from the figure in box 3 and enter in box 5. If the figure in box 3 is larger than that in box 4 then this total is the amount due to HMRC If the figure in box 3 is less than the figure in box 4 then the total is the amount that is due from HMRC.

Step 7 Fill in box 6 with the total of all sales less credit notes. This total is excluding VAT but should include the net amount of sales that are standard rated, zero-rated and exempt as well as any supplies to EU member countries.

Step 8 Fill in box 7 with the total of all purchases and other expenses – less any credit notes. Again this figure should be the total excluding any VAT and should include standard rated, zero-rated and exempt supplies. This total should also include any acquisitions from EU member countries.

Step 9 Fill in box 8 with the total value, excluding VAT of all supplies of goods and services to other EU member countries.

Step 10 Fill in box 9 with the total of all acquisitions of goods and related services, excluding VAT, from EU member countries.

Step 11 If a payment is due to HMRC then tick the relevant box at the bottom of the form

Step 12 Check that all of the figures and arithmetic are correct. Any errors should be crossed out and the correct figures inserted – any amendments should be initialled.

Step 13 Finally the form should be checked and authorised by the appropriate senior management figure in the organisation and should then be sent off in the envelope provided together with a cheque. Ensure that the form is received by VAT Central Unit by the due date.

Activity 2

How are acquisitions from other EU countries dealt with on the VAT return?

Not returning your VAT Form 100

If a business does not return the VAT return within the stated period, or month after the end of the tax period, then that trader is in default and SURCHARGE LIABILITY NOTICE will be sent. This warns the business that the business defaults in respect of an accounting period within the next 1 months then a default surcharge will be issued. The surcharge is based on percentage of the VAT that is unpaid ranging between 2% and 15%. If th business does not send in a VAT return then the amount of VAT that you ow will be assessed and the surcharge will be based upon this assessment.

Errors of more than £2,000

If a net error of more than £2,000 is discovered it cannot be adjusted for o the VAT return. Instead the local VAT Business Advice centre must be informed using Form VAT 652 or by letter – this is known as VOLUNTAR DISCLOSURE.

If any error is not reported in this way then this could mean a HMRC MISDECLARATION PENALTY which could be a 15% charge on any unpaic VAT.

SPECIAL SCHEMES

There are a number of special schemes which make VAT accounting easier for small businesses.

Annual accounting scheme

If a business has been registered for VAT for at least 12 months and the annual value of its taxable supplies, excluding VAT, is below £1,350,000 then they may be able to use the ANNUAL ACCOUNTING SCHEME.

In addition, businesses with an expected annual value of taxable supplies of up to £1,350,000 can join the scheme any time on or after the time when they apply to be registered for VAT - there is no 12 month restriction (until 2006 such businesses had to wait to join).

nder this scheme the business makes 9 (usually) monthly direct debit ayments based upon an estimate of the amount of VAT due. A VAT return ll then be prepared for the year and sent in with the tenth balancing ayment, within two months after the year end.

se of this annual accounting scheme is a great help to a small trader as it eans that he does not have to prepare a quarterly VAT return. However it oes mean that he must still keep accurate accounting records of the VAT formation for a whole year.

ll details of the annual accounting scheme can be found in VAT Notice 732 april 2002) VAT: Annual accounting.

Cash accounting scheme

the annual value of taxable supplies, excluding VAT, is less than £660,000 rovided that you have a clean record with HMRC you may be able to apply o use the CASH ACCOUNTING SCHEME.

he scheme allows the accounting for VAT to be based upon the date of eceipt or payment of money rather than the tax point on an invoice. This is articularly useful for a business which gives its customers a long period of redit but has to pay its suppliers promptly. The scheme also gives automatic elief from bad debts as if the customer does not pay the amount due the VAT eed not be accounted for to HMRC.

ull details of this scheme are set out in Notice 731 (April 2004) VAT: Cash accounting.

Retail schemes

There are a number of types of scheme to make accounting for VAT by shops easier. However the knowledge and understanding for Unit 7 does not require you to know about these in detail. However you may notice a further box on the VAT return for the appropriate code letter for any such scheme that is in use.

Flat rate scheme

This scheme applies to small businesses whose annual taxable turnover does not exceed £150,000. The scheme allows such businesses to account for VAT by applying a flat rate percentage to the business's total business supplies for a period, the result being the VAT owed to HMRC. This simplifies the administration considerably, as VAT does not have to be accounted for on each individual sales and purchase invoice. There are different flat rates set by HMRC for different trade sectors.

CONTACT WITH HMRC

The main contact with HMRC for a VAT-registered person is the local V٨ Office. They are responsible for the local administration of VAT and f providing advice to registered persons in the area. The address and telephor number of your local VAT Office can be found in the telephone directo under 'Customs and Excise' or 'HM Revenue & Customs.'.

The National Advice Bureau will be able to advise registered persons on mc VAT matters and they also keep stocks of VAT publications.

Whenever a registered person contacts the VAT Office either in writing or k telephone they should always quote their VAT registration number, and kee a note of the conversation and the call reference given.

In simulations you will typically be required to seek guidance from the VA office on some aspect of the organisation's affairs. The area that you have t enquire about may be very simple or it may be more complicated or obscure If it is a simple point then the task may require a brief explanation of the poir as well as seeking more detailed guidance from the VAT Office. If the poir is more complex then you will only be required to ask for guidance in a intelligent and professional manner, not to understand the sometime complex provisions of VAT law.

Visits from HMRC

From time to time an HMRC officer will visit a VAT-registered business ir order to examine the business records and accounting methods, and tc determine whether the correct amount of tax has been paid and whethe returns are being completed on time.

Usually there will be a set date agreed with the Customs officer for the visi but on occasion an officer may arrive unannounced in order to see the day to day operations of the business.

There is full detail about VAT visits in Notice 989 Visits by HMRC officers.

There is an important performance criterion for Element 7.3 which states that "Guidance is sought from the VAT Office when required, in a professional manner". Therefore whenever contact is made with the VAT Office or with Customs officers this must always be made in a polite and professional manner.

CHAPTER OVERVIEW

all VAT-registered persons must keep full records of the details of goods and services the business received on which VAT has been charged, any services received from abroad, details of all trade within the European Union, details of all supplies made by the business including zero-rated and exempt supplies and details of any goods exported

these records should normally be kept for 6 years and must be made available to a Customs officer if required

copies of sales invoices must be kept and the main accounting records for sales will be the sales day book, sales returns day book and cash receipts book

all invoices for purchases and expenses must be kept otherwise the input VAT cannot be reclaimed – the main accounting records for purchases and expenses are the purchases day book, the purchases returns day book and the cash payments book

the central record for recording VAT is the VAT control account which lists all of the VAT deductible, or input tax, on the debit side and all of the VAT payable, output tax, on the credit side – the balance on this account is the amount of VAT due to or from HMRC for the period

normally every quarter the VAT return, Form VAT 100 must be completed and sent back to HMRC together with any payment due within one month of the end of the tax period

the first five boxes of the VAT return can be completed from the figures in the VAT control account

boxes 6 to 9 must be completed from the other accounting records of the business showing sales and purchases, exports and acquisitions excluding VAT

if the VAT return for a quarter is not returned on time then a surcharge liability notice will be sent

KEY WORDS

VAT control account the ledger account in which is recorded all amounts of input tax and output tax

VAT return Form VAT 100 which must normally be completed to show the amount of VAT due or to be reclaimed for the quarter

VAT Central Unit the central VAT Office that sends out the VAT returns and to whom the completed VAT return and any payment due must be sent

Surcharge liability notice this warns a business that has not returned its VAT return in time that if the business defaults within the next twelve months a default surcharge will be issued

Voluntary disclosure the method of notifying HMRC of any error found from previous returns in excess of £2,000

Misdeclaration penalty a charge made by HMRC of up to 15% of any unpaid VAT if voluntary disclosure is not made

Annual accounting scheme a method of accounting for VAT which does not require quarterly returns and payments – instead 9 monthly direct debit payments and an annual return accompanied by the final payment

Cash accounting scheme a method of accounting for VAT which allows VAT to be dealt with according to the date of payment or receipt of cash rather than the tax point on the invoice

Flat rate scheme enables businesses to calculate their VAT payment as a percentage of total turnover

CHAPTER OVERVIEW cont.

- if a net error of more than £2,000 is discovered from a previous tax period this should not b adjusted in the VAT control account – instead voluntary disclosure should be made and the VA' Business Advice Centre must be informed, otherwise the business might have to pay misdeclaration penalty

- if a VAT-registered trader has a turnover of less than £1,350,000 excluding VAT, then he may be eligible for the annual accounting scheme – under this scheme 9 monthly direct debit payment are made based upon an estimate of the VAT liability for the year and the tenth and balancing payment is then made when the VAT return for the year is submitted within two months of the year end

- if a business has an annual turnover of less than £660,000, excluding VAT, then it may be eligible for the cash accounting scheme whereby VAT has to be accounted for to HMRC on the basis of cash payments received and made rather than on the basis of the tax point on the invoice

- if a business has an annual turnover of less than £150,000 they can simplify their VAT records by calculating their VAT payment as a percentage of total turnover instead of accounting for input and output tax on each individual purchase and sales invoice

- the main contact for advice and help for any VAT-registered business is the local VAT Business Advice Centre – on occasion the business may also receive a planned or unannounced visit from a Customs officer who will examine the business records and accounts in detail to ensure that VAT has not been underpaid or overpaid

OW MUCH HAVE YOU LEARNED?

1 How long do HMRC require relevant documents to be kept?

2 As far as VAT is concerned what would be the problem if:

    a) a business had not kept copies of sales invoices sent out
    b) a business had not kept suppliers' invoices received?

3 Given below is information about the VAT of a business that has been taken from the books of prime entry:

	£
VAT figures	
From the sales day book	7,589.60
From the sales returns day book	994.67
From the purchases day book	4,785.67
From the purchases returns day book	663.57
From the cash receipts book	1,662.78
From the cash payments book	936.58
EU acquisitions	1,558.36

Write up the VAT control account.

4 Given below is information about the VAT of a business taken from the books of prime entry:

From the sales day book	3,572.15
From the sales returns day book	662.70
From the purchases day book	1,825.67
From the purchases returns day book	310.56
From the cash receipts book	994.67
From the cash payments book	514.37
EU acquisitions	236.57
Bad debt relief	105.37
VAT underpaid in a previous period	44.79
VAT overpaid in a previous period	25.47

You are to write up the VAT control account.

5 Given below are extracts from the books of prime entry for a business Martin Trading, Blackn House, Jude Street, Clinford, CL3 6GH. The business's VAT registration number is 225 3756 and the tax period is January to March 2006.

Sales day book summary

	Zero-rated sales £	Standard rated sales £	VAT £	Total £
Total	13,447.67	45,267.44	7,921.80	66,636.91

Purchases day book summary

	Zero-rated purchases £	Standard rated purchases £	VAT £	Total £
Total	7,447.30	30,627.58	5,359.82	43,434.70

Sales returns day book summary

	Zero-rated sales £	Standard rated sales £	VAT £	Total £
Total	225.83	773.56	135.37	1,134.76

Purchases returns day book summary

	Zero-rated purchases £	Standard rated purchases £	VAT £	Total £
Total	215.61	714.20	124.98	1,054.79

Cash receipts book summary

	Net £	VAT £	Total £
Cash sales	5,054.63	884.56	5,939.19

Cash payments book summary

	Net £	VAT £	Total £
Cash purchases	3,352.75	586.73	3,939.48

As well as the purchases shown in the purchases day book there were also acquisitions from EU countries totalling £2,256.07 plus £394.81 of VAT.

You are required to complete the VAT return given.

Value Added Tax Return
For the period
01 03 06 to 30 06 06

For Official Use

Registration number   Period

You could be liable to a financial penalty if your completed return and all the VAT payable are not received by the due date.

Due date:

For Official Use	

If you have a general enquiry or need advice please call our National Advice Service on 0845 010 9000.

Before you fill in this form please read the notes on the back and the VAT Leaflet "*Filling in your VAT return*" and "*Flat rate schemes for small businesses*", if you use the scheme. Fill in all boxes clearly in ink, and write 'none' where necessary. Don't put a dash or leave any box blank. If there are no pence write "00" in the pence column. Do not enter more than one amount in any box.

For official use		£	p
	VAT due in this period on sales and other outputs **1**		
	VAT due in this period on acquisitions from other EC Member States **2**		
	Total VAT due (the sum of boxes 1 and 2) **3**		
	VAT reclaimed in this period on purchases and other inputs (including acquisitions from the EC) **4**		
	Net VAT to be paid to Customs or reclaimed by you (Difference between boxes 3 and 4) **5**		
	Total value of sales and all other outputs excluding any VAT. Include your box 8 figure **6**		00
	Total value of purchases and all other inputs excluding any VAT. Include your box 9 figure **7**		00
	Total value of all supplies of goods and related services, excluding any VAT, to other EC Member States **8**		00
	Total value of all acquisitions of goods and related services, excluding any VAT, from other EC Member States **9**		00

If you are enclosing a payment please tick this box.

DECLARATION: You, or someone on your behalf, must sign below.

I, _____ declare that the
(Full name of signatory in BLOCK LETTERS)
information given above is true and complete.

Signature_____ Date _____ 20 _____
A false declaration can result in prosecution.

6   Explain how the annual accounting scheme works and what are the benefits to a trader who uses this scheme for VAT.

7   Explain how the cash accounting scheme works and what are the benefits to a trader who uses this scheme for VAT.

CHAPTER 1 Management information

An extension to a building is an improvement to an existing fixed asset; it is like acquiring another building. It will increase the ability of the business to earn profits and is therefore a capital item. Repairs are treated as revenue expenditure as they only maintain the existing ability to earn profits.

a) Production cost

b) Administration cost – the Managing Director is involved in co-ordinating all areas of operations of a business

c) Selling and distribution cost

d) Administration cost, unless any part of this can be separately identified and attributed to another function

e) Production cost

f) Selling and distribution cost

g) Production cost

3 This is a direct cost as the painter is working on the product directly. Painters doing maintenance work in a factory which makes toys would be classified as indirect labour. This emphasises the importance of considering each case on its own merits; the same job is treated differently in two different situations.

4 a) £20
   b) £2
   c) £1
   d) £0.20

As the number of units increases, the fixed cost per unit decreases.

5

Output (units)		Total cost
		£
Highest	4,200	54,000
Lowest	2,900	41,000
High-low	1,300	13,000

$$\text{Variable cost per unit} = \frac{\text{High cost} - \text{low cost}}{\text{High output} - \text{low output}}$$

$$= \frac{£13,000}{1,300}$$

$$= £10$$

At 4,200 units

	£
Total cost	54,000
Less: variable cost (4,200 x £10)	42,000
= fixed cost	12,000

Or, at 2,900 units

	£
Total cost	41,000
Less: variable cost (2,900 x £10)	29,000
= fixed cost	12,000

6

	75,000	100,000	150,000
Units made:			
Costs:	£	£	£
Variable costs:			
Direct materials	375,000	500,000	750,000
£5 × 75,000/100,000/150,000			
Direct labour	1,687,500	2,250,000	3,675,000
3 × £7.50 × 75,000/100,000			
(3 × £7.50 × 150,000)+			
(3 × £2.00 × 50,000)			
Direct expenses	112,500	150,000	225,000
£1.50 × 75,000/100,000/150,000			
Prime cost	2,175,000	2,900,000	4,650,000
Fixed costs:			
Overhead	80,000	80,000	100,000
Production cost	2,255,000	2,980,000	4,750,000
Cost per unit	30.07	29.80	31.67

CHAPTER 2 Materials costs

Leather (upper)
Rubber (sole)
Plastic and card (insole)
Glue and thread (may be included in indirect materials due to their relatively small value)
Cardboard box and tissue (packaging)

These two documents are frequently mixed up, so make sure that you sort out the differences now!
To highlight the differences, this answer is set out in tabular form.

Purchase requisition	Materials requisition
A request to buy materials	A request to transfer materials out of stores to where they are needed
Raised by stores (or production if the items are not normally kept in stores e.g. for an individual job to customer's specifications)	Raised by the department needing the materials e.g. production for raw materials or administration for stationery
Sent to the purchasing department	Sent to the stores

3

STORES LEDGER ACCOUNT

Stock item Doggy bed   Maximum 200

Code D49802   Minimum 20

Date 2006	Receipts				Issues				Balance		
	GRN	Qty	Unit price £	£	Req No	Qty	Unit price £	£	Qty	Unit price £	£
1 Sept	Bal								50	10	500
3 Sept	G23	100	12	1,200					50	10	500
									100	12	1,200
									150		1,700
6 Sept					R55	50	10	500			
						60	12	720	40	12	480
9 Sept	G42	100	13	1,300					40	12	480
									100	13	1,300
									140		1,780
15 Sept					R98	40	12	480			
						40	13	520	60	13	780
21 Sept	G75	100	14	1,400					60	13	780
									100	14	1,400
									160		2,180

4

JOURNAL		
Code	DR (£)	CR (£)
1 Raw materials 500	1,250	
Creditors 700		1,250
2 Work in progress 600	750	
Raw materials 500		750

Reorder level   = buffer stock + (budgeted usage × maximum lead time)

                               = (2 × 5,000) + (5,000 × 3)

                               = 25,000 mands.

Maximum stock level is limited to 520.

520 = 72 + reorder quantity – (2 x 1)

Reorder quantity   = 520 – 72 + 2

                    = 450

The order is placed when stock falls to 72 units. 2 units is the minimum number used in the lead time, so that when the next delivery arrives there will be 70 units still in stock. Only 450 more can be fitted into the storage space to take the total to 520 units, so the reorder quantity must be limited to 450 units.

Perpetual inventory is the term used for the up-to-date record of the amount of each stock line on hand. The records are updated for every receipt and issue of stock so that, in theory, they will show the amount of goods on hand at any particular moment.

Continuous stocktaking is a check to ensure that the physical stock agrees with the perpetual inventory record. It is a system of stocktaking that counts stock lines on a rotational basis, ensuring that each stock line is counted at least once a year. Valuable and high-turnover items will be checked more often than this. The physical counts are compared with the stock records so that any discrepancies can be investigated. Continuous stocktaking is only of use if there is a perpetual inventory kept.

CHAPTER 3 Labour costs and expenses

1

	Direct cost £	Indirect cost £
Basic pay (37 x £10)	370	
Overtime: basic (4x £10)	40	
premium (4 x £5)		20
Total	410	20

2

	£
First 4,000 units: 4,000 x 10p	400.00
Next 500 units: 500 x 12p	60.00
Last 230 units: 230 x 14p	32.20
Gross pay	492.20

The major disadvantage of this method is that workers might increase their volume of output but not pay enough attention to the quality of their output. Quality control measures, such as increased inspection of output can reduce this problem, but at an extra cost. Another disadvantage is that idle time may arise due to the breakdown of machinery or a shortage of raw materials, leading to reduced pay. Some employers, however, pay idle time at a time rate so that workers are not penalised too heavily through no fault of their own. This is treated as indirect labour and charge to overheads. Sometimes the employer will set a guaranteed time rate which the employee will b paid if the piecework total is lower. It should already be obvious to you that the calculation involved can become quite complicated, another disadvantage.

3

	Time rate	Piecework rate
Easy/complicated to calculate an employee's pay	Easy	Complicated
Can/can't be used for all direct labour employees	Can	Can't
More efficient the workers are paid **more than/ the same as** less efficient workers	The same as	More than
The quality of the goods produced **is/is not** affected by workers rushing a job so that they earn more	Is not	Is
The employees' pay **fluctuates/remains the same** if output fluctuates	Remains the same	Fluctuates
More supervisors/more inspectors may be needed for this system	More supervisors	More inspectors
Production problems **can/cannot** lead to a cut in pay	Cannot	Can
Systems **do/do not** need to be set up to check the amount of work produced by each employee	Do not	Do

4 **Capital expenditure**   Purchases of fixed assets or the improvement of the earning capability of fixed assets

Revenue expenditure
- Purchase of goods for resale
- Maintenance of the existing earning capacity of fixed assets
- Expenditure incurred in conducting the business.

Direct costs   Can be directly identified with a unit of production or service

Indirect costs   Cannot be directly identified with a unit of production or service

Variable costs   Vary according to the level of production or activity

Fixed costs (period costs)   Do not vary with changes in production level or activity level. They are incurred in relation to a period rather than a product.

CHAPTER 4 Overheads

Overhead	a) Allocate or apportion?	b) Cost centre(s) charged?	c) Basis of apportionment?
Factory light & heat	Apportion	The four factory cost centres	Floor area or volume occupied
Rent	Allocate	Factory office (this is the only cost centre rented)	
Factory rates	Apportion	The four factory cost centres	Floor area
Office stationery	Allocate	Offices	
Cleaning of workers' overalls	Apportion	The four factory cost centres and the warehouse	Number of workers using overalls
Roof repair to warehouse	Allocate	Warehouse	

Cost Centre	Basis used	A £	B £	C £	Total £
Electricity	3:2:1	7,500	5,000	2,500	15,000
Rent	6:3:1	7,200	3,600	1,200	12,000
Supervisor	1:1:0	2,500	2,500		5,000
Licence	Allocated	–	–	2,000	2,000
		17,200	11,100	5,700	
Reapportion C		2,850	2,850	(5,700)	
Total		20,050	13,950	0	34,000

a) Separate departmental rates per direct labour hour

$$\text{Department X} = \frac{£20,000}{4,000h}$$

$$= £5 \text{ per direct labour hour}$$

$$\text{Department Z} = \frac{£40,000}{16,000h}$$

$$= £2.50 \text{ per direct labour hour}$$

b) Separate departmental rates per machine hour

$$\text{Department X} = \frac{£20,000}{12,000h}$$

$$= £1.67 \text{ per machine hour}$$

$$\text{Department Z} \quad = \quad \frac{£40,000}{100}$$

$$= \quad £400 \text{ per machine hour}$$

c)   It is obvious from these results that the two departments are very different. Department seems to utilise a lot of labour, but very little machinery in its production process, so a dire labour hour rate would be the best overhead absorption rate to use; the machine hour rat looks unreasonably high! Department X uses a lot more machine hours than labour hour so it may be more meaningful to use a machine hour rate in this department.

4   a)   Overhead absorption rate $= \quad \dfrac{£54,000}{60,000h}$ (budgeted direct labour hours)

$$= \quad £0.90 \text{ per direct labour hour}$$

b)

	£
Actual overheads	47,000
Absorbed overheads (55,000h x £0.90 per h)	49,500
Over absorption	2,500

The amount over absorbed will be an addition to profit.

CHAPTER 5 Absorption costing and marginal costing

1   a)   **Absorption costing - unit cost**

	£
Direct material	3.40
Direct labour	6.80
Variable overhead	1.20
Prime cost	11.40
Fixed overhead ((£340,000/100,000) x 2)	6.80
Absorption cost	18.20

b)   **Marginal costing - unit cost**

	£
Direct material	3.40
Direct labour	6.80
Variable overhead	1.20
Prime cost or marginal cost	61.40

Unit cost

	£
Direct material	6.40
Direct labour	15.00
Variable overhead ((120,000/24,000) x 2)	10.00
Marginal costing unit cost	31.40
Fixed overhead ((360,000/24,000) x 2)	30.00
Absorption costing unit cost	61.40

a) **Absorption costing - profit and loss account**

	£	£
Sales (11,600 x £65)		754,000
Less: cost of sales		
Opening stock (1,400 x £61.40)	85,960	
Production cost (12,000 x £61.40)	736,800	
	822,760	
Less: closing stock (1,800 x £61.40)	110,520	
		712,240
Profit		41,760

b) **Marginal costing - profit and loss account**

	£	£
Sales		754,000
Less: cost of sales		
Opening stock (1,400 x £31.40)	43,960	
Production cost (12,000 x £31.40)	376,800	
	420,760	
Less: closing stock (1,800 x £31.40)	56,520	
		364,240
Contribution		389,760
Less: fixed overheads		360,000
Profit		29,760

HAPTER 6 Costing systems

- Setting the price for the job
- Gathering the actual costs for the job
- Control of the job by the monitoring of variances between the actual cost and the expected cost of the job

If the overheads of the business are not included in the job quote then the overheads will never be covered by the income from jobs. Only by including the overheads before any profit element is added can the business be sure of earning enough to cover its overheads as well as the direct costs.

3 Cost per jacket $= \dfrac{£38,925}{450}$

$= £86.50$

4 a) <u>Step 1</u> Calculate the number of normal loss units:

16,000 ltr x 5% = 800 ltr

<u>Step 2</u> Calculate the expected output from the process:

16,000 ltr - 800 ltr = 15,200 ltr

<u>Step 3</u> Total the process costs:

£108,000 + £22,720 = £130,720

<u>Step 4</u> Calculate the cost per unit of expected output

$\dfrac{£130,720}{15,200\,\text{ltr}} = £8.60\ \text{per ltr}$

b)

Process account	ltr	£		ltr	£
Materials	16,000	108,000	Normal loss	800	-
Conversion costs		22,720	Output	15,200	130,720
	16,000	130,720		16,000	130,720

5 a) <u>Step 1</u> Calculate the number of normal loss units:

110,000 kg x 6% = 6,600 kg

<u>Step 2</u> Calculate the expected output from the process:

110,000 kg - 6,600 kg = 103,400 kg

<u>Step 3</u> Total the process costs:

£526,000 + £128,300 + £110,860 = £765,160

<u>Step 4</u> Calculate the cost per unit of expected output

$\dfrac{£765,160}{103,400\,\text{kg}} = £7.40\ \text{per kg}$

b)

Process account	kg	£		kg	£
Materials	110,000	526,000	Normal loss	6,600	-
Labour		128,300	Abnormal loss	3,000	22,200
Overheads		110,860	Output	100,400	742,960
	110,000	765,160		110,000	765,160

Abnormal loss account

	kg	£		kg	£
Process	3,000	22,200			

a) **Step 1** Calculate the number of normal loss units:

48,000 ltr x 10% = 4,800 ltr

Step 2 Calculate the expected output from the process:

48,000 ltr - 4,800 ltr = 43,200 ltr

Step 3 Total the process costs:

£164,200 + £56,120 = £220,320

Step 4 Calculate the cost per unit of expected output

$$\frac{£220,320}{43,200 \text{ ltr}} = £5.10 \text{ per litre}$$

b)

Process account

	ltr	£		ltr	£
Materials	48,000	164,200	Normal loss	4,800	-
Conversion costs		56,120	Output	44,000	224,400
Abnormal gain	800	4,080			
	48,800	224,400		48,800	224,400

Abnormal gain account

	ltr	£		ltr	£
			Process account	800	4,080

7   a) **Step 1** Calculate the number of normal loss units:

10,000 kg x 5% = 500 kg

Step 2 Calculate the expected output from the process:

10,000 kg - 500 kg = 9,500 kg

Step 3 Total the process costs and deduct the scrap value of the normal loss :

(£98,000 + £36,000 + £9,200) - (500 x £1.40) = £142,500

Step 4 Calculate the cost per unit of expected output

$$\frac{£142,500}{9,500\text{kg}} = £15 \text{ per kg}$$

b)

Process account

	kg	£		kg	£
Materials	10,000	98,000	Normal loss	500	700
Labour		36,000	Abnormal loss	400	6,000
Overheads		9,200	Output	9,100	136,500
	10,000	143,200		10,000	143,200

Abnormal loss account

	kg	£		kg	£
Process account	400	6,000	Scrap value	400	560
			Profit and loss a/c		5,440
	400	6,000		400	6,000

8

	Units	Materials Proportion complete	Materials Equivalent units	Labour/overheads Proportion complete	Labour/overheads Equivalent units
Completed units	4,000	100%	4,000	100%	4,000
Closing work in progress	600	75%	450	40%	240
Total equivalent units			4,450		4,240
Cost per equivalent unit			$\dfrac{£15,575}{4,450}$		$\dfrac{£8,480}{4,240}$
			= £3.50 per EU		= £2 per EU

Valuation

	£
Completed units	
Materials (4,000 x £3.50)	14,000
Labour/overheads (4,000 x £2)	8,000
	22,000
Closing work in progress	
Materials (450 x £3.50)	1,575
Labour/overheads (240 x £2)	480
	2,055

CHAPTER 7 Cost bookkeeping

1   An integrated cost bookkeeping system is one which combines the cost accounting and financial accounting functions in one system of ledger accounts. This means that there will be ledger accounts which relate to the cost accounting function such as materials control account, wages control account, production overheads control account and Work in Progress control account, as well as financial accounting ledgers such as the cash account and debtors and creditors control accounts.

DR   Materials control account
CR   Creditors control account

Production overheads control account

	£		£
Overheads incurred	3,690	Overheads absorbed	
		1,050 hours @ £3.24	3,402
		Under absorbed overhead	288
	3,690		3,690

The under absorbed overhead would be debited to the profit and loss account as an additional cost for the period.

Work in progress control account

	£		£
Opening balance	730	Transfer to finished goods	4,100
Direct materials	2,460		
Direct labour	1,070		
Production overhead			
140 hours @ £2.10	294	Closing balance	454
	4,554		4,554

CHAPTER 8 Short-term decision making

1   Break-even point $= \dfrac{£360,000}{£28-£19}$

$= 40,000$ units

2   Target profit output $= \dfrac{£250,000+£150,000}{£80-£60}$

$= 20,000$ units

3   Break-even point $= \dfrac{£480,000}{£32-£24}$

$= 60,000$ units

Margin of safety $= \dfrac{£75,000-60,000}{75,000} \times 100$

$= 20\%$

4   Profit volume ratio $= \dfrac{£36-£27}{£36} \times 100$

$= 25\%$

Break-even point $= \dfrac{£360,000}{0.25}$

$= £1,440,000$

5

	P	Q	R	S
Contribution per kg	£4.00	£3.75	£9.00	£7.00
Ranking	3	4	1	2

Production plan

	Units produced	Kgs used
R	1,000	1,000
S	4,000	8,000
P	2,000	6,000
Q (balance)	3,750	15,000
		30,000

Profit

	£
P (2,000 x £12)	24,000
Q (3,750 x £15)	56,250
R (1,000 x £9)	9,000
S (4,000 x £14)	56,000
Contribution	145,250
Less: fixed costs	30,000
Profit	115,250

CHAPTER 9 Long-term decision making

1   Time

Time	Cash flows	Cumulative cash flows
	£	£
31 Dec 06	30,000	30,000
31 Dec 07	40,000	70,000
31 Dec 08	40,000	110,000
31 Dec 09	20,000	130,000

The initial cost of the investment is fully covered after three year however as the cash inflows occur evenly throughout the year this can be calculated more accurately.

2 years + £30,000/£40,000 x 12 months = 2 years and 9 months

a) £7,100 x 0.8734   = £6,201.14
b) £380 x 0.6587   = £250.31
c) £2,030 x 0.9524   = £1,933.37

a) £1,000 x 3.6048   = £3,604.80
b) £1,000 + (£1,000 x 3.0374)   = £4,037.40

$$£240 \times \frac{1}{0.05} = 4,800$$

Year	Cash flows £	Discount factor @ 8%	Net present value £
0	(100,000)	1.00	(100,000)
1	30,000	0.9259	27,777
2	40,000	0.8573	34,292
3	40,000	0.7938	31,752
4	20,000	0.7350	14,700
Net present value			8,521

CHAPTER 10 Internal information

1 Decision making
    Planning
    Control

2 It should be relevant, reliable, consistent and prompt.

3

	£
Sales (157,388 + 104,734 – 31,267)	230,855
Cost of sales (96,365 + 77,446 – 31,267)	142,544
Gross profit	88,311

4
- revenue from each hotel
- costs of running each hotel
- number of rooms in each hotel
- number of rooms occupied each night
- revenue from distinct areas of the hotel such as restaurant or bar
- costs of any such distinct areas

CHAPTER 11 Performance measures

1 Quarter to June 2006 $\quad = 123/15$
$\quad\quad\quad\quad\quad\quad\quad\quad\quad\quad\quad\quad\ = 8.2$ advertisements per executive

Quarter to March 2006 $\quad = 88/12$
$\quad\quad\quad\quad\quad\quad\quad\quad\quad\quad\quad\quad\ = 7.3$ advertisements per executive

2 Productivity index $\quad\quad\ = 368,000/388,000 \times 100$
$\quad\quad\quad\quad\quad\quad\quad\quad\quad\quad\quad\quad\ = 94.8\%$

3 Cost per meal $\quad\quad\quad\quad = 66,500/3,600$
$\quad\quad\quad\quad\quad\quad\quad\quad\quad\quad\quad\quad\ = £18.47$

4 Labour utilisation $\quad\quad\ = 6,400/6,700 \times 100$
$\quad\quad\quad\quad\quad\quad\quad\quad\quad\quad\quad\quad\ = 95.5\%$

5 Machine utilisation (NBV) $= 316,800/280,000$
$\quad\quad\quad\quad\quad\quad\quad\quad\quad\quad\quad\quad\ = £1.13$ per £1 of NBV

Machine utilisation (hours) $= 316,800/12,200$
$\quad\quad\quad\quad\quad\quad\quad\quad\quad\quad\quad\quad\ = £25.97$ per machine hour

6 Asset turnover $\quad\quad\quad\ = 420,000/350,000$
$\quad\quad\quad\quad\quad\quad\quad\quad\quad\quad\quad\quad\ = £1.20$ per £1 of capital employed

7 Gross profit $\quad\quad\quad\quad\ = £442,000 - 278,000$
$\quad\quad\quad\quad\quad\quad\quad\quad\quad\quad\quad\quad\ = £164,000$

Gross profit margin $\quad\quad = 164,000/442,000 \times 100$
$\quad\quad\quad\quad\quad\quad\quad\quad\quad\quad\quad\quad\ = 37.1\%$

Net profit $\quad\quad\quad\quad\quad\ = £164,000 - 104,000$
$\quad\quad\quad\quad\quad\quad\quad\quad\quad\quad\quad\quad\ = £60,000$

Net profit margin $\quad\quad\quad = 60,000/442,000 \times 100$
$\quad\quad\quad\quad\quad\quad\quad\quad\quad\quad\quad\quad\ = 13.6\%$

8 Method 1 ROCE $\quad\quad = \dfrac{\text{Net profit after interest}}{\text{Owner's capital}} \times 100$

$\quad\quad\quad\quad\quad\quad\quad\quad\quad\quad = \dfrac{42,000}{380,000} \times 100$

$\quad\quad\quad\quad\quad\quad\quad\quad\quad\quad = 11.1\%$

Method 2 ROCE $\quad\quad = \dfrac{\text{Net profit before interest}}{\text{Owner's capital} + \text{long - term loan}} \times 100$

$\quad\quad\quad\quad\quad\quad\quad\quad\quad\quad = \dfrac{42,000 + 4,800}{380,000 + 80,000} \times 100$

$\quad\quad\quad\quad\quad\quad\quad\quad\quad\quad = 10.2\%$

CHAPTER 12 Writing a report

Title
Name and job title of person to whom report is sent
Name and job title of person writing the report
Date of report
Terms of reference
Summary
Findings
Conclusion
Recommendations
Appendices

REPORT

Report to: Philip Martin – Production director

Report from: Fred Harvey – Accounts assistant

Date: 22 June 2006

Terms of reference

This report has been prepared at the request of Philip Martin, Production director, in order to assess the performance of the company's three factories. The information for the report has been taken from the management accounting records for the three months ending 31 May 2006.

Summary

The Tamworth and Barnsley factories are performing well, but the Solihull factory is performing less well than the others in terms of productivity, resource utilisation and profitability. Consequently, the cost per unit at the Solihull factory is 5 to 8% higher than at the other two factories. Whilst Barnsley has the highest productivity and most efficient resource utilisation, a possible problem with the control of overheads has affected its profitability.

Findings

PRODUCTIVITY

Labour productivity is above the budgeted figure of 3.6 units per hour in both Tamworth and Barnsley but is significantly below target in Solihull.

Similarly both Tamworth and Barnsley have met or exceeded their budgeted production but Solihull's productivity index is only 92% meaning that production is well below the target figure.

However overall the productivity index for the total company shows a fairly healthy 98%.

In conclusion the productivity at Solihull should be investigated.

REPORT

COST PER UNIT

The cost per unit overall is £4.38 with both Tamworth and Barnsley products costing less than this figure.

Again there seems to be some problem at Solihull with the cost per unit being significantly higher than in the other two divisions.

RESOURCE UTILISATION

The labour utilisation indicates a significant amount of idle time in Solihull which will have an effect on the productivity of this branch.

The asset turnover figures are all very similar with all three divisions earning between 63 pence and 67 pence for every £1 of capital employed. Although there appears to be a problem with the production at Solihull the problem would appear to be restricted to production as the asset turnover shows that the sales level of the division is reasonable.

PROFITABILITY

The gross profit margins of Tamworth and Barnsley seem reasonable but the overall gross profit margin is pulled down by the performance of Solihull, probably due to the productivity and cost per unit problems there.

The net profit margin indicates a problem at Barnsley. Although Barnsley has a higher gross profit margin than Tamworth the net profit margin is lower. This might indicate that overheads at Barnsley should be investigated to find out why they are comparatively high.

The ROCE is reasonable for Tamworth and Barnsley but the poor performance of Solihull reduces the overall ROCE.

Conclusion

All of the divisions are profitable and they are all achieving reasonable levels of productivity and resource utilisation. However there are production problems at Solihull indicated by the low productivity and high cost per unit. The other problem is the net profit percentage of Barnsley which could perhaps be improved with more control over its overheads.

Recommendations

The production problems at Solihull should be investigated further. The other area to be considered is the net profit margin of Barnsley. The control over overheads at Barnsley should be investigated.

CHAPTER 13 Tables and diagrams

i)

	A	B	C	D
1		Sept	Oct	Nov
2	Actual units	102,000	108,000	110,000
3	Budgeted units	105,000	104,000	106,000
4	Productivity index	=(B2/B3)*100	=(C2/C3)*100	=(D2/D3)*100

ii)

	A	B	C	D
1		Sept	Oct	Nov
2	Actual units	102,000	108,000	110,000
3	Budgeted units	105,000	104,000	106,000
4	Productivity index	97%	104%	104%

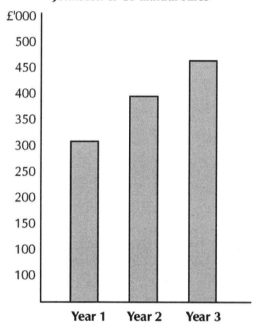

Johnston & Co annual sales

387

3   JOHNSTON & CO – ANNUAL SALES, GROSS PROFIT AND NET PROFIT

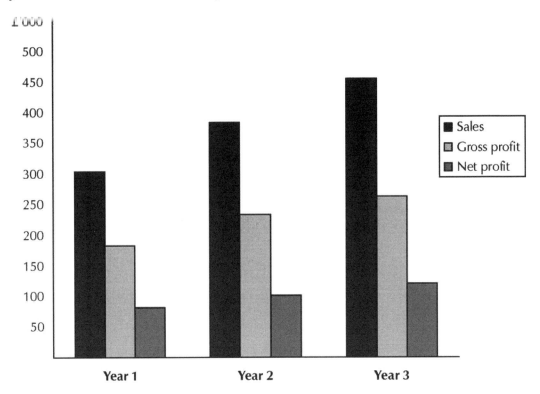

DIVISIONAL SALES

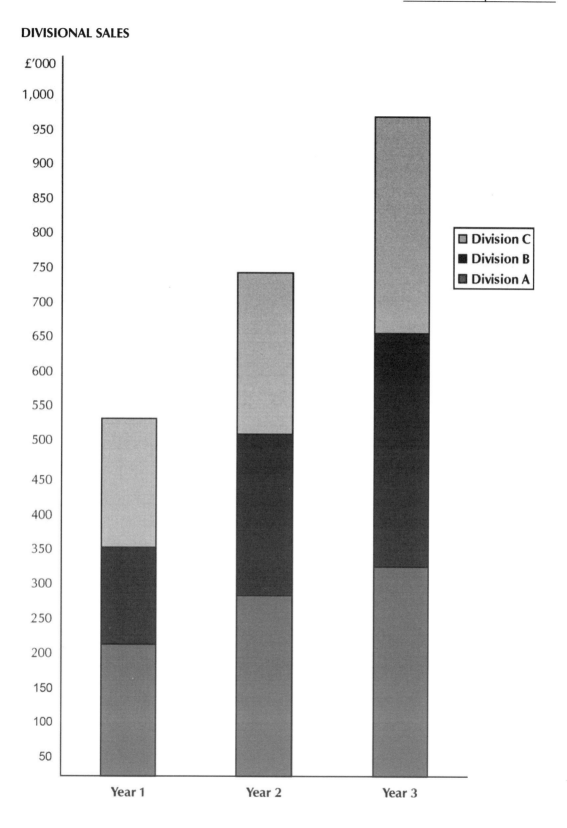

5   **DIVISIONAL SALES**

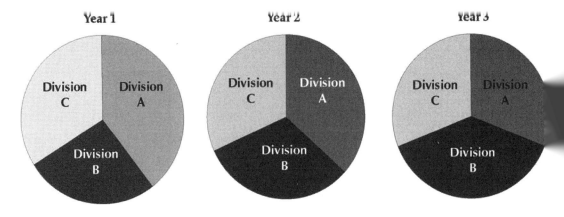

6   **MONTHLY SALES – APRIL TO JUNE**

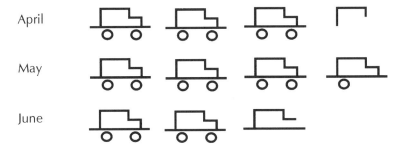

SALES, GROSS PROFIT AND NET PROFIT

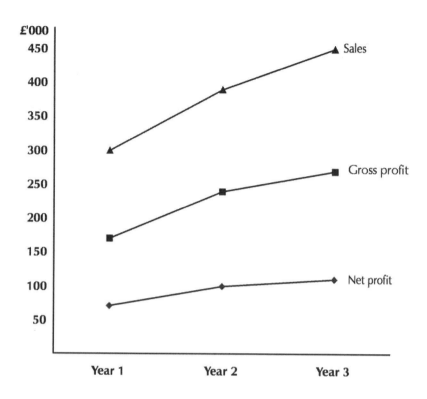

CHAPTER 14 Reporting figures over time

Average number of employees $= \dfrac{2,340 + 2,860 + 2,280}{3}$

$\qquad\qquad\qquad\qquad\quad = 2,493$

	£	Moving average £
March	125,600	–
April	135,800	130,200
May	129,200	132,867
June	133,600	133,900
July	138,900	138,367
August	142,600	–

3

		Moving average	Centred average Trend
	£	£	£
1998	226,700		–
1999	236,500		–
		236,500	
2000	240,300		238,175
		239,850	
2001	242,500		240,988
		242,125	
2002	240,100		243,038
		243,950	
2003	245,600		244,663
		245,375	
2004	247,600		
2005	248,200		

4

	A	B	C
1	January	47,600	
2	February	48,100	=(B1+B2+B3)/3
3	March	50,200	=(B2+B3+B4)/3
4	April	45,300	=(B3+B4+B5)/3
5	May	44,900	=(B4+B5+B6)/3
6	June	42,700	=(B5+B6+B7)/3
7	July	41,100	=(B6+B7+B8)/3
8	August	42,700	=(B7+B8+B9)/3
9	September	45,900	=(B8+B9+B10)/3
10	October	48,600	=(B9+B10+B11)/3
11	November	49,900	=(B10+B11+B12)/3
12	December	51,500	

5

		£	Index
2005	Quarter 1	35,600	100.0
	Quarter 2	32,100	90.2
	Quarter 3	38,700	108.7
	Quarter 4	33,400	93.8
2006	Quarter 1	36,500	102.5
	Quarter 2	31,400	88.2
	Quarter 3	40,200	112.9
	Quarter 4	36,800	103.4

		Sales £	RPI	Adjusted sales £
2005	June	33,100	171.1	33,100
	July	33,800	170.5	33,919
	Aug	33,600	170.8	33,659
	Sept	34,600	171.7	34,479
	Oct	35,800	171.6	35,696
	Nov	35,100	172.1	34,896
	Dec	35,600	172.1	35,393
2006	Jan	34,700	171.1	34,700
	Feb	35,900	172.0	35,712
	Mar	36,200	172.2	35,969
	Apr	36,500	173.1	36,078
	May	36,700	174.2	36,047

CHAPTER 15 External reporting

Population and migration

MASTER CRAFTSMAN'S GUILD

AGED DEBTOR QUESTIONNAIRE

Business name and address:

Total debtors at 30 April 2006   £37,364

Ageing of debtors:

Current   £17,668

30 to 60 days   £15,490

60 to 90 days   £3,669

More than 90 days   £537

Do you offer a settlement discount for early payment?   Yes / (No)

Please note that all information provided will be treated in the strictest confidence. Thank you for your co-operation.

CHAPTER 16 Value added tax

1 Input tax   –   Business B
     Output tax   –   Business A

2 20 May 2006

3

	£
Goods total	1,000
Less: trade discount	200
	800
Less: settlement discount	16
	784

VAT £784.00 x 17.5% = £137.20

4 VAT   =   £51.11 x 7/47
            =   £7.61

CHAPTER 17 VAT records

1 Expenditure on:

- telephone calls from public or private telephones
- purchases through coin operated machines
- car park charges

– provided that they are for £25 or less including the VAT

2 EU acquisitions are shown as both input tax and output tax on the VAT return.

HAPTER 1 Management information

Cost information is used in the management of an organisation. It is used in decision-making, particularly in deciding which products to make and what price should be charged. It is used in planning, particularly in the preparation of budgets which set out the future activities of the business in terms of costs and when they will arise. It is also used in control, which entails monitoring of actual costs, comparison with expected costs, and taking action when there are significant variances.

	Capital	Revenue
A new telephone system. This will be used within the business for several accounting periods. All the associated costs of installation can be capitalised.	✓	
Depreciation of vehicles. Depreciation can be thought of as the way in which part of a capital cost is converted to a revenue expense.		✓
Salesman's car. A company car is used by the salesman to obtain benefits for the business in the form of sales.	✓	
Road fund license for delivery van. Although the van is a capital item, the road fund license is a revenue expense of running the van.		✓
Telephone bill. The bill for rental and calls on the telephone system is a revenue expense.		✓
Computer software. Another example of something which is used by the business to bring benefits. The software might be used for the main business activity, such as in design of buildings by an architect, or in the processing of information necessary to administer the business	✓	
Repairs to the Managing Director's company car after an accident. This will not improve the earnings capacity of the car; it just restores it to what it was before.		✓

3 a) **Fixed costs**

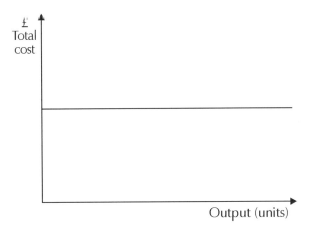

b) **Fixed cost per unit**

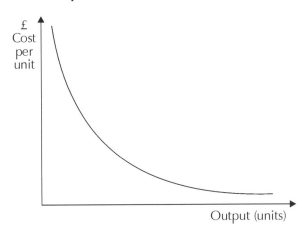

4

		Cost behaviour	
		Does fit the graph shape	**Does not fit th graph shape**
a)	Plastic used in the manufacture of moulded plastic furniture. A bulk-buying discount is given at point A on the graph.		✓
b)	Straight-line depreciation of a freehold factory. A new factory is bought at point A.	✓	
c)	Rent of a warehouse. A further warehouse is rented at point A.	✓	
d)	Electricity costs which have a standing charge and a cost per unit of power used. At point A the level of production reaches the point where a nightshift is required, which uses electricity at a cheaper rate.		✓

a) This is a variable cost. The bulk purchase discount would give a one-off kink in the graph at point A. The graph would appear as shown below.

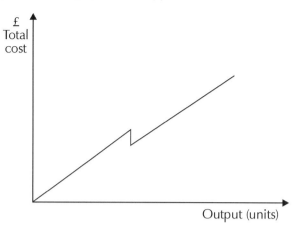

b) and c) are both step-fixed costs and will fit the graph shape.

d) This is a semi-variable cost. At point A, where the cheaper rate of electricity kicks-in, the graph will flatten as each unit of product will cost slightly less in electricity. This is illustrated in the graph below.

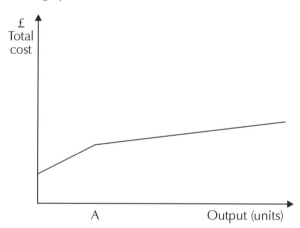

Output (units)		Total cost £
Highest	13,500	31,500
Lowest	6,500	17,500
High-low	7,000	14,000

$$\text{Variable cost per unit} = \frac{\text{High cost} - \text{low cost}}{\text{High output} - \text{low outpu}}$$

$$= \frac{£14,000}{7,000}$$

$$= £2$$

At 6,500 units

	£
Total cost	17,300
Less: variable cost (6,500 x £2)	13,000
= fixed cost	4,500

Using the fixed cost of £4,500 units, and the variable cost of £2 per unit, we can now estimate the total cost at 12,000 units:

	£
Fixed cost	4,500
Add: variable cost (12,000 x £2)	24,000
Total cost	28,500

6

COST CARD: Filing Cabinet

	£
Direct materials (3.8 + 1.8 + 0.9)	6.50
Direct labour	6.70
Prime cost	13.20
Production overheads (0.3 + 0.2)	0.50
Production cost	13.70
Non-production overheads	
– selling and distribution	3.00
Total cost	16.70

CHAPTER 2 Materials costs

1   The details that would be found on a purchase order are:

- Sequential number: so that all purchase orders can be accounted for and as a reference number for that particular order. If the purchase orders are filed sequentially it will be easy to find any order needed

- Date of the order: any long outstanding orders that have not been fulfilled can be chased up

- Delivery date required: this will usually be agreed with the supplier and may be crucial to ensure that production is not disrupted or customers are not inconvenienced

- Reference to the purchase requisition: so that the chain of events can be followed and to show that the purchase order was validly made in response to a requisition

- Name and address of the supplier: this is where the purchase order is sent

- Delivery address: as this is sometimes different from the address on the letterhead of the business

- The quantity, description and cost of the materials ordered: to confirm exactly what is required

	Raw materials	WIP	Finished goods
Bricks at a brick-making factory			✓
Bricks in stores at a building company	✓		
The ingredients for making bricks	✓*		
A brick that has been moulded but not fired in the kiln		✓	

* If the ingredients are stored separately in the stores, they are raw materials. However, if they have been requisitioned from stores and are assembled ready for mixing and making into bricks, they are WIP.

A materials requisition note is a document that is completed by the production department to request material from stores. It has to be signed by the foreman in charge of the relevant job or production line. It is therefore the authority stores need for issuing stock, but it is also used as the source document to charge the user department or job with that cost and to update the stock records (bin card and stores ledger card).

a)   **FIFO**

	Stock Record Card							
	Purchases			Sales			Balance	
Date	Quantity (kg)	Cost £	Total cost £	Quantity	Cost £	Total cost £	Quantity	Total cost £
3 Jan							100	880
16 Jan	400	9.00	3,600				500	4,480
27 Jan				100	8.80	880		
				150	9.00	1,350		
				250		2,230	250	2,250
5 Feb				180	9.00	1,620	70	630
9 Feb	400	9.30	3,720				470	4,350
17 Feb				70	9.00	630		
				350	9.30	3,255		
				420		3,885	50	465
25 Feb	500	9.35	4,675				550	5,140

Cost of material issues = £2,230 + £1,620 + £3,885
                        = £7,735

Value of closing stock   =£5,140

b) **LIFO**

Stock Record Card

Date	Purchases			Sales			Balance	
	Quantity (kg)	Cost £	Total cost £	Quantity	Cost £	Total cost £	Quantity	Total co £
3 Jan							100	88C
16 Jan	400	9.00	3,600				500	4,48C
27 Jan				250	9.00	2,250	250	2,23C
5 Feb				150	9.00	1,350		
				30	8.80	264		
				180		1,614	70	61€
9 Feb	400	9.30	3,720				470	4,33€
17 Feb				400	9.30	3,720		
				20	8.80	176		
				420		3,896	50	440
25 Feb	500	9.35	4,675				550	5,11£

Cost of material issues = £2,250 + £1,614 + £3,896
= £7,760

Value of closing stock = £5,115

c) **AVCO**

Stock Record Card

Date	Purchases			Sales			Balance	
	Quantity (kg)	Cost £	Total cost £	Quantity	Cost £	Total cost £	Quantity	Total cc £
3 Jan							100	88(
16 Jan	400	9.00	3,600				500	4,48(
27 Jan				250	8.96	2,240	250	2,24(
5 Feb				180	8.96	1,612.80	70	627.2
9 Feb	400	9.30	3,720				470	4,347..
17 Feb				420	9,249	3,884.58	50	462.6
25 Feb	500	9.35	4,675				550	5,137.•

Cost of material issues = £2,240.00 + £1,612.80 + £3,884.58
= £7,737.38

Value of closing stock = £5,137.62

5   The LIFO method of valuing materials has the advantage of being fairly easy to calculate a understand. Materials issues tend to be at current prices which makes managers more aware of prevailing prices.

There are several disadvantages of LIFO. Prices charged for issues will constantly change, wh makes managers' job of decision-making more difficult. The calculations are sometir cumbersome, as there may be part-batches of unused old prices that have to be carried forwa for when stocks run low and they are needed. The LIFO cost flow assumption, that the latest deliveries are used first, is rarely the case in practice, and it can therefore be argued that it is not appropriate. The Inland Revenue and Accounting Standards do not approve of LIFO for tax or financial reporting purposes.

Materials control account

		£			£
1 Mar	Opening balance	12,400	31 Mar	WIP	160,400
31 Mar	Bank/creditors	167,200	31 Mar	Production o/h control	8,300
			31 Mar	Closing balance	10,900
		179,600			179,600

Work in progress control account

		£		£
31 Mar	Materials control	160,400		

Production overhead control account

		£		£
31 Mar	Materials control	8,300		

Holding costs: warehouse rent, insurance, and cost of capital tied up.

Ordering costs: postage of order, wages for the checkers in the goods inwards department, salary of the clerk dealing with the order.

(Note. These are only suggestions. Refer to the section entitled 'Stock control for more examples.)

If the reorder quantity were increased, fewer orders would be needed each year to obtain the same overall quantity of stock, leading to a decrease in ordering costs. However, the amount of stock stored at any point in time would be greater so holding costs would increase.

$$EOQ = \sqrt{\frac{2cd}{h}}$$

$$= \sqrt{\frac{2 \times £50 \times (15 \times 52)}{£19.65}}$$

$$= \sqrt{3,969}$$

$$= 63 \text{ rolls}$$

Reorder level   = maximum usage x maximum lead time
     = 200 litres per day x 8 days
     = 1,600 litres

CHAPTER 3 Labour costs and expenses

1

OPERATION CARD				

Operator	Mary Dunnock		**Works order No** 1492	
Clock No	16		**Part No**	233
Week ending	7.7.06		**Description**	Wooden lids

Operation Sanding top and bottom surface using grade 2 sandpaper

Quantity produced	Quantity rejected	Good production	Rate £	£
Monday 350	12	338	0.14	47.32
Tuesday 428	21	407		56.98
Wednesday 483	2	481		67.34
Thursday 376	14	362		50.68
Friday 295	18	277		38.78

Employee number ....*LGS*............   Date ....*7.7.06*.........

Employee signature ......*PGL*..........

Supervisor's signature ......*M Dunnock*......

Gross pay =

	£
	47.32
	56.98
	67.34
	50.68
	38.78
	261.10

	J Sparrow	K Finch	M Swallow	B Cuckoo
Total hours	39.5	37.5	38.75	37.5
Basic pay (35 x £7)	£245.00	£245.00	£245.00	£245.00
Time and a half	(1.5 x £10.50) = £15.75	(2.5 x £10.50) = £26.25	(1.75 x £10.50) = £18.38	(0.5 x £10.50) = £5.25
Double time	(3 x £14 = £42.00		(2 x £14) = £28.00	(2 x £14) = £28.00
Total gross pay	£302.75	£271.25	£291.38	£278.25

Direct labour cost =   40h x £10 per h = £400
Indirect labour cost =   5h x   £4 per h =   £20

Alternatively:

£

Direct cost

Basic pay (35h x £10 per h)   350
Overtime: at basic rate (5h x £10 per h)   50
                                                                                          400

Indirect cost
Overtime: premium (5h x £4 per h)   20

Rather than paying just a time rate or a salary, an employer can make use of a bonus system to give employees an incentive to increase production. The bonus is paid if output is higher than a target level. The target set might be a certain time taken to do a job or a certain level of profit earned, or it might be judgmental, for example, management makes the decision as to who receives a bonus. Piecework, whereby employees are paid for each good unit of output, is another incentive scheme.

The major problem with these two methods of remuneration is that they reward quantity and not quality. Therefore, whilst output increases, there can be a consequent fall in quality and increased wastage. More inspectors will be needed to offset this problem, but this will add to costs. Other problems can arise from the complexity of the schemes adopted: they often involve more complex calculations and pay negotiations are more complicated. Bonus and piecework systems are not appropriate for all types of employees, and pay will be affected by production problems even when a guaranteed minimum amount is built into a piecework scheme.

Straight line method

$$\text{Charge for the year} = \frac{£20,000 - £1,000}{8}$$

$$= £2,375$$

Reducing balance method

Charge for the year = 20% x £20,000 (there is no accumulated depreciation at the end of the
first year)

= £4,000

Machine-hour method

$$\text{Charge for the year} = \frac{£20,000 - £1,000}{40,000} \times 8,000$$

Charge for the year = £3,800

The straight-line method does not reflect the use the asset gets and would therefore not
appropriate in this case. The reducing balance method would charge less depreciation as t
machine ages, which would give an approximation to a reduced usage as breakdowns increas
The best method, though, would be the machine hour method, which charges depreciation
proportion to the amount of use the machine actually has.

CHAPTER 4 Overheads

1 a)   Basis of apportionment

	Total £	Machine shop £	Assembly £	Painting £	Services £
Factory rent, rates and insurance (floor area) 5:2:3:2	9,000	3,750	1,500	2,250	1,500
Depreciation of machinery (value of machinery) 12:4:3:1	4,000	2,400	800	600	200
Supervisor's salary (number of employees) 8:9:5:2	8,000	2,667	3,000	1,667	666
Heat and light (floor area) 5:2:3:2	2,000	833	333	500	334
Apportionment to all departments	23,000	9,650	5,633	5,017	2,700

b)

Reapportionment of Services (40:30:30)	–	1,080	810	810	(2,700)
Total after reapportionment	23,000	10,730	6,443	5,827	Nil

a) **Basis of apportionment**

	Total	V	W	S1	S2
	£	£	£	£	£
Indirect materials	310,000	160,000	120,000	10,000	20,000
Indirect labour	1,125,000	400,000	650,000	40,000	35,000
Buildings depreciation and insurance (volume occupied) 60:30:8:2	100,000	60,000	30,000	8,000	2,000
Cleaning (volume occupied) 60:30:8:2	25,000	15,000	7,500	2,000	500
Machinery depreciation and insurance (value of machinery) 380:600:0:20	1,500,000	570,000	900,000	–	30,000
Supervision of production (supervisor hours) 15:20:0:0	70,000	30,000	40,000		
Power (% of power usage) 25:45:20:10	250,000	62,500	112,500	50,000	25,000
Heat and light (volume occupied) 60:30:8:2	20,000	12,000	6,000	1,600	400
Total after allocation and apportionment	3,400,000	1,309,500	1,866,000	111,600	112,900

b)

Reapportionment
(step-down method)

	Total	V	W	S1	S2
S2 first 40:50:10		45,160	56,450	11,290	(112,900)
				122,890	
S1 next 40:60		49,156	73,734	(122,890)	
Total after reapportionment	3,400,000	1,403,816	1,996,184	nil	nil

c) **Overhead absorption rates**

	V	W
$\dfrac{\text{Overheads}}{\text{Direct labour hours}} =$	$\dfrac{1,403,816}{200,000}$	$\dfrac{1,996,184}{500,000}$
	= £7.02 per direct labour hour	= £3.99 per direct labour hour

3   Department P1 = $\dfrac{£50,000}{2,500\,h}$

   = £20 per direct labour hour

   Department P2 = $\dfrac{£60,000}{4,000\,h}$

   = £15 per machine hour

Direct labour hours was chosen as the basis for absorption of the overheads of department P1
this department is labour intensive, and there is likely to be a link between the direct labour ho
worked and the overheads incurred. Similarly, with department P2, which is more mechanised a
less dependent upon direct labour, the use of the machinery is more likely to be related
overheads in that department.

4   a)

	£
Actual overheads	1,600
Absorbed overheads (650 units @ £3 per unit)	1,950
Over absorption	350

The over absorption of £350 would be added to profit (a credit) in the profit and I
account.

   b)

	£
Actual overheads	8,600
Absorbed overheads (590h x £15* per h)	8,850
Over absorption	250

   * Overhead absorption rate = $\dfrac{£9,000}{600\ \text{direct labour hours}}$ = £15 per direct labour hou

The over absorption of £250 would be added to profit (a credit) in the profit and I
account.

   c)

	£
Actual overheads	3,500
Absorbed overheads (552h x £5)	2,760
Under absorption	740

The under absorption of £740 would be deducted from profit (a debit) in the profit a
loss account.

CHAPTER 5 Absorption costing and marginal costing

In an absorption costing system all fixed production overheads are absorbed into the cost of the products and are included in unit cost. In a marginal costing system the fixed production overheads are written off in the profit and loss account as a period cost.

a) Absorption costing - unit cost

	£
Direct materials	12.50
Direct labour assembly (4 x £8.40)	33.60
finishing	6.60
Assembly overheads (£336,000/(60,000 x 4) x 4)	5.60
Finishing overheads (£84,000/60,000)	1.40
	59.70

b) Marginal costing - unit cost

	£
Direct materials	12.50
Direct labour assembly (4 x £8.40)	33.60
finishing	6.60
Assembly overheads $\dfrac{£336,000 \times 60\%}{240,000}$ x 4	3.36
Finishing overheads $\dfrac{£84,000 \times 75\%}{60,000}$	1.05
	57.11

Unit cost

	£
Direct materials	12.00
Direct labour	8.00
Variable overhead (£237,000/15,000)	15.80
Marginal costing unit cost	35.80
Fixed overhead (£390,000/15,000)	26.00
Absorption costing unit cost	61.80

a) i) Absorption costing - profit and loss account

	November £	November £	December £	December £
Sales (12,500/18,000 x £75)		937,500		1,350,000
Less: cost of sales				
Opening stock				
(2,000 x £61.80)	123,600			
(4,500 x £61.80)			278,100	
Production costs				
(15,000 x £61.80)	927,000		927,000	
	1,050,600		1,205,100	
Less: closing stock				
(4,500 x £61.80)	278,100			
(1,500 x £61.80)			92,700	
		772,500		1,112,400
Profit		165,000		237,600

ii) Marginal costing - profit and loss account

	November £	November £	December £	December £
Sales (12,500/18,000 x £75)		937,500		1,350,000
Less: cost of sales				
Opening stock				
(2,000 x £35.80)	71,600			
(4,500 x £35.80)			161,100	
Production costs				
(15,000 x £35.80)	537,000		537,000	
	608,600		698,100	
Less: closing stock				
(4,500 x £35.80)	161,100			
(1,500 x £35.80)			53,700	
		447,500		644,400
Contribution		490,000		705,600
Less: fixed overheads		390,000		390,000
Profit		100,000		315,600

b)

	November £	December £
Absorption costing profit	165,000	237,600
Increase in stocks x fixed cost per unit		
((4,500 - 2,000) x £26)	(65,000)	
Decrease in stocks x fixed cost per unit		
((4,500 - 1,500) x £26)		78,000
Marginal costing profit	100,000	315,600

HAPTER 6 Costing systems

	£
Direct materials – fabric	590.00
– lining	175.00
Labour 27 hours @ £7.70	207.90
Overheads 27 hours @ £8.70	234.90
a) **Cost of production**	1,207.80
Profit 15% x 1,207.80	181.17
	1,388.97
VAT at 17.5%	243.06
b) **Final quote to the customer**	1,632.03

	£
Job costing schedule	
Materials	12,500.00
Direct labour – fitting 23 hours @ £8.60	197.80
– decorating 5 hours @ 6.50	32.50
Overheads 28 hours @ £12.40	347.20
Total costs	13,077.50
Profit 25% x 13,077.50	3,269.38
	16,346.88
VAT at 17.5%	2,860.70
Cost to the customer	19,207.58

3

	£
Ingredients	840.00
Labour 7 hours @ £6.50	45.50
Overheads 7 hours @ £1.20	8.40
	893.90

Cost per pie $= \dfrac{£893.90}{1,200}$

$\qquad\quad = \quad$ 74.5 pence

4 Step 1 Calculate the number of normal loss units:

50,000 kg x 5% = 2,500 kg

Step 2 Calculate the expected output from the process:

50,000 kg - 2,500 kg = 47,500 kg

Step 3 Total the process costs:

£350,000 + £125,000 + £57,000 = £532,000

Step 4   Calculate the cost per unit of expected output

$$\frac{£532,000}{47,500kg} = £11.20 \text{ per kg}$$

Process account

	kg	£		kg	£
Materials	50,000	350,000	Normal loss	2,500	–
Labour		125,000	Abnormal loss	1,500	16,800
Overheads		57,000	Output	46,000	515,200
	50,000	532,000		50,000	532,000

Abnormal loss account

	kg	£		kg	£
Process account	1,500	16,800			

5   **Step 1**   Calculate the number of normal loss units:

6,000 ltr x 10% = 600 ltr

Step 2   Calculate the expected output from the process:

6,000 ltr - 600 ltr = 5,400 ltr

Step 3   Total the process costs:

£14,300 + £7,200 + £11,980 = £33,480

Step 4   Calculate the cost per unit of expected output

$$\frac{£33,480}{5,400 \text{ ltr}} = £6.20 \text{ per litre}$$

Process account

	ltr	£		ltr	£
Materials	6,000	14,300	Normal loss	600	–
Labour		7,200			
Overheads		11,980			
Abnormal gain	200	1,240	Output	5,600	34,720
	6,200	34,720		6,200	34,720

Abnormal gain

	ltr	£		ltr	£
			Process account	200	1,240

Step 1   Calculate the number of normal loss units:

40,000 kg x 8% = 3,200 kg

Step 2   Calculate the expected output from the process:

40,000 kg - 3,200 kg = 36,800 kg

Step 3   Total the process costs and deduct the scrap proceeds for the normal loss :

(£158,200 + £63,500 + £31,740) - (3,200 x £1) = £250,240

Step 4   Calculate the cost per unit of expected output

$$\frac{£250,240}{36,800 \text{ kg}} = £6.80 \text{ per kg}$$

Process account

	kg	£		kg	£
Materials	40,000	158,200	Normal loss	3,200	3,200
Labour		63,500	Abnormal loss	1,800	12,240
Overheads		31,740	Output	35,000	238,000
	40,000	253,440		40,000	253,440

Abnormal loss account

	kg	£		kg	£
Process account	1,800	12,240	Scrap	1,800	1,800
			Profit and loss a/c	1,800	10,440
	1,800	12,240		1,800	12,240

	Units	**Materials**		**Labour/overheads**	
		Proportion complete	**Equivalent units**	**Proportion complete**	**Equivalent units**
Completed units	2,000	100%	2,000	100%	2,000
Closing work in progress	400	60%	240	50%	200
Total equivalent units			2,240		2,200
Cost per equivalent unit			$\frac{£8,960}{2,240}$		$\frac{£4,290}{2,200}$
			= £4.00 per EU		= £1.95 per EU

Valuation £

Completed units
    Materials (2,000 x £4.00)   8,000
    Labour/overheads (2,000 x £1.95)   3,900
            11,900

Closing work in progress
    Materials (240 x £4.00)   960
    Labour/overheads (200 x £1.95)   390
            1,350

Process account

	£		£
Materials	8,960	Completed units	11,900
Labour/overheads	4,290	Closing work in progress	1,350
	13,250		13,250

CHAPTER 7 Cost bookkeeping

1

Materials control account

	£		£
Creditors control	4,380	WIP control	4,190

Wages control account

	£		£
Bank	4,140	WIP control	3,200
		Production overhead control	940

Production overhead control account

	£		£
Bank	1,200	WIP control 480 hours @ £3.10	1,488
Wages control	940	Under absorbed overhead	652

Work in progress control account

	£		£
Materials control	4,190	Finished goods	7,900
Wages control	3,200		
Production overhead control	1,488		

Production overhead control account

	£		£
Overhead incurred	3,800	Overhead absorbed	
		550 @ £6.80	3,740
		Under absorbed overhead	60
	3,800		3,800

The balance on the account, representing under absorbed overheads, is debited to the profit and loss account.

Materials control account

	£		£
Opening balance	550	WIP control	4,670
Creditors control	5,300	Administration overhead	760
		Closing balance	420
	5,850		5,850

Wages control account

	£		£
Bank (2,520 + 640)	3,160	WIP control	2,520
		Production overhead control	640
	3,160		3,160

Production overhead control account

	£		£
Wages control	640	WIP control 360 @ £7.80	2,808
Bank	2,700	Under absorbed overhead	532
	3,340		3,340

Work in progress control account

	£		£
Opening balance	680	Finished goods	10,000
Materials control	4,670		
Wages control	2,520		
Production overhead control	2,808	Closing balance	678
	10,678		10,678

Finished goods control account

	£		£
Opening balance	1,040	Cost of sales (bal fig)	9,030
WIP control	10,000	Closing stock	2,010
	11,040		11,040

Debtors control account

	£		£
Opening balance	3,700	Bank	11,000
Sales	12,000	Closing balance	4,700
	15,700		15,700

Creditors control account

	£		£
Bank	5,140	Opening balance	2,100
Closing balance	2,260	Materials control	5,300
	7,400		7,400

Cash at bank account

	£		£
Opening balance	2,090	Wages control	3,160
Debtors control	11,000	Creditors control	5,140
		Production overhead control	2,700
		Administration overhead control	1,580
		Closing balance	510
	13,090		13,090

Administration overheads account

	£		£
Materials control	760	Profit and loss	2,340
Bank	1,580		
	2,340		2,340

Sales account

	£		£
		Debtors control	12,000

4   Profit and loss account

	£
Sales	12,000
Cost of sales	9,030
Gross profit	2,970
Administration overhead	(2,340)
Under absorbed production overhead	(532)
Net profit	98

CHAPTER 8 Short-term decision making

As activity levels increase the fixed costs will be split amongst more units, and the amount of fixed cost in unit cost will get smaller. With no change in selling cost or variable cost the total unit cost will decrease.

Break-even point $= \dfrac{£360,000}{£57 - £45}$

$= 30,000$ units

Margin of safety $= \dfrac{38,000 - 30,000}{38,000}$

$= 21\%$

Target profit sales $= \dfrac{£910,000 + £500,000}{£24 - £17}$

$= 201,429$ units

Profit volume ratio $= \dfrac{£(40 - 32)}{£40} \times 100$

$= 20\%$

Target profit sales revenue $= \dfrac{£100,000 + £200,000}{0.20}$

$= £1,500,000$

Resource requirements for maximum demand

	R	S	T	Total
Materials	80,000 kg	120,000 kg	25,000 kg	225,000 kg
Labour hours	20,000 hours	80,000 hours	5,000 hours	105,000 hours
Machine hours	60,000 hours	80,000 hours	15,000 hours	155,000 hours

Therefore the machine hours available are the limiting factor.

Contribution per machine hour

	R	S	T
Contribution	£6	£12	£6
Machine hours	6	4	3
Contribution/machine hour	£1.00	£3.00	£2.00
Ranking	3	1	2

Production plan

	Units produced	Machine hours used
S	20,000	80,000
T	5,000	15,000
R (balance)	4,166	24,996
		119,996

Profit

	£
R (4,166 x £6)	24,996
S (20,000 x £12)	240,000
T (5,000 x £6)	30,000
	294,996
Less: fixed costs	50,000
Profit	244,996

CHAPTER 9 Long-term decision making

1 a) **Payback period - Investment A**

Date	Cash flow £	Cumulative cash flow £
30 June 2007	43,000	43,000
30 June 2008	51,000	94,000
30 June 2009	52,000	146,000

$$2 \text{ years } + \frac{£26,000}{£52,000} \times 12 \text{ months}$$

= 2 years and 6 months

Payback period - Investment B

Date	Cash flow £	Cumulative cash flow £
30 June 2007	21,000	21,000
30 June 2008	21,000	42,000
30 June 2009	21,000	63,000
30 June 2010	21,000	84,000
30 June 2011	40,000	124,000

$$4 \text{ years } + \frac{£16,000}{£40,000} \times 12 \text{ months}$$

= 4 years and 5 months

Therefore only Investment A would be accepted.

b)   The payback period method is only concerned with how quickly the initial cost of the investment is repaid from cash inflows. It ignores any cash flows after the payback period. In this case only Investment A would be accepted under the payback method; however, overall, Investment B has greater total cash flows and a lower initial investment than Investment A.

a)   £3,100 x 0.7312   =   £2,266.72

b)   £15,000 x 1.000   =   £15,000.00

c)   £1,000 x 1.6901   =   £1,690.10

d)   £4,400 x 0.8734   =   £3,842.96

Net present value   =   (£80,000 x 5.5348) - £500,000

                     =   - £57,216

As this is a negative net present value then the business should not invest in the new production line.

Present value = $\dfrac{£80}{0.08}$

                = £1,000

Year	Cash flows £	Discount factor @ 7%	Present value £
0	(340,000)	1.000	(340,000)
1	80,000	0.9346	74,768
2	70,000	0.8734	61,138
3	90,000	0.8163	73,467
4	120,000	0.7629	91,548
5	60,000	0.7130	42,780
Net present value			3,701

Remember that depreciation is not a cash flow and is therefore excluded from the net present value calculations.

a)

Year	Cash flows £	Discount factor @ 11%	Present value £
0	(90,000)	1.000	(90,000)
1	23,000	0.9009	20,721
2	31,000	0.8116	25,160
3	40,000	0.7312	29,248
4	18,000	0.6587	11,857
Net present value			(3,014)

b)   As the investment in the new plant and machinery has a negative net present value at the cost of capital of 11% then the investment should not take place.

CHAPTER 10 Internal information

1   a)   Production supervisor

- hours worked in total
- overtime hours worked
- labour costs for the month
- absentee levels
- productivity levels

b)   Managing director

- total labour cost for the period
- any significant variances from budget for labour hours or costs

The reason for the different information required by the two people is due to the different nature of their roles within the organisation. The production supervisor is concerned with the daily detail of the production labour force. The managing director however will only require information regarding any significant variances from budget for control purposes and any other specific information that might be required for decision making.

2   The type of information that management are likely to require to take this decision will include:

- the cost of manufacturing the Hedgit
- the selling price of the Hedgit
- market demand
- the resources used in manufacture of the Hedgit – labour, machinery etc
- any alternative uses for the resources used by the Hedgit

3   a)   Manufacturer of double glazed window units:

- materials cost of the units
- labour cost
- production overheads
- sales revenue
- number of employees
- number of units manufactured

b)   Private nursing home

- revenue
- staff costs
- other costs
- number of rooms
- number of occupants

c)   Firm of solicitors

- revenue
- staff costs
- other overheads
- chargeable hours
- non-chargeable hours
- number of qualified and non-qualified staff

d)   Transport organisation

- revenue
- transport costs
- staff costs
- other overheads
- number of lorries
- number of drivers
- number of miles travelled

	£
Sales (163,500 + 104,700 + 126,500)	394,700
Cost of sales (101,400 + 64,500 + 78,400)	244,300
Gross profit	150,400
Other expenses (35,900 + 23,000 + 27,800)	86,700
Net profit	63,700

	£
Sales (368,900 + 286,300 − 31,600)	623,600
Cost of sales (236,700 + 183,200 − 31,600)	388,300
Gross profit	235,300
Production overheads (88,500 + 71,500)	160,000
Net profit	75,300

CHAPTER 11   Performance measures

		February	March	April	May
a)	**Productivity per labour hour** Output/hours worked – units per hour	10.4	10.6	10.6	10.2
b)	**Productivity index** Output/budgeted output x 100	97.6%	106.3%	101.8%	97.1%

		April	May	June	Total
a)	**Productivity per labour hour** Output/hours worked	10.8	10.2	10.6	10.5
b)	**Productivity index** Actual output/budgeted output	100.4%	97.9%	86.8%	94.8%
c)	**Labour utilisation** Hours worked/hours available	93.3%	96.4%	91.3%	93.8%
d)	**Cost per unit** Production costs/output	£3.46	£3.30	£3.50	£3.41
e)	**Machine utilisation** Revenue/machine hours	£75.00	£65.83	£67.13	£69.09

3

	July – Sept	Oct – Dec	Jan – March	April – June	Total
a) **Productivity** Holidays sold/7	1,185	886	1,400	1,029	4,500
b) **Productivity index** Holidays sold/budgeted holidays	110.7%	88.6%	89.1%	90.0%	94.0%
c) **Cost per holiday**	£12.59	£17.77	£11.89	£15.14	£13.97

The cost per holiday ranges from £11.89 to £17.77. The main reason for this is probably that m
of the costs of the business are fixed costs. This means that they are expenses that will be incur
no matter how many holidays are sold, such as rent of the shop and salaries of the s
representatives. Therefore the cost per holiday will depend almost totally on the number
holidays sold in the quarter – if the holidays sold are high then the cost per holiday will be f
low and vice versa.

4

a)	July – Sept	Oct – Dec	Jan – March	April – June
Productivity index Actual hours/standard hours	109.4%	118.8%	105.0%	102.5%
Productivity per employee Cases/employees	10.5	11.25	11.5	12.0
Productivity per hour Cases/hours	0.24	0.24	0.27	0.29
Asset turnover Sales/capital	£2.26	£2.41	£2.02	£2.08

b) The introduction of the additional capital has caused a reduction in the asset turnove
although revenue has increased since January there is also a £30,000 increase in capital.
introduction of the two new qualified staff has however had a positive effect in term
productivity. The additional staff has meant that less overtime has been worked in the sec
half of the year with the productivity index reducing. This was one of the aims of
additional employees in order to ease the workload in the first 6 months. The number of c
completed by employees each quarter is increasing and the number of cases completed e
hour is also increasing.

5

	Jan £000	Feb £000	Mar £000	April £000	May £000	June £000
Gross profit margin Gross profit/sales x 100	48.0%	43.3%	42.9%	37.5%	40.0%	38.2%
Net profit margin Net profit/sales x 100	14.0%	13.3%	11.4%	10.9%	12.0%	10.3%
Return on capital employed Net profit/capital	23.3%	26.7%	18.8%	18.4%	21.0%	17.5%
Asset turnover Sales/capital	£1.67	£2.00	£1.65	£1.68	£1.75	£1.70

Clearly over the last six months sales have increased significantly. However this appears to have been at the expense of profitability. The gross profit percentage has decreased from 48% to 38.2% and the net profit margin has fallen in line with this from 14% to 10.3%. This fall in profitability has affected the return on capital employed which has fallen from a high of 26.7% to 17.5%. However having said that, an 17.5% return on capital is still a healthy figure. The asset turnover, other than a sharp increase in February, has remained fairly constant showing that the sales revenue is still in line with the capital. If the problems with the gross profit margin can be solved then the business should be able to return to its former levels of profitability.

	July – Sept	Oct – Dec	Jan – March	April – June
Gross profit margin				
Gross profit/sales	45.2%	46.9%	48.5%	50.0%
Net profit margin				
Net profit/sales	14.5%	15.4%	17.4%	18.6%
Return on capital employed				
Net profit/capital	30.0%	33.3%	31.9%	36.1%
Asset turnover				
Sales/capital	£2.07	£2.17	£1.83	£1.94

Sales have increased by 12.9% over the year but the outstanding feature is the 28.3% increase in gross profit margin. This has almost been matched by an increase in net profit margin. This increased profitability is reflected in the increase in the return on capital employed even though the capital was increased in the third quarter. Asset turnover dropped when the additional capital was initially introduced but by the fourth quarter is rising again. Overall the business looks to be in a healthy state.

CHAPTER 12 Writing a report

REPORT

Report to: John Hartman – Sales Director

Report from: Philip Oliver – Accounts Assistant

Date: 15 July 2006

Terms of reference

This report has been written at the request of John Hartman, Sales Director, for the purpose of comparing the performance of the three stores in Worksop, Mansfield and Newark for the first six months of 2006.

Summary

All three stores are profitable although there is a wide range of gross profit margins. The most profitable store is Worksop although this store does have relatively high overheads. Mansfield makes the best use of its limited floor space and its employees.

Findings

All three stores have been profitable during the first six months of 2006. However there is a wide range of gross profit margins. Worksop has a gross profit margin of 60% whereas that of Mansfield is only 50%. If all three stores could achieve the gross profit margin of Worksop then this could improve the overall profitability.

However despite the range of gross profit margins the three net profit margins are fairly similar with Worksop achieving the highest at 13.3%. Similarly the return on capital employed of the three stores are all fairly similar ranging from 9.8% in Mansfield to 10.9% in Worksop. Clearly, despite the much better gross profit margin in Worksop, much of this is wiped out by higher overheads than the other two stores.

In terms of resource utilisation it would appear that Worksop may be incurring additional overheads due to over staffing. The sales per employee and sales per hour worked are both significantly lower than those of the other two stores.

Mansfield is the store which makes the best use of its space with the highest figure for sales per square metre. If the Mansfield store is lacking in floor space then this may be one of the reasons for its lower gross profit margin. If there is not enough space for high stock levels then Mansfield may not be able to take advantage of bulk purchase discounts that are available to the other two stores.

In terms of labour utilisation, Mansfield again has the highest sales per employee but the sales per hour are below those of Newark indicating that Mansfield may be paying its staff to work for too many hours.

Conclusion

All three stores are profitable with Worksop showing the highest gross and net profit margins, return on capital employed and asset turnover. Worksop is clearly using its capital well. There is however a wide range of gross profit margins. If the gross profit margins of the other two stores can be increased to that of Worksop then this could have a significant effect on their profitability.

Despite its profitability Worksop has the poorest labour utilisation figures, indicating that it may be overstaffed. Mansfield has the highest sales per square metre and the lowest floor space indicating that more floor space may be required here.

Recommendations

The range of gross profit margins should be investigated further in order to try to increase the gross profit margins of Mansfield and Newark to that of Worksop.

The overheads of Worksop should be investigated to discover why they are relatively high in comparison to the other two stores. In particular the staffing levels should be investigated.

The amount of floor space that Mansfield has should be investigated, as this may be causing problems leading to this store being the least profitable despite making the best use of its floor space and employees.

APPENDIX – PERFORMANCE INDICATORS

	Worksop	Mansfield	Newark
Gross profit margin	60.0%	50.0%	54.9%
Net profit margin	13.3%	12.1%	12.7%
Return on capital employed	10.9%	9.8%	10.0%
Asset turnover (per £ of capital employed)	£0.82	£0.80	£0.78
Sales per sq metre	£225	£236	£204
Sales per employee	£18,750	£22,000	£21,250
Sales per hour worked	£21.63	£23.57	£25.50

REPORT

Report to: Janis Robbins – Sales director

Report from: Kevin Burne – Accounts assistant

Date: 22 April 2006

Terms of reference

This report was requested by Janis Robbins, Sales director, in order to comment on the results of the business for the six months ending 31 March 2006.

Summary

The business still has a healthy return on capital employed but due to the substantial increase in sales there has been a sharp drop in profitability. The decrease in gross profit margin is the major problem and if this decline can be reversed then the business should be able to return to its earlier levels of profitability.

Findings

The sales have increased significantly over the six month period from £300,000 in October to a high of £420,000 in February. However this increase in turnover has been at the expense of profitability. As sales have increased the gross profit margin has fallen from 50% to 37.5%. The net profit margin has also fallen in line with this from almost 17% to about 9%.

This has had a similar effect on the return on capital employed which has dropped from 28% to 14.6%. However the 14.6% in March is still a reasonable level of return and in the earlier months the return was considerably higher than this.

Asset turnover has remained reasonably constant over the period and therefore the increased sales are still in line with the capital base.

Conclusion

The large increase in sales has been accompanied by a significant decline in the gross profit margin which in turn has led to a decrease in net profit margin and return on capital employed.

If the gross profit problems can be sorted out then there should be no reason why the business should not return it its former levels of profitability.

APPENDIX – PERFORMANCE INDICATORS

	Oct	Nov	Dec	Jan	Feb	Mar
Gross profit margin	50.0%	44.4%	44.1%	36.8%	40.5%	37.5%
Net profit margin	16.7%	13.9%	13.2%	10.5%	11.9%	8.8%
Return on capital employed	27.8%	27.8%	22.5%	17.4%	20.8%	14.6%
Asset turnover (per £ of capital employed)	£1.67	£2.00	£1.70	£1.65	£1.75	£1.67

CHAPTER 13 Tables and diagrams

1 i)

	A	B	C	D	E
1		February	March	April	May
2	Output - units	136,700	154,200	144,600	139,800
3	Budgeted output - units	140,000	145,000	142,000	144,000
4	Hours worked	13,200	14,600	13,600	13,700
5	Productivity per labour hour	=B2/B4	=C2/C4	=D2/D4	=E2/E4
6	Productivity index	=B2/B3*100	=C2/C3*100	=D2/D3*100	=E2/E3*100

Productivity per labour hour $= \dfrac{\text{Output in units}}{\text{Hours worked}}$

For February $= B2/B4$

Productivity index $= \dfrac{\text{Actual output}}{\text{Budgeted output}} \times 100$

For February $= B2/B3*100$

ii)

	A	B	C	D	E
1		February	March	April	May
2	Output - units	136,700	154,200	144,600	139,800
3	Budgeted output - units	140,000	145,000	142,000	144,000
4	Hours worked	13,200	14,600	13,600	13,700
5	Productivity per labour hour	10.4	10.6	10.6	10.2
6	Productivity index	97.6	106.3	101.8	97.1

a)

	A	B	C	D	E
1		April	May	June	Total
2	Production costs £	416,400	452,300	425,500	Sum(B2:D2)*
3	Output - units	120,500	137,000	121,500	Sum(B3:D3)
4	Hours worked	11,200	13,400	11,500	Sum(B4:D4)
5	Budgeted output	120,000	140,000	140,000	Sum(B5:D5)
6	Hours available	12,000	13,900	12,600	Sum(B6:D6)
7	Sales revenue £	765,000	790,000	725,000	Sum(B7:D7)
8	Machine hours	10,200	12,000	10,800	Sum(B8:D8)
9	Productivity per labour hour	=B3/B4	=C3/C4	=D3/D4	=E3/E4
10	Productivity index	=B3/B5*100	=C3/C5*100	=D3/D5*100	=E3/E5*100
11	Labour utilisation	=B4/B6*100	=C4/C6*100	=D4/D6*100	=E4/E6*100
12	Cost per unit £	=B2/B3	=C2/C3	=D2/D3	=E2/E3
13	Machine utilisation £	=B7/B8	=C7/C8	=D7/D8	=E7/E8

Productivity per labour hour $=$ $\dfrac{\text{Output in units}}{\text{Hours worked}}$

For April $=$ B3/B4

Productivity index $=$ $\dfrac{\text{Output in units}}{\text{Budgeted output}}$ x 100

For April $=$ B3/B5*100

Labour utilisation $=$ $\dfrac{\text{Hours worked}}{\text{Hours available}}$ x 100

For April $=$ B4/B6*100

Cost per unit $=$ $\dfrac{\text{Production costs}}{\text{Output in units}}$

For April $=$ B2/B3

Machine utilisation $=$ $\dfrac{\text{Sales revenue}}{\text{Machine hours}}$

For April $=$ B7/B8

*Alternatively totals can be found from the formula B2+C2+D2 etc.

b)

	A	B	C	D	E
1		April	May	June	Total
2	Production costs £	416,400	452,300	425,500	1,294,200
3	Output - units	120,500	137,000	121,500	379,000
4	Hours worked	11,200	13,400	11,500	36,100
5	Budgeted output	120,000	140,000	140,000	400,000
6	Hours available	12,000	13,900	12,600	38,500
7	Sales revenue £	765,000	790,000	725,000	2,280,000
8	Machine hours	10,200	12,000	10,800	33,000
9	Productivity per labour hour	10.8	10.2	10.6	10.5
10	Productivity index	100.4	97.9	86.8	94.8
11	Labour utilisation	93.3	96.4	91.3	93.8
12	Cost per unit £	3.46	3.30	3.50	3.41
13	Machine utilisation £/hr	75.00	65.83	67.13	69.09

3 a)

	A	B	C	D
1		January	February	March
2	Sales	250,000	300,000	280,000
3	Cost of sales	130,000	170,000	160,000
4	Gross profit	=B2-B3	=C2-C3	=D2-D3
5	Overheads	85,000	90,000	88,000
6	Net profit	=B4-B5	=C4-C5	=D4-D5
7	Capital	150,000	150,000	170,000
8	Gross profit margin	=B4/B2*100	=C4/C2*100	=D4/D2*100
9	Net profit margin	=B6/B2*100	=C6/C2*100	=D6/D2*100
10	Return on capital employed	=B6/B7*100	=C6/C7*100	=D6/D7*100
11	Asset turnover	=B2/B7	=C2/C7	=D2/D7

Gross profit margin = $\dfrac{\text{Gross profit}}{\text{Sales}} \times 100$

For January = B4/B2*100

Net profit margin = $\dfrac{\text{Net profit}}{\text{Sales}} \times 100$

For January = B6/B2*100

Return on capital employed = $\dfrac{\text{Net profit}}{\text{Capital}} \times 100$

For January = B6/B7*100

Asset turnover = $\dfrac{\text{Sales}}{\text{Capital}}$

For January = B2/B7

b)

	A	B	C	D
1		January	February	March
2	Sales	250,000	300,000	280,000
3	Cost of sales	130,000	170,000	160,000
4	Gross profit	120,000	130,000	120,000
5	Overheads	85,000	90,000	88,000
6	Net profit	35,000	40,000	32,000
7	Capital	150,000	150,000	170,000
8	Gross profit margin	48.0	43.3	42.9
9	Net profit margin	14.0	13.3	11.4
10	Return on capital employed	23.3	26.7	18.8
11	Asset turnover	1.67	2.00	1.65

LATHAM PRODUCTS – PRODUCTION COSTS – MARCH TO JUNE

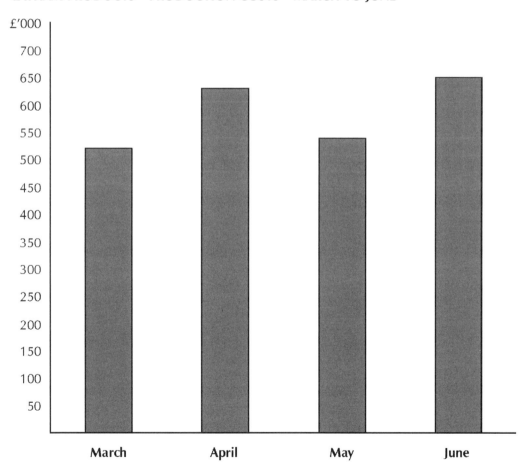

5   LATHAM PRODUCTS – PRODUCTION COSTS – MARCH TO JUNE

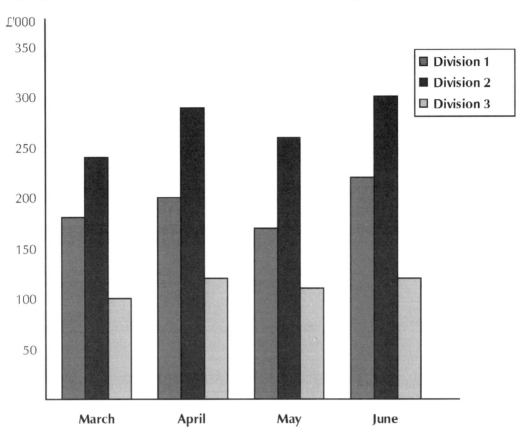

LATHAM PRODUCTS – PRODUCTION COSTS – MARCH TO JUNE

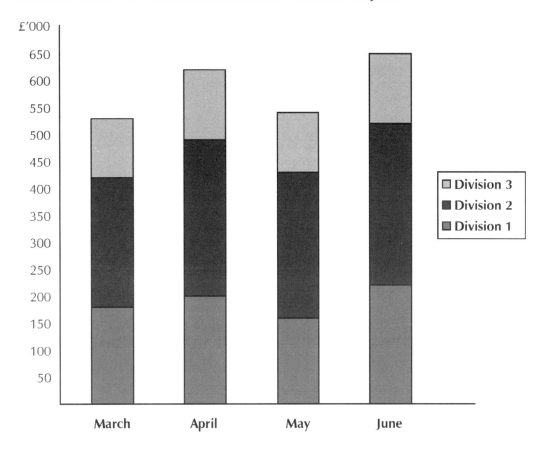

7   LATHAM PRODUCTS – SALES – MARCH TO JUNE

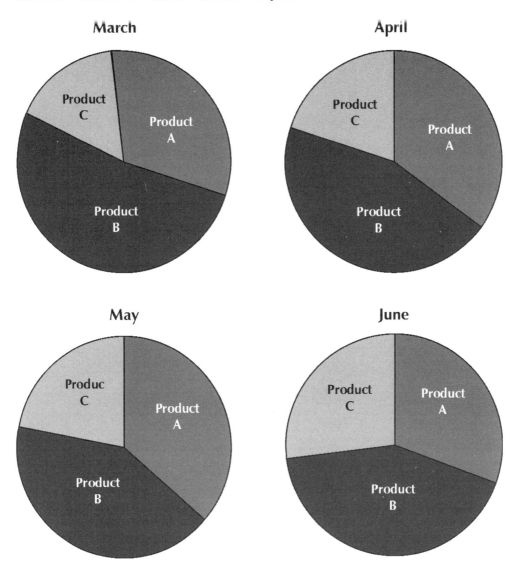

March

Product C
Product A
Product B

April

Product C
Product A
Product B

May

Produc C
Product A
Product B

June

Product C
Product A
Product B

LATHAM PRODUCTS – SALES – MARCH TO JUNE

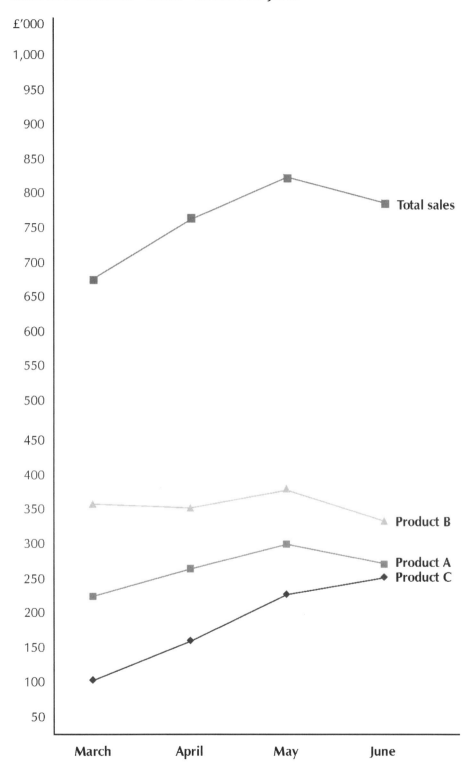

CHAPTER 14 Reporting figures over time

1

	£	Moving average £
July	305,800	–
August	310,600	308,000
September	307,600	310,000
October	311,800	310,600
November	312,400	312,800
December	314,200	313,467
January	313,800	314,567
February	315,700	316,500
March	320,000	317,833
April	317,800	319,767
May	321,500	321,267
June	324,500	–

2

		£	Moving average £	Trend £
2004	Quarter 1	479,600		
	Quarter 2	484,600		
			456,800	
	Quarter 3	452,200		457,150
			457,500	
	Quarter 4	410,800		458,238
			458,975	
2005	Quarter 1	482,400		457,525
			456,075	
	Quarter 2	490,500		457,675
			459,275	
	Quarter 3	440,600		460,300
			461,325	
	Quarter 4	423,600		462,713
			464,100	
2006	Quarter 1	490,600		466,675
			469,250	
	Quarter 2	501,600		470,113
			470,975	
	Quarter 3	461,200		
	Quarter 4	430,500		

QUARTERLY SALES AND TREND

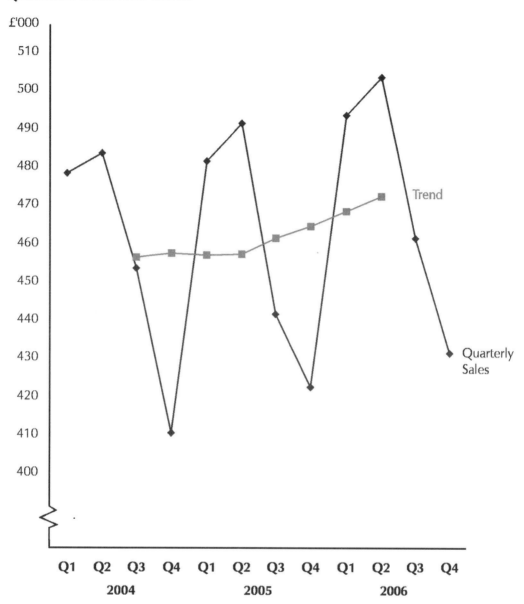

4

	A	B	C	D	E
1	2004	Quarter 1	479,600		
2					
3		Quarter 2	484,600		
4				=(C1+C3+C5+C7)/4	
5		Quarter 3	452,200		=(D4+D6)/2
6				=(C3+C5+C7+C9)/4	
7		Quarter 4	410,800		=(D6+D8)/2
8				=(C5+C7+C9+C11)/4	
9	2005	Quarter 1	482,400		=(D8+D10)/2
10				=(C7+C9+C11+C13)/4	
11		Quarter 2	490,500		=(D10+D12)/2
12				=(C9+C11+C13+C15)/4	
13		Quarter 3	440,600		=(D12+D14)/2
14				=(C11+C13+C15+C17)/4	
15		Quarter 4	423,600		=(D14+D16)/2
16				=(C13+C15+C17+C19)/4	
17	2006	Quarter 1	490,600		=(D16+D18)/2
18				=(C15+C17+C19+C21)/4	
19		Quarter 2	501,600		=(D18+D20)/2
20				=(C17+C19+C21+C23)/4	
21		Quarter 3	461,200		
22					
23		Quarter 4	430,500		

5

	£	Index
January	59,700	100.0
February	62,300	104.4
March	56,900	95.3
April	60,400	101.2
May	62,400	104.5
June	66,700	111.7

6

		Adjusted sales £
January	127,600 x 171.1/171.1	127,600
February	129,700 x 171.1/172.0	129,021
March	130,400 x 171.1/172.2	129,567
April	131,600 x 171.1/173.0	130,155
May	130,500 x 171.1/172.1	129,742
June	131,600 x 171.1/171.3	131,446

	RPI adjusted sales figure	Index
	£	£
January	127,600	100.0
February	129,021	101.1
March	129,567	101.5
April	130,155	102.0
May	129,742	101.7
June	131,446	103.0

	A	B	C	D	E
1	January	127,600	171.1	=B1*(C1/C1)	=(D1/D1)*100
2	February	129,700	172.0	=B2*(C1/C2)	=(D2/D1)*100
3	March	130,400	172.2	=B3*(C1/C3)	=(D3/D1)*100
4	April	131,600	173.0	=B4*(C1/C4)	=(D4/D1)*100
5	May	130,500	172.1	=B5*(C1/C5)	=(D5/D1)*100
6	June	131,600	171.3	=B6*(C1/C6)	=(D6/D1)*100

CHAPTER 15 External reporting

NORTHERN BANK

LOAN MONITORING

Month: June 2006

	Budget	Actual	Variance
	£	£	£
Sales	140,000	135,700	4,300 ADV
Costs	110,000	108,400	1,600 FAV

WINE MERCHANTS ASSOCIATION

QUARTERLY PROFIT SURVEY

Please provide the following information for the quarter ended 30 June 2006 – all information provided will be treated with the strictest confidentiality.

Gross profit percentage	34.0%
Net profit percentage	11.7%
Return on capital employed	12.3%

435

CHAPTER 16 Value Added Tax

1   HM Revenue and Customs (HMRC)

2   Output VAT is the VAT charged by a supplier on the sales that are made by his business. Input V
is the VAT suffered by the purchaser of the goods which will be reclaimed from HMRC if t
purchaser is VAT registered.

3   VAT is collected by HMRC throughout the manufacturing chain for goods. Each business that buy
processes and then sells the goods pays the difference between the VAT on their sale and the V/
on their purchase over to HMRC.

4   VAT = £384.00 x 17.5%
       = £67.20

Business C – output tax
Business D – input tax

5   Standard rate   17.5%
    Zero rate   0%
    Reduced rate for domestic fuel and power   5%

6   Any four from:

- young children's clothes and shoes
- food purchased in shops
- bus and train fares
- books
- newspapers and magazines

7   Any four from:

- Post Office postal services
- education
- healthcare
- insurance
- betting and gambling

8   Refer to Appendix A of the VAT Guide

9   If exempt services are supplied then the business is not able to reclaim the VAT on its purchases
and expenses from HMRC. If zero-rated goods are supplied then no VAT is charged on sales but
the VAT incurred on purchases and expenses can be reclaimed.

10
- if the taxable turnover for a business for twelve month period exceeds the registration limit of
  £61,000 then the business must apply to register within 30 days of the end of that twelve
  month period
- if the taxable turnover is expected to exceed £61,000 within the next 30 days then the
  business must apply to register for VAT.

11
- business entertainment expenses
- cars purchased for use within the business

i)   22 June 2006 – actual tax point
ii)   23 June 2006 – actual tax point
iii) 27 June 2006 – actual tax point

i)   £356.79 x 17.5%   = £62.43
ii)   (£269.00 – £40.35) x 17.5%   = £40.01
iii) (£250.00 – £6.25) x 17.5%   = £42.65
iv)   (£300.00 – £30.00 – £8.10) x 17.5%   = £45.83

i)   £42.88 x 7/47   = £6.38
ii)   £96.35 x 7/47   = £14.35
iiii) £28.20 x 7/47   = £4.20
iv)   £81.07 x 7/47   = £12.07

5 A pro-forma invoice is one which is sent out to a customer in order to offer them the chance to purchase the goods detailed. A pro-forma invoice cannot be used by the purchaser if they do purchase the goods to reclaim the VAT so a pro-forma invoice must always include the words "This is not a VAT invoice".

6 The VAT on a bad debt can be reclaimed from HMRC when the following three conditions are met:

  ■ the debt is more than 6 months overdue
  ■ the original VAT on the invoice has been paid to HMRC
  ■ the debt is written off in the accounts of the business

7 The goods will be treated as zero rated in the UK provided that there is documentary evidence of the export and that this has been obtained by the supplier within three months of the supply.

CHAPTER 17 VAT records

1 Normally 6 years

2 a) there is no evidence of output tax charged
   b) there is no evidence of input tax incurred and therefore it cannot be reclaimed

3   VAT ACCOUNT

VAT deductible – input tax	£	VAT payable – output tax	£
Purchases day book	4,785.67	Sales day book	7,589.60
Cash payments book	936.58	Cash receipts book	1,662.78
EU acquisitions	1,558.36	EU acquisitions	1,558.36
	7,280.61		10,810.74
Less: credit notes received	663.57	Less: credit notes issued	994.67
Total VAT deductible	6,617.04	Total VAT payable	9,816.07
		Less: VAT deductible	6,617.04
		Due to HMRC	3,199.03

4   **VAT ACCOUNT**

VAT deductible – input tax	£	VAT payable output tax	£
Purchases day book	1,825.67	Sales day book	3,572.15
Cash payments book	514.37	Cash receipts book	994.67
EU acquisitions	236.57	EU acquisitions	236.57
Bad debt relief	105.37	Net undercharge	
		(44.79 – 25.47)	19.32
	2,681.98		4,822.71
Less: credit notes received	310.56	Less: credit notes issued	662.70
Total VAT deductible	2,371.42	Total VAT payable	4,160.01
		Less: VAT deductible	2,371.42
		Due to HMRC	1,788.59

5   WORKINGS   £

Box 1
VAT on sales from the sales day book	7,921.80
VAT on sales from the cash receipts book	884.56
Less: VAT on credit notes issued	(135.37)
	8,670.99

Box 4
VAT on purchases from purchases day book	5,359.82
VAT on purchases from cash payments book	586.73
VAT on EU acquisitions	394.81
Less: VAT on credit notes received	(124.98)
	6,216.38

Box 6
Zero-rated credit sales	13,447.67
Standard rated credit sales	45,267.44
Cash sales	5,054.63
Less: zero-rated credit notes	(225.83)
standard rated credit notes	(773.56)
	62,770.35

Box 7
Zero-rated credit purchases	7,447.30
Standard rated credit purchases	30,627.58
Cash purchases	3,352.75
EU acquisitions	2,256.07
Less: zero rated credit notes	(215.61)
standard rated credit notes	(714.20)
	42,753.89

Value Added Tax Return

For the period
01 03 06 to 30 06 06

For Official Use

Registration number

225 3756 12

Period

0606

You could be liable to a financial penalty if your completed return and all the VAT payable are not received by the due date.

Due date: 31 July 2006

MARTIN TRADING
BLACKNESS HOUSE
JUDE STREET
CLINFORD
CL3 6GH

For Official Use

If you have a general enquiry or need advice please call our National Advice Service on 0845 010 9000.

Before you fill in this form please read the notes on the back and the VAT Leaflet "*Filling in your VAT return*" and "*Flat rate schemes for small businesses*", if you use the scheme. Fill in all boxes clearly in ink, and write 'none' where necessary. Don't put a dash or leave any box blank. If there are no pence write "00" in the pence column. Do not enter more than one amount in any box.

For official use			£	p
	VAT due in this period on sales and other outputs	**1**	8,670	99
	VAT due in this period on acquisitions from other EC Member States	**2**	394	81
	Total VAT due (the sum of boxes 1 and 2)	**3**	9,065	80
	VAT reclaimed in this period on purchases and other inputs (including acquisitions from the EC)	**4**	6,216	38
	Net VAT to be paid to Customs or reclaimed by you (Difference between boxes 3 and 4)	**5**	2,849	42
	Total value of sales and all other outputs excluding any VAT. Include your box 8 figure	**6**	62,770	00
	Total value of purchases and all other inputs excluding any VAT. Include your box 9 figure	**7**	42,754	00
	Total value of all supplies of goods and related services, excluding any VAT, to other EC Member States	**8**	NONE	00
	Total value of all acquisitions of goods and related services, excluding any VAT, from other EC Member States	**9**	2,256	00

If you are enclosing a payment please tick this box

☑

DECLARATION: You, or someone on your behalf, must sign below.

I, _____ declare that the
(Full name of signatory in BLOCK LETTERS)
information given above is true and complete.

Signature_____ Date .... 20 ....

A false declaration can result in prosecution.

6   If you have been registered for VAT for at least 12 months and the annual value of your taxab
     supplies, excluding VAT, is below £660,000 then you may be able to use the annual accountir
     scheme. This also applies if your taxable supplies total less than £150,000, regardless of the leng
     of time since registration.

     Under this scheme you make 9 monthly direct debit payments based upon an estimate of th
     amount of VAT due. You must then prepare a VAT return for the year and send it in with the tent
     balancing payment, by two months after the year end.

     Use of this annual accounting scheme is a great help to a small trader as it means that he does nc
     have to prepare a quarterly VAT return. Only one VAT return is to prepared each year obvious
     reducing the amount of time that a small trader must spend on this task. However it does mea
     that he must still keep accurate accounting records of the VAT information for a whole year.

7   If the annual value of taxable supplies, excluding VAT, is less than £660,000 and provided that
     trader has a clean record with HMRC, he may be able to apply to use the cash accounting scheme

     The scheme allows the accounting for VAT to be based upon the date of receipt or payment o
     money rather than the tax point on an invoice. This is particularly useful for a business which give
     its customers a long period of credit but has to pay its suppliers promptly. This means that VAT or
     sales need only be paid to HMRC when the debt has been received but the VAT on payment tc
     suppliers can be reclaimed as soon as the payment is made.

     The scheme also gives automatic relief from bad debts as if the customer does not pay the amoun
     due then the VAT need not be accounted for to HMRC.

Present value table

Present value of £1 ie, $\dfrac{1}{(1+r)^n} = (1+r)^{-n}$

where r = discount rate
       n = number of periods until payment

Discount rates (r)

Periods

(n)	1%	2%	3%	4%	5%	6%	7%	8%	9%	10%
1	0.990	0.980	0.971	0.962	0.952	0.943	0.935	0.926	0.917	0.909
2	0.980	0.961	0.943	0.925	0.907	0.890	0.873	0.857	0.842	0.826
3	0.971	0.942	0.915	0.889	0.864	0.840	0.816	0.794	0.772	0.751
4	0.961	0.924	0.888	0.855	0.823	0.792	0.763	0.735	0.708	0.683
5	0.951	0.906	0.863	0.822	0.784	0.747	0.713	0.681	0.650	0.621
6	0.942	0.888	0.837	0.790	0.746	0.705	0.666	0.630	0.596	0.564
7	0.933	0.871	0.813	0.760	0.711	0.665	0.623	0.583	0.547	0.513
8	0.923	0.853	0.789	0.731	0.677	0.627	0.582	0.540	0.502	0.467
9	0.914	0.837	0.766	0.703	0.645	0.592	0.544	0.500	0.460	0.424
10	0.905	0.820	0.744	0.676	0.614	0.558	0.508	0.463	0.422	0.386
11	0.896	0.804	0.722	0.650	0.585	0.527	0.475	0.429	0.388	0.350
12	0.887	0.788	0.701	0.625	0.557	0.497	0.444	0.397	0.356	0.319
13	0.879	0.773	0.681	0.601	0.530	0.469	0.415	0.368	0.326	0.290
14	0.870	0.758	0.661	0.577	0.505	0.442	0.388	0.340	0.299	0.263
15	0.861	0.743	0.642	0.555	0.481	0.417	0.362	0.315	0.275	0.239

Periods

(n)	11%	12%	13%	14%	15%	16%	17%	18%	19%	20%
1	0.901	0.893	0.885	0.877	0.870	0.862	0.855	0.847	0.840	0.833
2	0.812	0.797	0.783	0.769	0.756	0.743	0.731	0.718	0.706	0.694
3	0.731	0.712	0.693	0.675	0.658	0.641	0.624	0.609	0.593	0.579
4	0.659	0.636	0.613	0.592	0.572	0.552	0.534	0.516	0.499	0.482
5	0.593	0.567	0.543	0.519	0.497	0.476	0.456	0.437	0.419	0.402
6	0.535	0.507	0.480	0.456	0.432	0.410	0.390	0.370	0.352	0.335
7	0.482	0.452	0.425	0.400	0.376	0.354	0.333	0.314	0.296	0.279
8	0.434	0.404	0.376	0.351	0.327	0.305	0.285	0.266	0.249	0.233
9	0.391	0.361	0.333	0.308	0.284	0.263	0.243	0.225	0.209	0.194
10	0.352	0.322	0.295	0.270	0.247	0.227	0.208	0.191	0.176	0.162
11	0.317	0.287	0.261	0.237	0.215	0.195	0.178	0.162	0.148	0.135
12	0.286	0.257	0.231	0.208	0.187	0.168	0.152	0.137	0.124	0.112
13	0.258	0.229	0.204	0.182	0.163	0.145	0.130	0.116	0.104	0.093
14	0.232	0.205	0.181	0.160	0.141	0.125	0.111	0.099	0.088	0.078
15	0.209	0.183	0.160	0.140	0.123	0.108	0.095	0.084	0.074	0.065

Annuity table

Present value of an annuity of 1 ie, $\dfrac{1-(1+r)^{-n}}{r}$

where r = discount rate

n = number of periods

Periods

(n)	1%	2%	3%	4%	5%	6%	7%	8%	9%	10%
1	0.990	0.980	0.971	0.962	0.952	0.943	0.935	0.926	0.917	0.909
2	1.970	1.942	1.913	1.886	1.859	1.833	1.808	1.783	1.759	1.736
3	2.941	2.884	2.829	2.775	2.723	2.673	2.624	2.577	2.531	2.487
4	3.902	3.808	3.717	3.630	3.546	3.465	3.387	3.312	3.240	3.170
5	4.853	4.713	4.580	4.452	4.329	4.212	4.100	3.993	3.890	3.791
6	5.795	5.601	5.417	5.242	5.076	4.917	4.767	4.623	4.486	4.355
7	6.728	6.472	6.230	6.002	5.786	5.582	5.389	5.206	5.033	4.868
8	7.652	7.325	7.020	6.733	6.463	6.210	5.971	5.747	5.535	5.335
9	8.566	8.162	7.786	7.435	7.108	6.802	6.515	6.247	5.995	5.759
10	9.471	8.983	8.530	8.111	7.722	7.360	7.024	6.710	6.418	6.145
11	10.368	9.787	9.253	8.760	8.306	7.887	7.499	7.139	6.805	6.495
12	11.255	10.575	9.954	9.385	8.863	8.384	7.943	7.536	7.161	6.814
13	12.134	11.348	10.635	9.986	9.394	8.853	8.358	7.904	7.487	7.103
14	13.004	12.106	11.296	10.563	9.899	9.295	8.745	8.244	7.786	7.367
15	13.865	12.849	11.938	11.118	10.380	9.712	9.108	8.559	8.061	7.606

Periods

(n)	11%	12%	13%	14%	15%	16%	17%	18%	19%	20%
1	0.901	0.893	0.885	0.877	0.870	0.862	0.855	0.847	0.840	0.833
2	1.713	1.690	1.668	1.647	1.626	1.605	1.585	1.566	1.547	1.528
3	2.444	2.402	2.361	2.322	2.283	2.246	2.210	2.174	2.140	2.106
4	3.102	3.037	2.974	2.914	2.855	2.798	2.743	2.690	2.639	2.589
5	3.696	3.605	3.517	3.433	3.352	3.274	3.199	3.127	3.058	2.991
6	4.231	4.111	3.998	3.889	3.784	3.685	3.589	3.498	3.410	3.326
7	4.712	4.564	4.423	4.288	4.160	4.039	3.922	3.812	3.706	3.605
8	5.146	4.968	4.799	4.639	4.487	4.344	4.207	4.078	3.954	3.837
9	5.537	5.328	5.132	4.946	4.772	4.607	4.451	4.303	4.163	4.031
10	5.889	5.650	5.426	5.216	5.019	4.833	4.659	4.494	4.339	4.192
11	6.207	5.938	5.687	5.453	5.234	5.029	4.836	4.656	4.486	4.327
12	6.492	6.194	5.918	5.660	5.421	5.197	4.988	4.793	4.611	4.439
13	6.750	6.424	6.122	5.842	5.583	5.342	5.118	4.910	4.715	4.533
14	6.982	6.628	6.302	6.002	5.724	5.468	5.229	5.008	4.802	4.611
15	7.191	6.811	6.462	6.142	5.847	5.575	5.324	5.092	4.876	4.675

NDEX